The Complete Guide to CERAMIC TILE

Third Edition

Updated with New Products & Techniques

Creative Publishing international

MINNEAPOLIS, MINNESOTA
www.creativepub.com

Creative Publishing international

Creative Publishing international, Inc.
400 First Avenue North, Suite 300
Minneapolis, Minnesota 55401
1-800-328-0590
www.creativepub.com

Printed in USA.

10 9 8 7 6 5 4 3 2

Library of Congress Cataloging-in-Publication Data

The complete guide to ceramic tile. -- 3rd ed., with DVD.
p. cm.
At head of title: Black & Decker.
Includes index.
Rev. ed. of: The complete guide to ceramic & stone tile.
Summary: "Provides information for do-it-yourself tile projects for the home, including floors, walls, bathrooms, kitchens, and outdoors"--Provided by publisher.
ISBN-13: 978-1-58923-563-2 (soft cover)
ISBN-10: 1-58923-563-0 (soft cover)
1. Tile laying--Amateurs' manuals. 2. Tiles--Amateurs' manuals. I. Creative Publishing International. II. Black & Decker Corporation (Towson, Md.) III. Complete guide to ceramic & stone tile.

TH8531.C65 2010
698--dc22

2010020980

President/CEO: Ken Fund

Home Improvement Group

Publisher: Bryan Trandem
Managing Editor: Tracy Stanley
Senior Editor: Mark Johanson

Creative Director: Michele Lanci-Altomare
Art Direction/Design: Jon Simpson, Brad Springer, James Kegley

Lead Photographer: Joel Schnell
Set Builder: James Parmeter
Production Managers: Laura Hokkanen, Linda Halls

Edition Editor: Carter Glass
Page Layout Artist: Danielle Smith
Copy Editor: Betsy Matheson Symanietz
Proofreader: Drew Siqveland

The Complete Guide to Ceramic Tile
Created by: The Editors of Creative Publishing international, Inc., in cooperation with Black & Decker.

NOTICE TO READERS

For safety, use caution, care, and good judgment when following the procedures described in this book. The publisher and Black & Decker cannot assume responsibility for any damage to property or injury to persons as a result of misuse of the information provided.

The techniques shown in this book are general techniques for various applications. In some instances, additional techniques not shown in this book may be required. Always follow manufacturers' instructions included with products, since deviating from the directions may void warranties. The projects in this book vary widely as to skill levels required: some may not be appropriate for all do-it-yourselfers, and some may require professional help.

Consult your local building department for information on building permits, codes, and other laws as they apply to your project.

Contents

The Complete Guide to Ceramic Tile

8

8

8

8

56

56

56

Contents (Cont.)

90

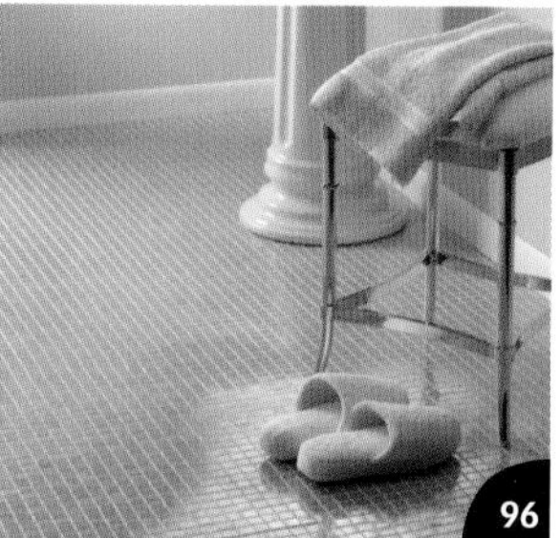
96

106

123

124

138

169

184

188

193

194

212

223

230

Introduction

Building materials evolve and change very quickly in the do-it-yourself world. New formulations, advanced installation systems, and a host of "plug-and-play" gimmicks make keeping pace with the things we put into our houses a constant battle. But ceramic tile is different. Although trends, colors, and shapes may look slightly different from year to year, tiling is a lifelong skill that will serve you well as long as you own your home.

Laying tile is a very popular DIY project for a number of reasons, but the primary appeal is that tile is a manageable material that yields beautiful, long-lasting floors for a relatively small investment. Because of the nature of the material and the installation process, you can work at your own pace. If you make an error, it is not difficult to back up and re-do the work.

In *The Complete Guide to Ceramic Tile,* you will discover clear, beautifully photographed information that shows you, step-by-step, exactly how to work with tile. Layout, installing subbases, cutting and fitting, setting, grouting, and sealing are just some of the techniques you will learn.

The projects featured in this book show tile in just about every usage you'll find around the home. By far, floors are the most popular spot for tiling, and here you'll get the full picture of how to lay out a floor grid and set tile like a pro. Walls are also popular spots for tile, particularly in bathrooms, showers, and kitchen backsplashes. Tiled countertops have many advantages over other countertop material, whether in the kitchens, the bathroom, or even in your outdoor food preparation areas. Horizontal patio surfaces are also good candidates for tile in many climates, and you'll see how to approach these projects as well.

Because tile is a highly decorative material, it can be used to create fun items that may not have any practical purpose other than to delight. Mirror frames, mosaic wall hangings, and tile-covered garden planting pots are just a few of these. You'll even find a complete how-to sequence on making your own fired ceramic tiles from raw clay.

Finally, any tile surface will require occasional repair and maintenance. From re-grouting a shower receptor to replacing a broken wall tile, the last chapter in this books gives the essential information you need to keep your tile looking its best for years to come.

Gallery of Tile Projects

In this alcove, decorative tiles grace a fireplace surround topped by a brick mantel. The floor combines large quarry tile with interesting accent tiles that emphasize the Mediterranean feeling of the patio. Accessories scattered throughout the area echo the blue-and-white theme set by the fireplace and accent tiles.

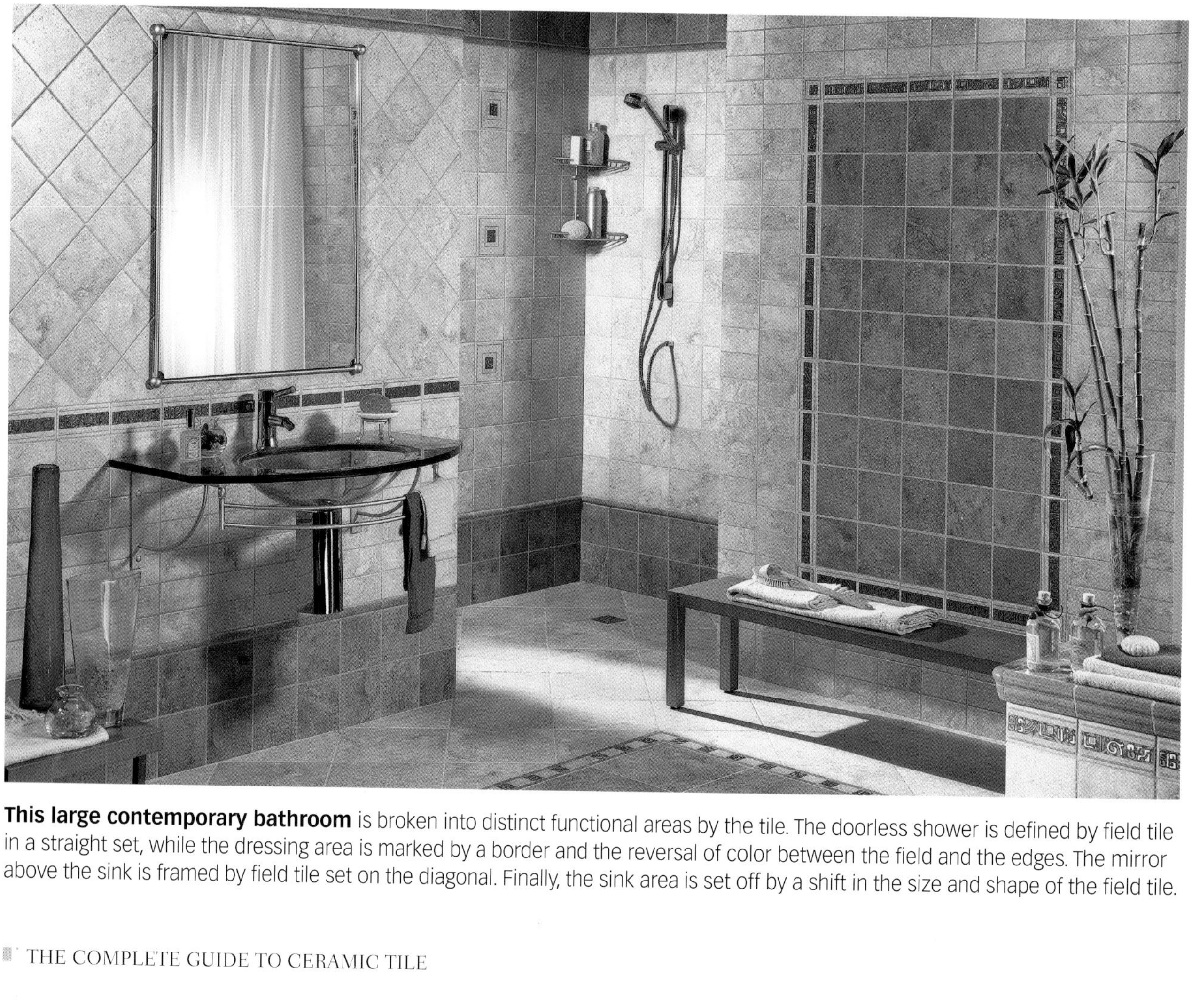

This large contemporary bathroom is broken into distinct functional areas by the tile. The doorless shower is defined by field tile in a straight set, while the dressing area is marked by a border and the reversal of color between the field and the edges. The mirror above the sink is framed by field tile set on the diagonal. Finally, the sink area is set off by a shift in the size and shape of the field tile.

Lush floral photo murals sparkle against white tile backgrounds in this exotic bathroom.

Small mosaic tile in two colors provides a dramatic backdrop for a contemporary entryway.

With a view like this, the best design is one that gets out of its own way. This blue mosaic tile echoes the color of the mountains without competing for attention.

Mosaic tile, with its multitude of grout lines, is highly slip-resistant. A border defines the edges of this hallway and leads the eye toward the next room.

Stair risers are typically invisible. With their colorful handpainted tile, these risers are anything but typical and are certainly not invisible.

Borders liven up walls and break up otherwise boring expanses of solid color.

Stones cut to resemble river rocks make an unusual bathroom floor. The stones, which are attached to a mesh backing, are remarkably easy to install. Coordinating grout blends the tiles; contrasting grout would emphasize the individual stones.

Terra-cotta ("baked earth") tile is made by pressing unrefined clay into molds and baking it. Its color is determined by minerals unique to the soil from which it is made. Machine-made terra-cotta tile can be laid like standard tile, but traditional terra-cotta, with its irregularities and uneven shapes, requires more care during installation. Unglazed terra-cotta, which is porous and absorbent, should be treated with sealant before being installed in potentially wet locations, such as entries.

Creative tilework can have a big impact in a very small space. These custom, handmade backsplash tiles bring a real shot of life to a small half bath where there are few opportunities for making a design statement.

The golden color of this home's exterior is reflected in the mottled tones of the tile patio and accented by the sunny yellow patio furniture.

Subway tile, or simple rectangular tile, blends the shower into its surroundings. The room is brightened considerably by a backsplash of colorful mosaic tile. A niche, cleverly sized and placed, creates the appearance that the backsplash continues behind the shower, and a mosaic floor provides a visual anchor.

Artistic tile installations can go well beyond a nicely balanced mosaic and into bold abstract or contemporary designs. Here, natural stone tiles are presented to depict a mountainous staircase rising up from the tub rim in a brightly lit bathroom alcove.

Plain wall tile in solid colors makes a bold statement when combined with accessories in similar or complementary colors.

Combining mosaic tile in a variety of colors and sizes produces elegant designs. Elaborate patterns can be deceptively easy to create with tile mounted to mesh backings. Even pre-arranged borders are widely available. Mosaic tile of any material is quite slip-resistant because of the many grout lines.

Mosaic tile—small, colorful tiles made of ceramic, porcelain, terra-cotta, or cement—can be installed on walls and floors to form patterns and pictures or just to add a splash of color. Mosaic tile can be expensive, but covering the few square feet of a backsplash, such as this one, creates exciting decoration at a reasonable price.

Ceramic Tile Basics

Tile is a simple material: a piece of clay that's glazed and fired. But visiting a tile store and choosing the tile that's right for you is hardly a simple act. Ceramic or porcelain? Wall or floor? Squares or mosaic sheets? With accents or without? Before you even start to think about things like color and design, there are many questions you'll need to answer. The following pages are a basic introduction to the wide array of tile shapes, sizes, and functions you'll encounter at your average tile store. By studying up a bit, you can pre-make some decisions and greatly simplify your tile-buying experience.

Following the information on tile products, you'll find basic tile-handling skills needed for any tile, regardless of type or style. Primarily, this means learning to cut your tiles to fit. Additional skills are undoubtedly required for any tile installation project, but because these vary by degree they will be covered as each project type is discussed.

In this chapter:

Floor Tile

Floor tile needs to be more than just attractive—it needs to be strong and durable as well. After all, floors bear the weight of furniture, foot traffic, and the sudden impact of every one and every thing that falls on them. Floor tile is engineered to tolerate these stresses. Most floor tile is also suitable for countertops. And although it's generally thicker and heavier than wall tile, many styles of floor tile can be used on walls. The trim pieces necessary for counters and walls aren't always available, though, which may limit your options.

When shopping for tile, look for ratings by the American National Standards Institute or the Porcelain Enamel Institute (see below). If ratings aren't available, check with your dealer to make sure the tile you're considering is suitable for your project.

Before you start shopping, consider where the tile will be used and what you want it to accomplish. Will it be exposed to moisture? Should it be a focal point or a subtle background? Do you want the floor to establish the room's color scheme or blend into it? The range of options is truly mind-boggling, so establish some guidelines before you go shopping to simplify the selection process.

Floor tiles are thicker and almost always larger than wall tiles. Ceramic floor tiles are usually between ¼ and ½" thick.

Floor Tile Ratings ▸

Floor tile often comes labeled with water absorption and Porcelain Enamel Institute (PEI) ratings. Ratings indicate how a tile can be used and whether or not it needs to be sealed against moisture. Absorption is a concern because tile that soaks up water is susceptible to mildew and mold and can be difficult to clean. Tile is rated non-vitreous, semi-vitreous, vitreous, or impervious, in increasing order of water resistance. Non-vitreous tile is quite porous; semi-vitreous is used in dry-to-occasionally-wet locations; vitreous tile can be used without regard to its exposure to moisture. Impervious tile is generally reserved for restaurants, hospitals, and commercial applications where sanitation is a special concern.

The PEI number is a wear rating that indicates how the tile should be used. Ratings of 1 and 2 indicate tile is suitable for walls only; tile rated 3 and 4 is suitable for all residential applications—walls, counters, and floors. Most tile carries absorption and PEI ratings, but some, especially imported and art tiles, may not. Ask the retailer if you're not sure.

Depending on the retailer, tile may also have other ratings. Some tile is graded 1 to 3 for the quality of manufacturing. Grade 1 indicates standard grade; 2 indicates minor glaze and size flaws; 3 indicates major flaws; use for decoration only. Tile suitable for outdoor use is sometimes rated with regard to its resistance to frost. Finally, coefficient of friction numbers may be included with some tile. The higher the coefficient, the more slip resistant the tile. A dry coefficient of .6 is the minimum standard established by the Americans with Disabilities Act.

Wall Tile

Wall tile, unlike floor tile, doesn't have the burden of bearing weight or withstanding heavy traffic, so it can be thinner, have finer finishes, and, in some cases, be less expensive. Wall tile layouts tend to have more exposed edges, so manufacturers often offer matching trim and border pieces with finished edges. Wall tile is generally self spacing—individual tiles have small flanges on each edge to help keep the spacing even. You can use floor tile on walls, but since it is heavier, it tends to slide down during installation. Using battens while installing can help solve this problem. Fewer styles of matching trim tile are available for floor tile, which may make it difficult to conceal unfinished edges.

Wall tile should not be used on floors or countertops, however, because it will not stand up to much weight or sudden impacts. If you have concerns about a tile's suitability for your application, ask your retailer or look for ratings by the American National Standards Institute or the Porcelain Enamel Institute. Wall tile can be a fairly inconspicuous wall covering or, if used in an elaborate design, can become the focal point of a room. As with floor tiles, there are styles for every effect from subtle to bold, so envision the effect you want before you head to the tile store or home improvement center.

Wall tiles are usually less than ¼" thick and no larger than 6 × 6", with 4 × 4" tiles the most common. Lightweight tiles are less likely to sag during installation.

Wall Tile Ratings ▸

Most tile intended for walls comes labeled with a water absorption rating. As with floor tile, absorbent wall tile will be susceptible to mildew and mold and be difficult to clean. Tiles are rated non-vitreous, semi-vitreous, vitreous, and impervious, in increasing order of water resistance. Practically speaking, these ratings tell you whether your tile may require sealant or if it can be left as is. Non-vitreous and semi-vitreous do absorb noticeable amounts of water and may need to be sealed in damp rooms like bathrooms. Sealant can alter a tile's appearance, so test before you buy.

There are a few other ratings to consider when purchasing wall tile. Depending on where you buy tile, it may be graded from 1 to 3 for the quality of manufacturing. Grade 1 indicates standard grade, suitable for all installations. Grade 2 indicates minor glaze and size flaws, but the tile is structurally standard. Grade 3 tiles may be slightly irregular in shape and are decorative, suitable only for walls. Tiles with manufacturing irregularities may be more difficult to lay out and install precisely. If you live in a freeze zone and are looking for tile for outdoor walls, you'll also want tile rated resistant to frost. If the frost-resistance rating is not on the package, the retailer should be able to tell you. Some colored tile may come with a graphic to indicate the degree of color variation from tile to tile—in most cases it will vary somewhat.

Types of Tile

Porcelain tile is produced by pressing refined clay into shape and then firing it in a kiln at very high temperatures. The resulting tile is extremely hard, absorbs very little or no water, and doesn't stain or mildew. Porcelain tile is manufactured in all shapes and sizes, and, because its white base color accepts dye beautifully, a virtually unlimited range of colors and finishes are available. Tile makers can also imprint textures when the tile is pressed to create a slip-resistant surface well suited for floors in wet locations. Porcelain tile is colored by mixing dye into the clay rather than applying it in a glaze, which means the color extends through the full thickness of the tile. Because of this process, tile makers can press finer, more intricate textures and patterns into the tile. Porcelain tile can even be pressed so that it's nearly indistinguishable from cut stone, which tends to be more expensive but less durable. For ease of care, porcelain is hard to beat. Its smooth finish and imperviousness to moisture keep soil and stains from setting in, making it easy to maintain. *Note: grout can stain porous material, so take great care in grouting and be sure to follow manufacturer instructions.*

Glazed ceramic tile is made from clay pressed into a shape by a machine, glazed, and then fired in a kiln. The glaze, made up of a number of glass and metal elements, provides color and creates a hard, shiny surface. To make floor tile slip-resistant, the surface can be textured, given a slightly raised design, or the glaze itself may include materials added to create a non-skid surface. Glazed tile generally absorbs very little or no water, making it both easy to maintain and mildew resistant. If the glaze is hard and scratch-resistant and the tile is properly installed and maintained, glazed ceramic tile can last for decades.

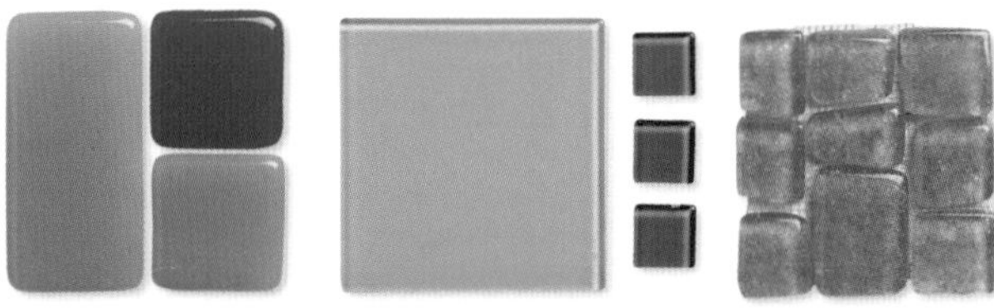

Glass tile is an especially interesting option for walls, although in some applications it can be used on floors as well. It is available in a variety of colors, degrees of translucency, shapes, and sizes. Because most glass tile is translucent to some degree, it's important to use a white tile adhesive that won't affect the appearance of the tiles once they are installed. Glass is impervious to moisture, but can be scratched and cracked, so it shouldn't be installed where it will get hit by swinging doors or scratched by general traffic. See pages 24 to 25 to learn more about glass tile.

Metal tiles are quite expensive per square foot, but adding just a few to an installation of glazed or porcelain tiles can have a big impact. Metal tiles are installed just like standard tiles, and they are available in shapes and thicknesses to work in most layouts. They are available with smooth finishes, polished or unpolished, and with embossed designs. Some metals may weather and discolor with time and exposure to moisture.

Natural stone tile is marble, granite, slate, and other more exotic stones cut very precisely into tiles of various sizes that can be installed just like manufactured tile. Because stone is a natural material, variations in color, texture, and markings must be expected. Manufacturers do offer stone tiles with some added finish. In addition to polished tile, suppliers offer a variety of distressed and textured finishes that can be very attractive as well as slip-resistant. With the exception of granite, natural stone tends to be quite porous and requires periodic sealing to prevent staining. Also, not all types are uniformly abrasion-resistant, so check before making a purchase. Some stone is so soft that it can be very easily scratched by normal use.

Terra-cotta tile evokes images of rustic patios in Mexico or perhaps sunny piazzas on the Mediterranean. These images are quite appropriate because terra-cotta tile originated in these regions. The tile is traditionally made by pressing unrefined clay into molds of various shapes and firing it (terra-cotta literally means "baked earth"). The color of the tile, from brown to red to yellow, is largely a result of the minerals unique to the local soil. Machine-made terra-cotta tile is regular in shape and can be laid like standard tile, but traditional terra-cotta, especially handmade Mexican saltillo tile, has irregularities and uneven shapes and thus requires more care during installation. The variability and rustic character of the tile make up much of its appeal—and terra-cotta can be quite slip-resistant. Unglazed terra-cotta, which is porous and absorbent, should be treated with sealant before being used in wet locations.

Mosaic tiles are ceramic, porcelain, terra-cotta, stone, or other tile cut into small pieces. Individual small tiles are often mounted on a mesh backing so that large squares of many tiles can be installed at once. These squares may be a solid color or contain a pattern or image. Individual mosaic tiles are also available for making custom accents and mosaics. Mosaic tile can be very low maintenance or it can require periodic application of sealant, depending on the material. Mosaic tile is generally quite slip-resistant because of the large number of grout lines in an installation.

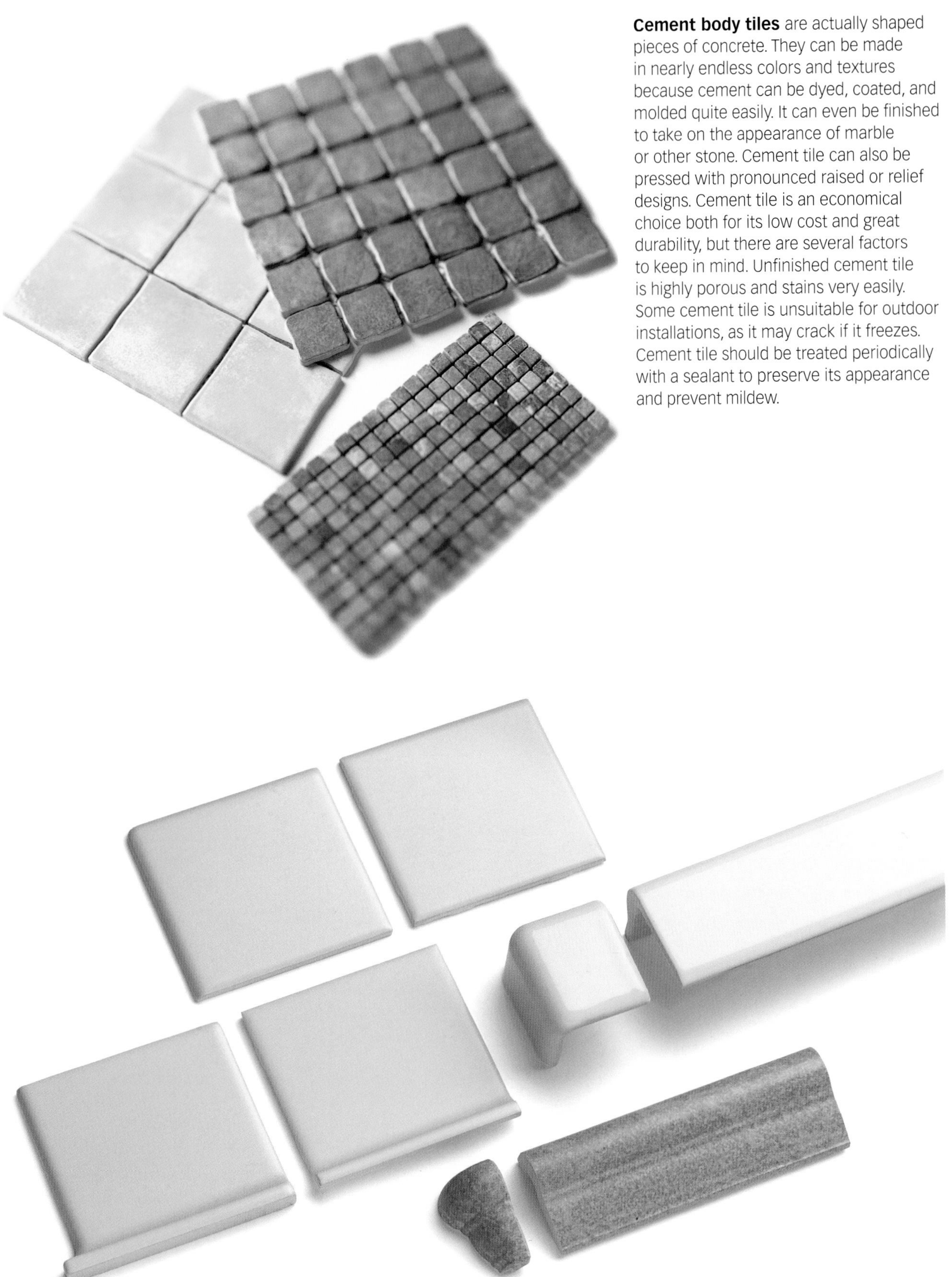

Cement body tiles are actually shaped pieces of concrete. They can be made in nearly endless colors and textures because cement can be dyed, coated, and molded quite easily. It can even be finished to take on the appearance of marble or other stone. Cement tile can also be pressed with pronounced raised or relief designs. Cement tile is an economical choice both for its low cost and great durability, but there are several factors to keep in mind. Unfinished cement tile is highly porous and stains very easily. Some cement tile is unsuitable for outdoor installations, as it may crack if it freezes. Cement tile should be treated periodically with a sealant to preserve its appearance and prevent mildew.

Trim tiles are designed to conceal exposed edges of field tile, especially on wall and counter installations. Bullnose tile is used to finish the edges of partial walls; cove and corner tile shields curves and corners; chair rail tile accents a wall of field tile or functions as an accent around edges. When planning a wall project, investigate available trim as part of the planning process.

Buying Tile & Tiling Materials

Before you can select or purchase materials, you'll need to figure out exactly what you need and how much. Start by drawing a room layout, a reference for you and for anyone advising you about the project.

To estimate the amount of tile you need for a floor project, calculate the square footage of the room and add five percent for waste. For example, in a 10-foot × 12-foot room, the total area is 120 square feet. Add five percent, six square feet, for breakage and other waste. You'll need to purchase enough tile to cover 126 square feet.

Tile cartons generally indicate the number of square feet one carton will cover. Divide the square footage to be covered by the square footage contained in a carton in order to determine the number of cartons required for your floor project. For example, if a carton holds 10 square feet, you will need 13 cartons to cover the 10 × 12 floor in our example.

Estimating tile for a wall project is slightly more complex. Start by deciding how much of each wall will be tiled. In a shower, plan to tile to at least six inches above the showerhead. It's common for tile to extend four feet up the remaining bathroom walls, although it's possible and sometimes very attractive for full walls to be tiled.

To calculate the amount of field tile required, measure each wall and multiply the width times the height of the area to be covered. Subtract the square footage of doors and windows. Do this for each wall, then add all the figures together to calculate the total square footage. Add five percent for waste. Calculate the number of cartons necessary (square footage of the project divided by the square footage contained in a carton).

Trim for floors and walls is sold by the lineal foot. Measure the lineal footage and calculate based on that. Plan carefully—the cost of trim tile adds up quickly. See page 21 for further information on trim types and styles.

Before buying the tiles, ask about your dealer's return policy. Most dealers allow you to return unused tiles for a refund. In any case, think of it this way: buying a few too many tiles is a small problem. Running out of tiles before the job's done could turn into disaster if you can no longer get the tile or the colors don't match.

A specialty tile shop or a larger home center will carry all or most of the materials you'll need for your tiling project. It's always a good idea to bring a few samples home to compare them and see how the color and scale work in the actual room in which they'll be installed.

ESTIMATING TILE NEEDS EXAMPLE

Wall 1:	8 × 8 ft.	64.00 sq. ft.
	– door 2.5 × 6.5	16.25 sq. ft.
	=	47.75 sq. ft.
+ Wall 2:	8 × 10 ft.	80.00 sq. ft.
+ Wall 3:	8 × 8 ft.	64.00 sq. ft.
	– window 2 × 4 ft.	8.00 sq. ft.
	=	56.00 sq. ft.
+ Wall 4:	4 × 10 ft.	40.00 sq. ft.
	Total wall coverage	223.75 sq. ft.
	+ 5% waste	11.18 sq. ft.
	New total tile needs	235.00 sq. ft.
	÷ Amount of tile per carton (carton sizes vary)	10 sq. ft.
	= Number of cartons needed	24 cartons

Suggestions for Buying Tile

Use your room drawing to identify all the types of trim that will be necessary (above). Evaluate the trim available for the various tiles you're considering and select a combination that meets the specifications of your project.

Buy all necessary tile, tools, and materials before you begin to avoid wasted trips and to make sure all the elements are appropriate for one another and the project.

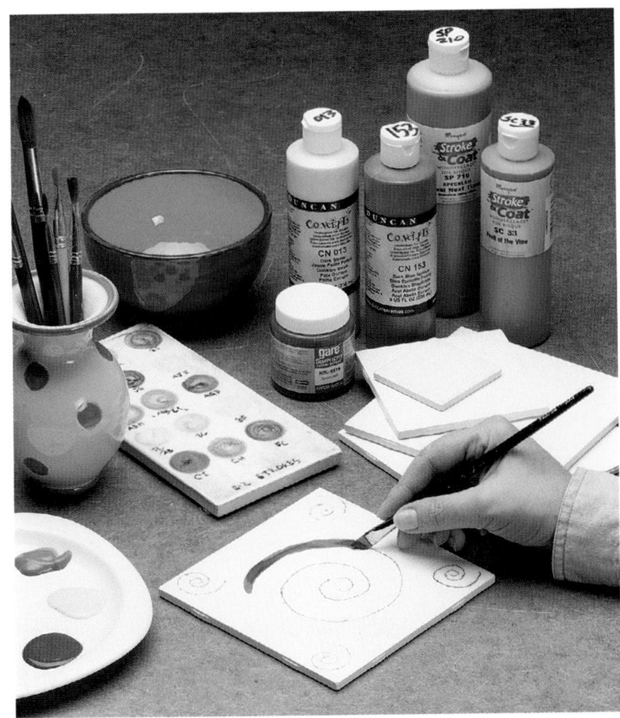

You can design and paint your own custom tiles at many specialty ceramic stores. Order tile of the right size, bisque-fired but not glazed. You can then paint or stencil designs on the tile and have them fired.

Mix tile from carton to carton. Slight variations in color won't be as noticeable mixed throughout the project as they would be if the color shifts from one area to another.

Glass Tile ▸

Largely lost in the bounty of ceramic and stone choices, glass tile deserves serious consideration for the dynamic impact it can make in a kitchen or bathroom. Boasting elegant, jewel-like colors, this type of tile can create a truly unique and stunning floor.

The secret of glass tile's attraction is the color. Pigment is added during the actual production of the glass, meaning that the color is inherent in the material—it won't fade, wear off, or otherwise change. Of course, as durable as the color is, the glass surface itself can be chipped. Still, the thickness of the tiles themselves ensures that they won't crack under normal wear.

Installing glass tiles is just slightly more challenging than laying a floor of stone or ceramic tile. The goal is to create a bright white background against which the color of the tile will pop. To this end, some manufacturers back their glass with a white base. All specify the use of a white crack suppression membrane under the tile and bright white thinset mortar to bed the tiles. Glass tiles are cut on a wet saw just like many stone tiles, but the saw must be equipped with a diamond blade made for cutting glass. The finished floor is grouted in the same way that a ceramic tile floor would be.

The white subsurface and backing give glass tile floors an almost luminous quality, as if the floor were lit from within. It's a clean, sophisticated, modern look that calls attention to itself. This type of floor is therefore best suited to simple, uncluttered, and largely monochromatic color schemes that won't compete with the bright hues of the floor. But used in the right space, glass floor tiles offer a design element that is a feast for the eyes.

Relatively plain ceramic floor tiles take on new life when framed with a border of glass tiles. Here, the glass tile border also makes a stunning transition from the ceramic tile floor to a carpeted area.

Hexagonal glass mosaic tiles hearken back the Art Deco era of the early- to mid-Twentieth Century, but the texture, the luminescence, and the contemporary wasabi color clearly identify this as a modern floor. The floor pairs beautifully with the reproduction vitreous china lavatory with its round steel legs. Accent tiles in a floral display create a highlight near the door.

The glass wall tile is definitely the star of this bathroom, but the effect succeeds largely because of the rustic slate tile floor. Not infrequently, mosaic glass tile is carried through to the floor as well. This can be effective, but if not handled with some design skill it can quickly become dizzying.

Glass tiles come in unlimited color options. Choosing a few and blending them together adds a lot of visual interest to the floor and creates opportunities to pull out color from neighboring surfaces, fixtures, and decorative elements. Because glass tile is installed on a white substrate, even very muted colors read instantly; this allows you to mix and match with much less risk than if the colors were bolder.

Custom glass tile designs make a bold statement. This sophisticated arrangement of hexagons, squares, and triangles is created in mosaic sheets at the tile manufacturing facility. Creating your own unique design and color scheme is great fun, but it does add considerably to the cost.

Cutting Tile

Careful planning will help you eliminate unnecessary cuts, but most tile jobs require cutting at least a few tiles and some jobs require cutting a large number of tiles, no matter how carefully you plan. For a few straight cuts on light- to medium-weight tile, use a snap cutter. If you're working with heavy tile or a large number of cuts on any kind of tile, a wet saw greatly simplifies the job. When using a wet saw, wear safety glasses and hearing protection. Make sure the blade is in good condition and the water container is full. Never use the saw without water, even for a few seconds.

Other cutting tools include nippers, hand-held tile cutters, and rod saws. Nippers can be used on most types of tile, but a rod saw is most effective with wall tile, which is generally fairly soft.

A note of caution: hand-held tile cutters and tile nippers can create razor-sharp edges. Handle freshly cut tile carefully, and immediately round over the edges with a tile stone.

Before beginning a project, practice making straight and curved cuts on scrap tile.

How to Use a Snap Cutter

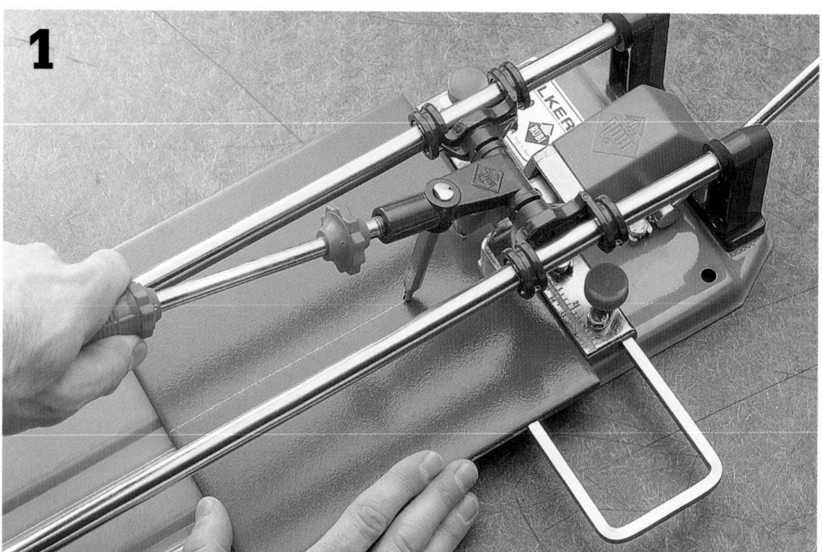

Mark a cutting line on the tile with a pencil, then place the tile in the cutter so the cutting wheel is directly over the line. While pressing down firmly on the wheel handle, run the wheel across the tile to score the surface. For a clean cut, score the tile only once.

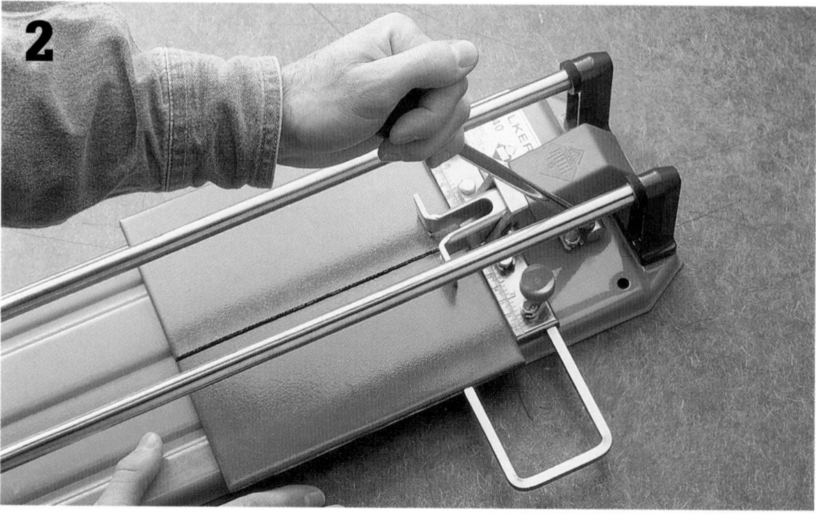

Snap the tile along the scored line, as directed by the tool manufacturer. Usually, snapping the tile is accomplished by depressing a lever on the tile cutter.

How to Use a Wet Saw

Individual saws vary, so read the manufacturer's directions for use and make sure you understand them. Refer any questions to the rental center. Wear safety glasses and hearing protection; make sure water is reaching the blade at all times.

Place the tile on the sliding table and lock the fence to hold the tile in place, then press down on the tile as you slide it past the blade.

How to Mark Square Notches

Place the tile to be notched over the last full tile on one side of the corner. Set another full tile against the ½" spacer along the wall and trace along the opposite edge onto the second tile.

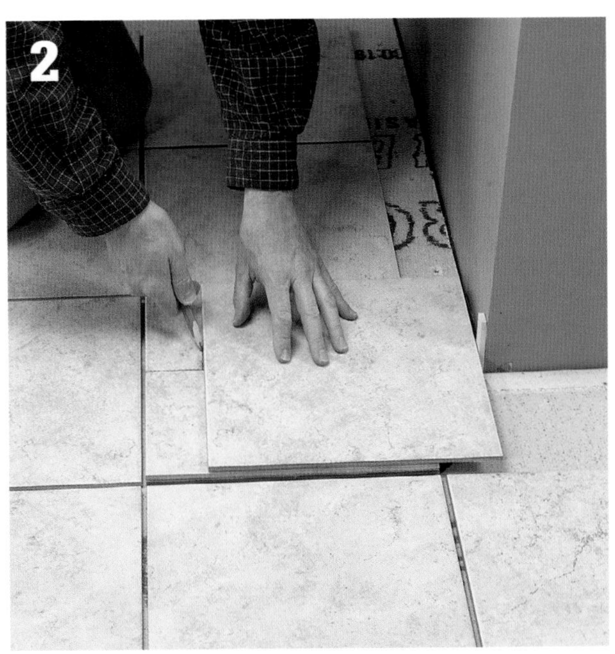

Move the top two tiles and spacer to the adjoining wall, making sure not to turn the tile that is being marked. Make a second mark on the tile as in step 1. Cut the tile and install.

How to Cut Square Notches

Cut along the marked line on one side of the notch. Turn the tile and cut along the other line to complete the notch. To keep the tile from breaking before you're through, slow down as you get close to the intersection with the first cut.

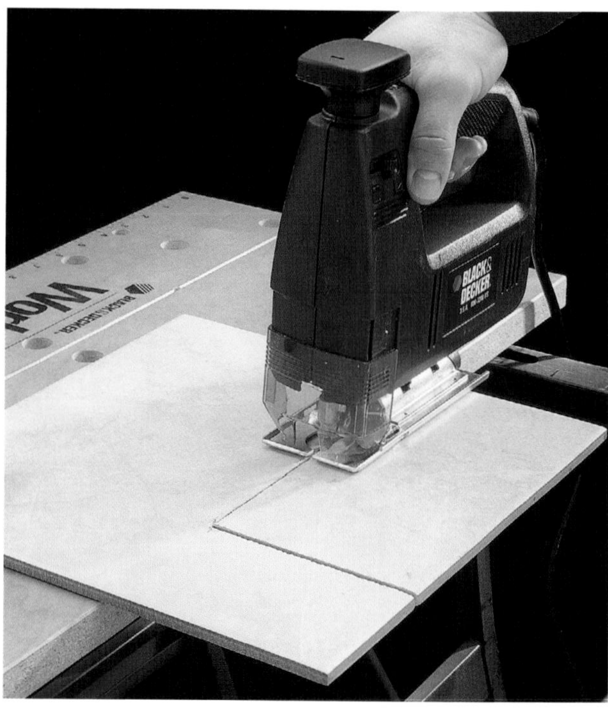

To cut square notches in a small number of wall tiles, clamp the tile down on a worktable, then use a jigsaw with a tungsten carbide blade to make the cuts. If you need to notch quite a few tiles, a wet saw is more efficient.

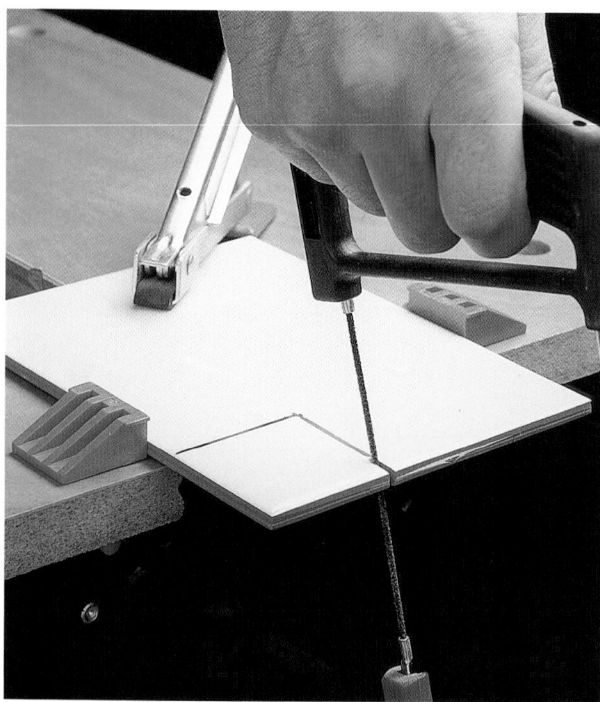

To make a small number of cuts in wall tile, you can use a rod saw. Fit a tungsten carbide rod saw into a hacksaw body. Firmly support the tile and use a sawing motion to cut the tile.

To make a very small notch, use tile nippers. Score the lines and then nibble up to the lines, biting very small pieces at a time.

How to Mark & Cut Irregular Notches

Make a paper template of the contour or use a contour gauge. To use a contour gauge, press the gauge onto the profile and trace it onto the tile.

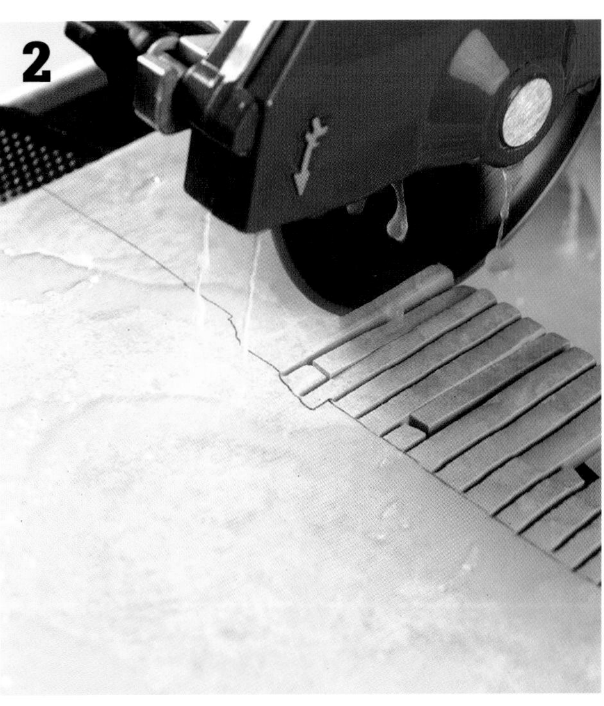

Use a wet saw to make a series of closely spaced, parallel cuts, then nip away the waste.

How to Cut Tile with Tile Nippers

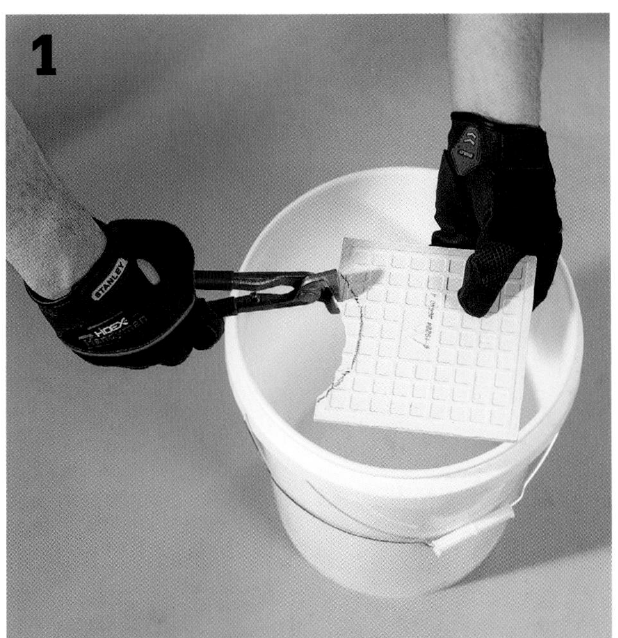

Tile nippers have sharp carbide tipped jaws that are used to firmly grip the leading edge of a tile and snap off small fragments of unwanted material. They are primarily used to make irregular cuts in tile.

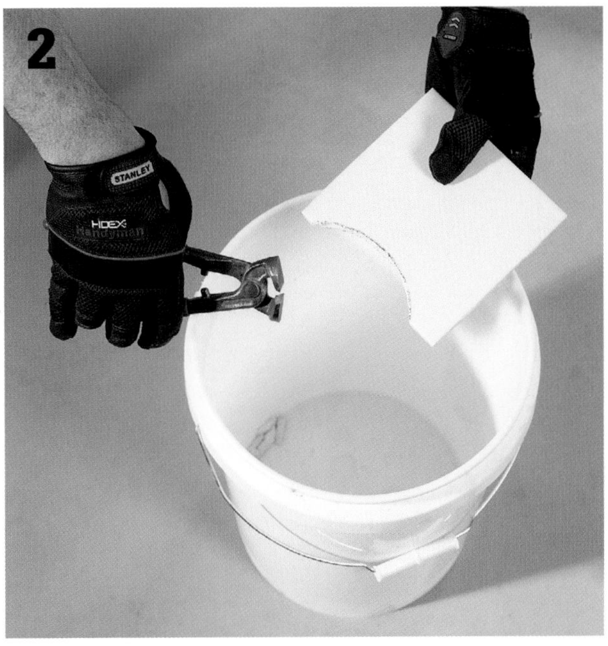

To avoid breaking the tile, use the tile nippers to take very small bites out of the cut. Afterwards, use a rubbing stone to smooth the sharp edges of exposed cuts.

How to Mark Tile for Cutting Holes

Align the tile to be cut with the last full row of tile and butt it against the pipe. Mark the center of the pipe onto the front edge of the tile.

Place a ¼" spacer against the wall and butt the tile against it. Mark the pipe center on the side edge of the tile. Using a combination square, draw a line through each mark to the edges of the tile.

Starting from the intersection of the lines at the center, draw a circle slightly larger than the pipe or protrusion.

Cutting Mosaic Tile ▸

Score cuts on mosaic tiles with a tile cutter in the row where the cut will occur. Cut away excess strips of mosaics from the sheet, using a utility knife, then use a handheld tile cutter to snap tiles one at a time. *Note: Use tile nippers to cut narrow portions of tiles after scoring.*

Options for Cutting Holes in Tile

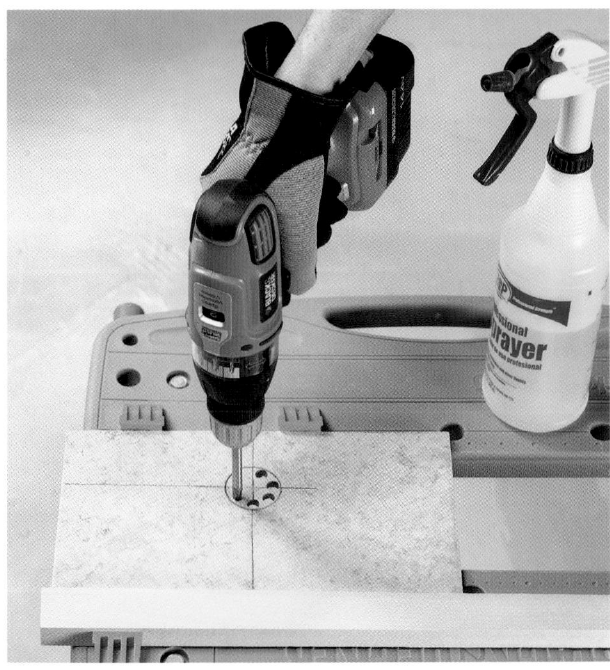

Drill around the edges of the hole using a ceramic tile bit. Gently knock out the waste material with a hammer. The rough edges of the hole will be covered by a protective plate (called an escutcheon).

Variation: Score and cut the tile so the hole is divided in half, using the straight-cut method, then use the curved-cut method to remove waste material from each half of the circle.

How to Cut a Hole with a Hole Saw

Make a dimple with a center punch to break through the glaze, to keep the drill bit from wandering.

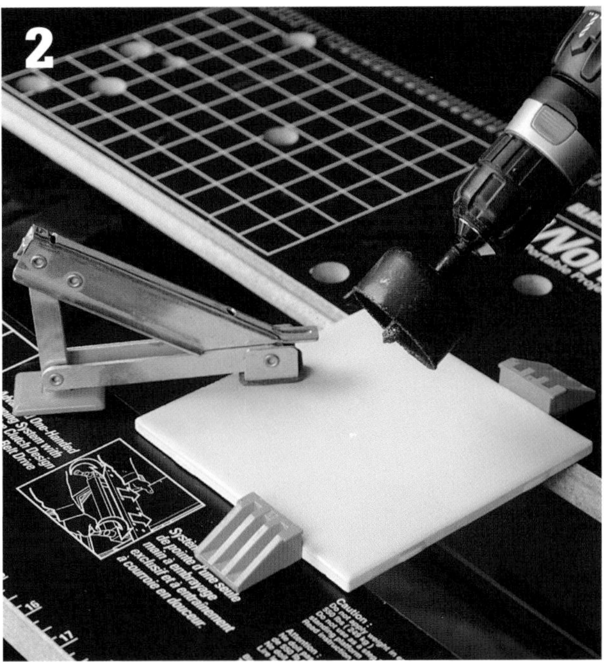

Select a tungsten carbide hole saw in the appropriate size and attach it to a power drill. Place the tip at the marked center and drill the hole.

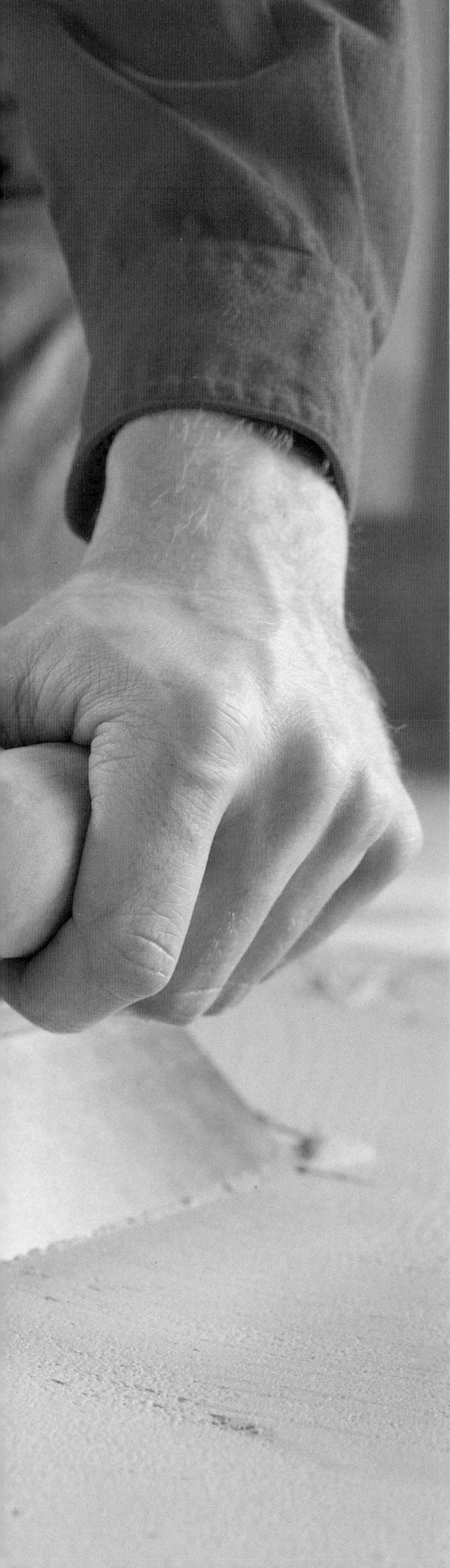

Materials & Tools

This chapter describes and illustrates the tools and materials necessary for the tile projects presented throughout the book. Most homeowners, especially those who enjoy do-it-yourself projects, already own many of the tools and materials necessary for tile projects. From the saws and flat bars necessary for removing old surfaces to the drills and utility knives handy for repairing and installing substrates, many are basic components of a standard toolkit. Others, such as a snap cutter, are not common, but neither are they expensive or difficult to use.

There are a few less common and more expensive tools that, while not strictly necessary, will simplify large projects to such a degree that you may want to add them to your arsenal. A wet saw, for example, cuts even heavy tile easily and simplifies tricky cuts. For small projects you may want to rent a tile saw; for large projects you may want to purchase the saw.

Materials for tile projects range from cementboard to cork, from thinset mastic to grout. These materials are widely available and reasonably priced. The important issue is matching the product to the project. This chapter will help you do exactly that.

In this chapter:

Safety

Working safely includes such obvious but important factors as wearing the right protective gear and staying alert. But it also means taking the time to think about what you're doing. Most people have watched a home improvement show on the topic of renovation and the first tool to be put into use is a sledge hammer, swung haphazardly into the nearest available wall. A competent renovator would not begin a demolition in this fashion. What if there had been a gas line, electrical junction box, or water pipe behind that wall? The consequences of such impetuous actions could be quite costly, if not deadly.

Before attempting to open up any wall or floor for repairs, visually inspect all sides of the structure you will be working on. Check for evidence of plumbing, electrical wiring, phone lines, gas lines, or anything else that may look out of place. Make a note of any locations you find and exercise care when working around them.

If the project requires you to work around exposed electrical wiring, turn the power off at the main breaker box and verify it is off by using a circuit tester or voltage meter to individually test each outlet. Turn the water off before working around plumbing pipes but remember to turn it back on later to check for leaks before the work is covered back up.

More importantly, invest in high quality safety gear. Remodeling is a very dusty job, so protect your lungs by wearing a NIOSH approved respirator rated type N-95 or higher when working around fine particles such as airborne dust from cut tiles. Keep the work area well ventilated. A pair of heavy-duty work gloves is essential for protecting your hands while carrying heavy materials and jagged work debris. Take extra care when handling broken shards of tile. Latex gloves will protect your hands from the high-alkalinity and abrasiveness of wet cementitious mortar. Safety glasses will protect your eyes from the dust and shards of tile. You will be spending a fair amount of time crawling around on your knees, often over a fair amount of sharp rubble, so pick out a pair of comfortable knee pads and wear them.

As a rule, take your time and keep your work area clean and uncluttered. Whenever possible, divide each task into portions you can easily manage within a short time frame. Your confidence to take on bigger projects will grow as you gain experience, as will the quality of your work.

Basic safety equipment for use when working with tile includes: Ear protection to be worn when operating power tools (A); knee pads for comfort (B); safety goggles (C) or glasses (D); a NIOSH N-95 rated particle mask (E) or respirator to be worn when cutting tiles with a tile saw; work gloves for handling materials and working with sharp objects (F); rubber gloves (G) or latex gloves (H) to be worn when handling cementitious products such as thinset mortar.

First Aid Kits ▸

Assemble a first aid kit. Cuts from a hand or power tool can be serious and require prompt and thoughtful attention. Be prepared for such situations with a well-equipped first aid kit that is easy to find. Record any emergency telephone numbers on the first aid kit or by the nearest phone so they are available in an emergency.

Equip your kit with a variety of items, including bandages, needles, tweezers, antiseptic ointment, cotton swabs, cotton balls, eye drops, a first aid handbook, a chemical-filled cold pack, elastic bandages, first aid tape, and sterile gauze.

For puncture wounds, cuts, burns, and other serious injuries, always seek medical attention as soon as first aid—such as washing and wrapping of cuts—has been provided.

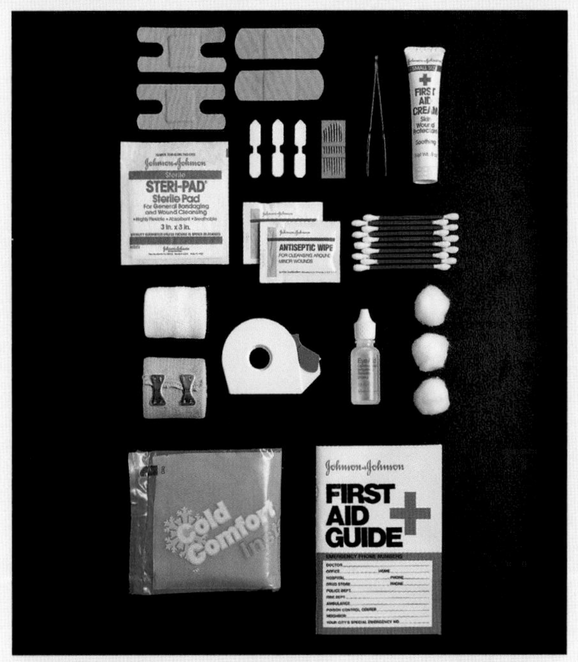

Always keep a well-equipped first aid kit close at hand when doing any home improvement work.

Working Safely

Keep your tools sharp and clean. Accidents are more likely to occur when blades are dull and tools are filled with sawdust and dirt.

Use a GFCI receptacle, adapter, or extension cord to reduce the risk of shock while operating a power tool outdoors or in wet conditions.

Check outlets with a circuit tester to make sure the power is off before removing cover plates, exposing wires, or drilling or cutting into walls that contain wiring.

Materials: Levelers & Resurfacers

Self-leveling underlayment, otherwise referred to as self-leveling cement, is applied over uneven surfaces, such as cementitious backers and concrete slabs, to make them level prior to tile application. A similar product called concrete resurfacer accomplishes essentially the same thing. Levelers and resurfacer have fairly liquid viscosities. They are poured onto uneven surfaces, where gravity directs them to fill in the low areas of a subfloor. One 50-pound bag of floor leveler will typically cover a surface area of approximately 50 square feet, at ⅛-inch thick. Leveler can be applied in layers as thin as a feather edge and as thick as one inch, depending on the specific product you buy. Self-leveling underlayment cures very quickly, usually within a few hours of application. In some cases, multiple applications are required to build up to the desired thickness.

A coat of paint-like primer should be applied prior to the leveler in almost all cases. This is usually rolled onto the substrate using a short-nap roller. The primer seals the substrate, which helps keep it from absorbing the moisture in the cement mixture too rapidly. It also improves the adhesive bond between the self-leveling cement and the surface it is applied to.

The leveler compound is best mixed using a ½-inch corded drill fitted with a mixing paddle. A garden rake and a trowel will also be necessary to spread the batch over the area in need of repair.

Cement-based tile products such as this floor leveler must be mixed well with water. A ½" power drill with a mixing paddle attachment is a great help in this regard.

Floor levelers and resurfacers are applied prior to installing tile backer to address dips, valleys, and other uneven areas in a concrete floor. An acrylic or latex fortifier helps the product flow more smoothly and gives it some extra flex, without sacrificing hardness.

How to Apply Leveler

Patch any major cracks or large popouts with concrete patching compound before you apply the leveler. Once the patch dries, wash and rinse the floor according to the instructions on the leveler package. This may include the use of grease cutters and pressure washers.

Apply an even layer of concrete primer to the entire surface using a long-nap paint roller. Let the primer dry completely.

Following the manufacturer's instructions, mix the floor leveler with water. The batch should be large enough to cover the entire floor area to the desired thickness (up to 1"). Pour the leveler over the floor.

Distribute the leveler evenly, using a rake or spreader. Work quickly: the leveler begins to harden in 15 min. Use a trowel to feather the edges and create a smooth transition with an uncovered area. Let the leveler dry for 24 hrs.

Materials: Tile Backer

Tile backer is any approved sheet panel that is installed on subfloor, countertop, or wall surface to serve as underlayment for the installation of tiles. Most commonly today, that means cementboard. Cementboard was invented in the early 1960s by Paul Dinkel, a tile contractor determined to develop a tile substrate to replace drywall, which is prone to deterioration in wet areas. His solution was a thin, precast, strong concrete-base panel that has come to be known as cementboard.

The projects in this book employ cement and fiber/cement backer boards. They are commonly sold in three-by-five-foot panels in thickness of ½-inch or ¼-inch. For walls, ½-inch-thick backer board is installed over wall studs spaced 16 inches on center. For horizontal applications (floors, countertops, and tub decks), either ¼- or ½-inch-thick cementboard may be used. For floors, the joists should be spaced 16 inches on center and there should be a subbase of ¾-inch thick sheathing. Unless otherwise allowed by the manufacturer, use ½-inch-thick cementboard for all other applications.

On horizontal surfaces, the backer board panel may be laminated to the subbase using a dry-set or modified thinset mortar bed and then fastened with screws or nails. This setting bed is required by some local codes, but may not be required in your area. It is a good idea regardless, as it eliminates voids under the panels and provides a dimensionally stable surface for the application of tile. This greatly reduces tile cracking.

Tile backer board is designed to retain its rigidity when damp—whether the dampness is from the thinset mortar during the application or the conditions of the room. Cement or fiber/cement base backer (cementboard) is made in ¼ and ½" thicknesses. Other fiberglass-base tile backers are lighter than cementboard and some installers find them easier to work with.

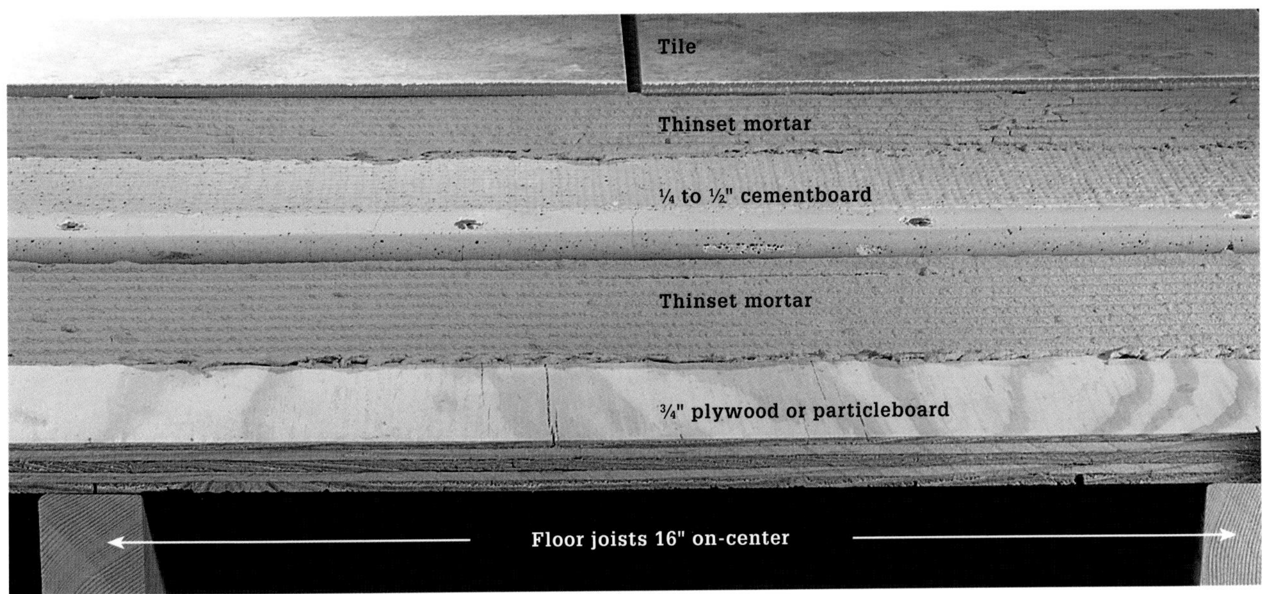

A typical tile floor has floor joists spaced 16" on center, topped with a subbase of ¾" plywood or particleboard sheathing. A layer of cementboard (you may use ¼ or ½") is set into a bed of thinset mortar (in most cases) and fastened down with cementboard screws. The tile flooring is laid into another bed of thinset on top of the cementboard.

Proper fastener selection is critical for the long-term success of any backer board installation. Use 1¼-inch, corrosion-resistant backer board screws with a minimum of a ⅜-inch diameter head. A full-sized backer board panel installed over a floor or countertop will require up to 60 screws. Wall applications will require up to 30 screws per panel, and ceiling applications will require up to 42 screws per panel.

Alkaline resistant, two-inch-wide fiberglass mesh tape is used in conjunction with a modified thinset mortar to reinforce the adjoining edges between backer board panels. Fiberglass tapes that are not alkaline resistant will degrade over time, become brittle, and lose their reinforcing strength.

Cementboard screws are specially designed to penetrate the cementitious material without cracking it.

Cementboard mesh tape is used to cover and reinforce the seams between cementboard panels. Don't use regular mesh tapes for this job: they are not alkali-resistant and will degrade.

Cutting Cementboard

Even though cementboard is a rigid material that breaks or crushes fairly easily, with the right tools, it can be cut to fit with little difficulty. The most low-tech way to make straight cuts in cementboard is to use a carbide scoring knife for cutting shallow guidelines in the panel, which can then be snapped and broken accurately. With practice and patience, L-cuts and cutouts are also possible using this tool. This method generates no dust.

Carbide and diamond-tipped hole saws are useful for boring smaller diameter holes in tile and cementboard in order to accommodate items such as water pipe and valve protrusions. Spraying the bit with water while you are drilling will help to reduce dust and lubricate the cutting edge of the bit.

A jigsaw fitted with a carbide tungsten grit blade is a versatile power tool capable of making curved and straight cuts in cementboard. Purchase some extra blades though, as they tend to wear out quickly.

A rotary tool fitted with a tile-cutting bit is useful for making round cutouts for toilet flanges. These saws are often supplied with a circular cutting guide for making custom-sized radial cuts. With a little practice, a rotary tool (also called a spiral-cutting tool) can be used to make L-cuts and rectangular cutouts for electrical boxes. The tile cutting bits are prone to breakage due to heat and the high torque generated by the saw, so set it to a low working speed and periodically lubricate the bits with all-purpose oil.

An angle grinder fitted with a four-inch dry-cutting diamond blade is an all purpose tile saw useful for making a wide range of linear cuts in tile and backer board, including square cutouts for water valves and electrical boxes.

Although the blade is too large to make small cutouts, circular saws fitted with a carbide tipped fiber cement blade are useful for making linear cuts in backer board panels.

Safety Tip ▸

Dry-cutting tile or cementboard with any power tool will produce harmful silica dust. Wear a respirator and safety glasses while cutting and make tile and cementboard cuts outdoors in a well-ventilated area whenever possible. A fan is recommended to provide additional ventilation and to help blow dust away from the workspace.

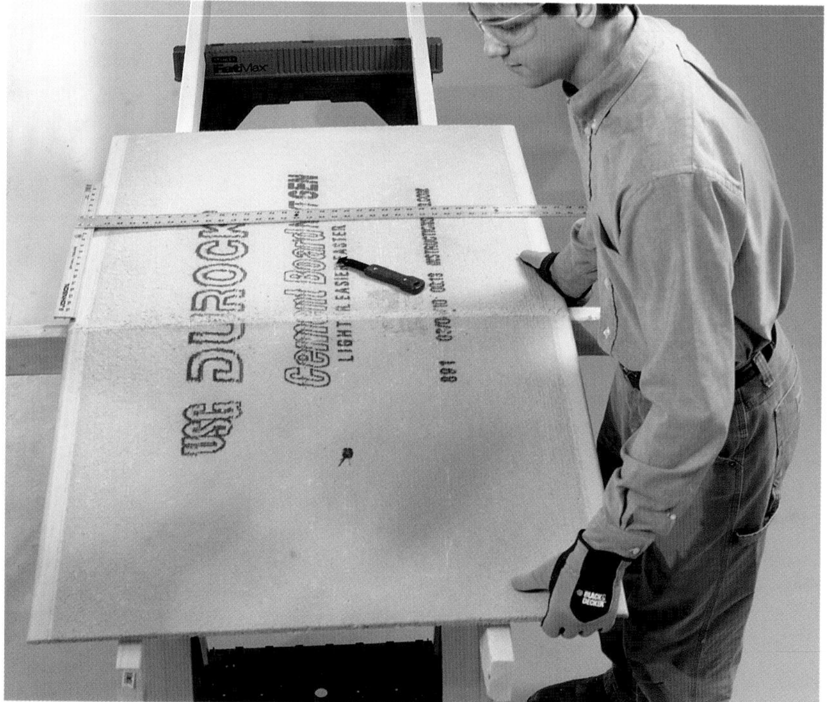

To score and snap cementboard using a scoring tool, measure and mark the rough side of the cement board to the desired size. Using a straightedge as a guide, score the board with a carbide scoring tool, then snap the panel evenly along the scored line. Score the panel deep enough to penetrate the glass-fiber mesh layer just below the surface of the cement board.

Tools for Cutting Cementboard

Angle grinder. Snap reference lines using chalkline and cut along the line with an electric angle grinder equipped with a diamond blade. Use this tool only in a well-ventilated area and be sure to wear full safety protection.

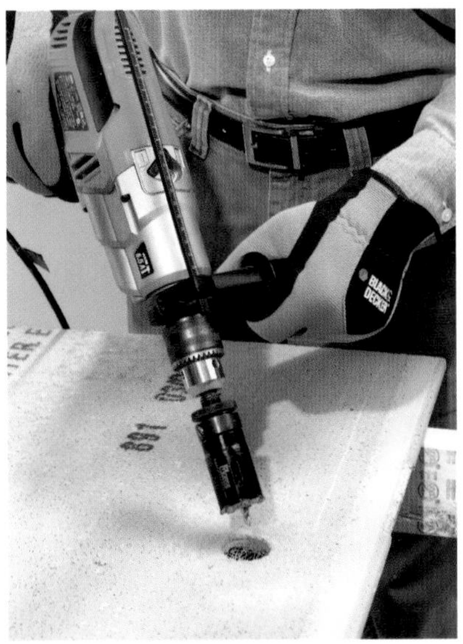

Hole saw. To make round and curved cutouts in cementboard, try using a power drill fitted with a carbide or diamond-tipped hole saw. Mark the centerpoint of the cut on the panel and bore the hole at low speed. To improve performance, use a spray bottle filled with water to periodically moisten the cutting edge of the bit.

Rotary tool/spiral cutting saw. To make round cuts in cementboard using a rotary saw fitted with a tile cutting bit, adjust the circle cutter guide to the desired hole size and drill a pilot hole in the center point and perimeter of the desired cut. Insert the pivot foot of the guide and the bit into the pilot holes and complete the cut.

Scoring tool. To make L-cuts in cementboard with a carbide scoring tool, mark the outline of the cut on both sides of the panel. Using a straightedge as a guide, score both sides of the panel and punch the waste material out from the back side of the panel using a hammer.

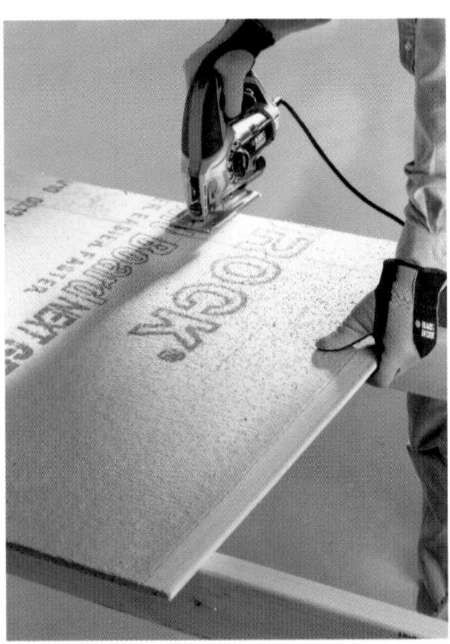

Jigsaw for straight cuts. To make L-cuts in cementboard with a jigsaw, mark the outline of the desired cut on the panel with a pencil. Fit the jigsaw with an abrasive blade and cut out and remove the waste material.

Jigsaw for rounds cuts. To make round cuts in cementboard using a jigsaw fitted with a carbide grit blade, mark the center point of the cut on the panel and drill a starter hole. Insert the jigsaw blade into the pilot hole and complete the cut.

Materials: Tile Membranes

Tile membranes are thin, flexible tile underlayment materials designed to isolate tile installations from problematic substrates, provide for sound abatement, or waterproof and vapor-proof tile installations in wet areas and steam rooms. There are dozens of different types of tile membranes on the market. Please refer to the manufacturer for specific information pertaining to the limitations, benefits, and installation of the membrane selected.

Waterproofing membranes are installed in wet areas and are designed to prevent the migration of water beyond the membrane. They often provide additional benefits, including crack suppression. Tile installed in steam rooms, wet saunas, and steam showers requires the installation of a membrane that is both vapor-proof and waterproof.

Sound isolation membranes are designed to reduce the transmission of impact sounds from hard surface flooring to lower level living spaces. This type of membrane is usually installed in apartment dwellings and condominiums (and behind drywall in home theaters).

Crack isolation and anti-fracture membranes, also called crack suppression membranes, isolate tile installations from tile substrates that are susceptible to stresses that produce horizontal movement. They can absorb movement of as much as $\frac{1}{8}$-inch to $\frac{3}{8}$-inch. Some membranes are liquid applied to the substrate with a trowel or roller, others are sheet applied. There are even anti-fracture thinset mortars, eliminating the need in some cases, for a separate sheet or liquid applied membrane.

Uncoupling membranes isolate the finished tile installation from the substrate while allowing both to move independently. This type of membrane is typically installed over problematic sub-floors and newly installed or problematic concrete slabs.

Note: Crack suppression and uncoupling membranes are not intended to be a substitution for sound building practices. Tile installations that exceed structural recommendations may see little benefit with the installation of these types of products. Likewise, marginal installations will benefit more from structural reinforcement or repairs. Whenever possible, reinforce weak wall framing and floor joists with wood blocking and install an additional layer of plywood over wood sub-floors if needed.

Membranes used for laying tile include: Roll-on waterproofing and crack prevention membrane (A); multi-purpose membrane for uncoupling, waterproofing and vapor management (B); 40-mil thick PVC shower pan liner (C); 40-mil thick ($\frac{1}{16}$") self-bonding membrane designed for use under floor tile requiring protection from structural movement (D); crack prevention mat (E).

Tile Transitions Strips ▸

Available in numerous materials and profiles, transition strips are installed to create a smooth bridge from one floor covering to another. They are typically installed in doorways or in any open area where a newly installed tile floor will abut another floor covering. The type of profile required will depend largely on the floor surfaces being transitioned. Height reducing thresholds, or reducer strips, have a profile with a beveled edge and are used to transition between two floors of differing height. Gradual transition strips have a sloped profile, making them wheelchair friendly. T-molding is used to transition between two floors of even height. Transition strips can often be omitted on transitions between carpet and tile.

Usually found in doorways, transition strips are installed after the tile layout is completed to create a bridge between floor coverings. Individual strips are engineered for specific transitions: for example, ceramic tile to hardwood or tile to carpeting.

Carpet is usually tucked right up to the edge of a tile installation.

Carpet can also be tucked into a threshold, as shown here.

T-molding is used to transition between two floors of even height.

Transition strips with an edge profile do not have a height adjusting profile. They are used to protect the edges of exposed tile.

Height reducing thresholds are used to transition between two floors of differing heights.

To make a room accessible to wheelchair users, use a gradual transition strip with a sloped profile.

Materials: Thinset Mortar

Introduced in the early 1950s, thinset is an adhesive mortar consisting of Portland cement, a water retentive agent, sand or aggregate (optional), and other additives. Prior to thinset, tiles were installed with a thick paste consisting of Portland cement and water. Unless they were soaked in water prior to installation, absorbent tiles would quickly soak up the moisture in the paste and fail to bond to the substrate. Thinset mortar made it possible for installers to install tile over a variety of cementitious substrates without needing to soak the tile beforehand.

Thinset mortars have improved substantially in quality and ease of use over the years. Because no two products are exactly alike, you should always read the package label carefully to make sure the product you select is an appropriate adhesive for the tile and the substrate to which it will be applied.

The adhesive mortars used for the projects in this book include dry-set thinset mortar, polymer-modified thinset mortar, and latex-modified thinset mortar. Modified thinset, the most common adhesive used, is widely employed to adhere a variety of different types of tile to cementboard and concrete substrates. Use gray thinset for darker grout selections and white thinset for lighter grout selections.

Dry-set mortars are mixed with potable water and used as a setting bed to seat backer board panels. In special circumstances, it can also be used as an adhesive to set tile.

Thinset mortar is applied in a thick layer to make a bed for setting tile. It is sold in premixed tubs and in dry powder forms—most professionals prefer to mix their own. If the product you buy has not been modified with polymer additive, you can mix in latex additive yourself. Different thinset mortars have different ratios of additives and fortifiers for specific purposes. You will also find some color variation. Most is cement gray, but white thinset intended for use with glass tile is also available. You can also use white thinset to reduce the chance of color bleedthrough if you are applying a light-colored grout.

Polymer-modified thinset mortar contains dry-polymer additives. It also should be mixed with potable water. Latex-modified thinset is prepared by mixing dry-set thinset mortar with a liquid latex additive. Although more costly and difficult to work with than conventional modified blends, liquid latex modified mortars usually offer higher bond strengths, higher flexural values, and increased water and chemical resistance.

Small quantities of mortar can be mixed by hand to a smooth and creamy consistency using a margin trowel. Larger batches of mortar can be mixed at speeds of less than 300 rpm, using a ½-inch drill fitted with a mixing paddle.

Cementboard setting beds are applied using a ¼-inch square notch trowel. Use a ¼-inch V-notch trowel to install mosaic tiles two inches square or less. Most varieties of larger tile can be installed using a ¼-inch or ⅜-inch square or U-notch trowel. Very large tiles and certain types of stone may require larger trowel sizes.

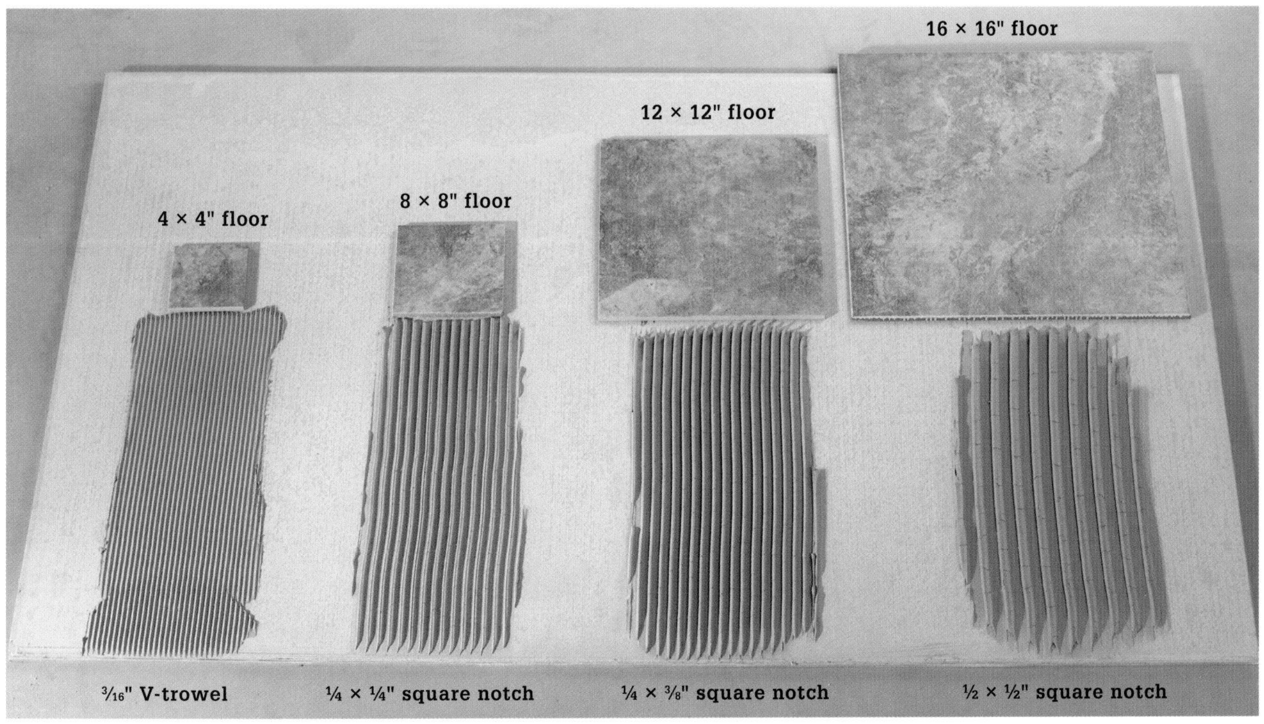

The type of trowel used to apply thinset is dictated mostly by the size of the tile being installed.

Premixed Thinset Mortar ▸

Most professionals prefer to mix their own thinset mortar because it is considerably cheaper than premixed material. But homeowners who are only tiling a small area should consider purchasing tubs of premixed thinset mortar. Not only is it a convenience, you are assured that the material contains an adequate ratio of latex additive and is blended to the proper consistency.

Materials: Grout

Grout (or "grout mortar") is available in dozens of stock colors and can be tinted to an unlimited variety of tones. Beyond color, grout has several other features that differ, making some types more appropriate for various applications than others.

The projects in this book use polymer-modified grout or dry-set grout mixed with a liquid latex additive. Polymer-modified grout contains an additive in dry form that is activated when mixed with water. Latex-modified grout is prepared by mixing a dry-set grout with a liquid latex additive. These additives aid in increasing the water and chemical resistance, bonding, and compressive strength of the grout.

To apply grout to floor or wall tile installations, a rubber grout float is needed, along with a minimum of one or two large grout sponges for every 150 square feet of tile installed. A margin trowel is also useful for spreading grout under kitchen or bathroom cabinet toe kicks and other hard-to-reach areas.

Grouting Tips ▸

- The spacing of the tiles will determine the type of grout to be applied. Unsanded grout is used with grout joints ⅛" wide or narrower. Sanded grout is used for grout joints that will be wider than ⅛".
- Remember to treat any gaps between the tile and walls, tubs, cabinets, and other hard surfaces as expansion joints. Do not apply grout in these areas. Instead, cover them with molding or fill them with a flexible, mildew-resistant silicone, urethane, or latex caulk.

A few days after installation, a water-based silicone grout sealer may be applied to finished grout joints. Keep in mind, these types of sealers will not waterproof the grout. They are designed to be vapor transmissive and allow moisture to evaporate from the surface of the grout joint. Grout sealers do help to prevent some mild blemishing and, at the very least, they allow for a little leeway for cleaning up spills before they have time to permanently stain the grout.

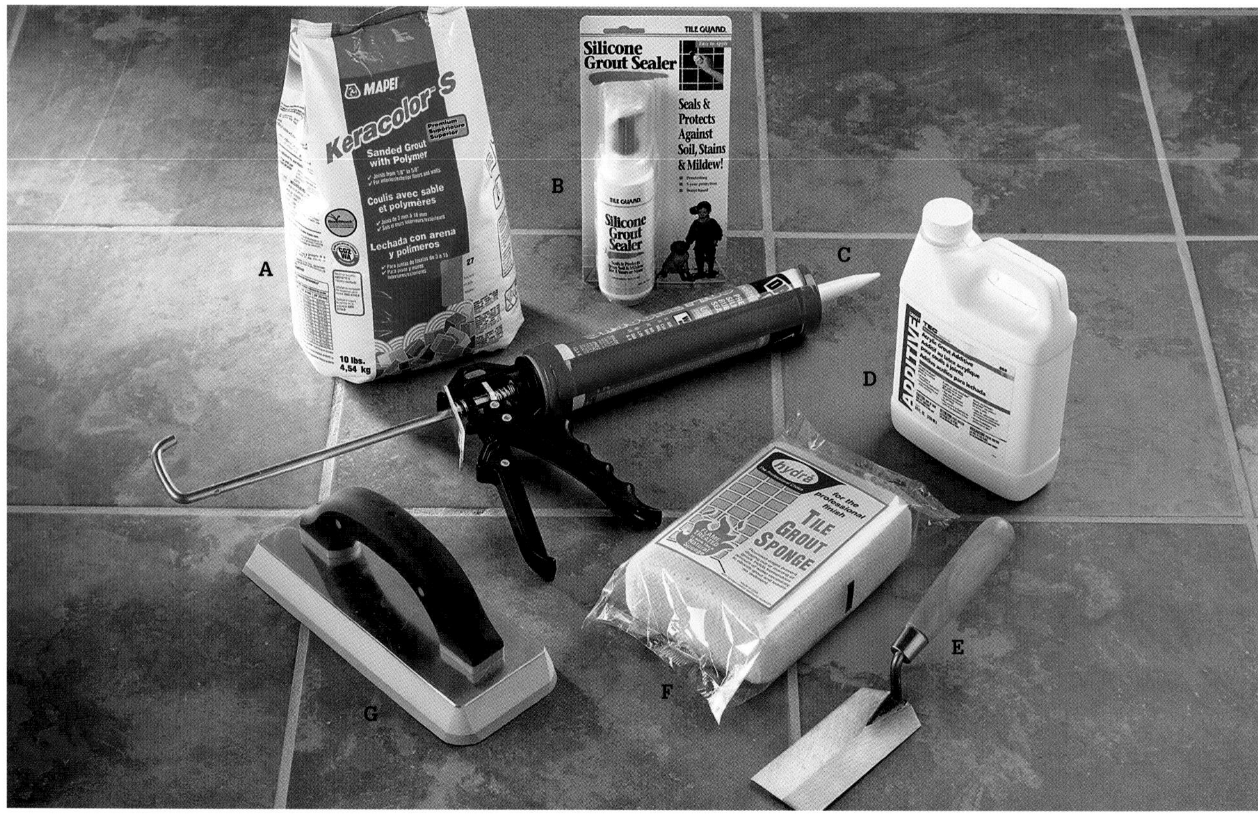

Materials and tools for grouting tile joints include: Dry mix, sanded grout (A); silicone grout sealer (B); tub-and-tile caulk (C); latex grout fortifier (D); margin trowel (E); grout sponge (F); grout float (G).

How to Mix Thinset & Grout

On the back of each bag of thinset mortar or grout you will find instructions detailing the amount of water or liquid additive required, slake time, mixing speeds, and other important guidelines. These recommendations should always be followed carefully. Any variation in the mixing guidelines can create problems, ranging from uneven or washed out grout colors, to weakened mortars that lack compressive strength or fail to adequately bond to tile and substrates.

To mix a full bag of mortar, add one half of the amount of potable water or liquid additive recommended by the manufacturer to a five gallon bucket. Slowly add a half bag of mortar while mixing the water and dry mix together with a ½-inch (chuck capacity) electric drill fitted with a mixing paddle. Keep the paddle turning at a low rate. Repeat the process, mixing the entire batch thoroughly and uniformly for several minutes to a smooth, paste-like consistency.

If recommended by the manufacturer, allow the batch to slake. This is simply a waiting period that allows the dry mortar to more thoroughly absorb the liquid that was added to it. After the batch has slaked for the appropriate amount of time, mix the mortar once more and it will be ready for use.

Stiffened batches of thinset and grout mortars that have become too difficult to work with may be mixed again to loosen them up. However, this should be done without adding additional water or liquid additives.

Options for Mixing Thinset Mortar & Grout

To make a small batch of mortar, add the proper ratio of water or liquid additive and dry powder to a container and stir by hand.

A heavy duty ½" drill fitted with a mixing paddle is useful for mixing large quantities of mortar at one time.

Tools for Removing Old Surfaces

Quality tools remove old surfaces faster and leave surfaces ready to accept new tile. Home centers and hardware stores carry a variety of products for surface removal. Look for tools with smooth, secure handles and correctly weighted heads for safety and comfort.

End-cutting nippers allow you to pull out staples remaining in the floor after carpeting is removed. This plier-like tool can also be used to break an edge on old tile so a chisel or pry bar can be inserted.

Heat guns are used to soften adhesives so vinyl base cove moldings and stubborn tiles can be pryed away from the wall. They are also used to remove old paint, especially when it is heavily layered or badly chipped.

Hand mauls are often used in combination with pry bars and chisels to remove old flooring and prepare surfaces for tile. They are helpful for leveling high spots on concrete floors and separating underlayments and subfloors.

Flat pry bars are used to remove wood base moldings from walls and to separate underlayments and floor coverings from subfloors. This tool is also effective for removing tiles set in mortar.

Chisels come in a variety of sizes for specific jobs. Masonry chisels are used with hand mauls to remove high spots in concrete. Cold chisels are used with hand mauls or hammers to pry tiles from mortar.

Floor scrapers are used to scrape and smooth patched areas on concrete floors, and to pry up flooring, and scrape adhesives and backings from underlayments.

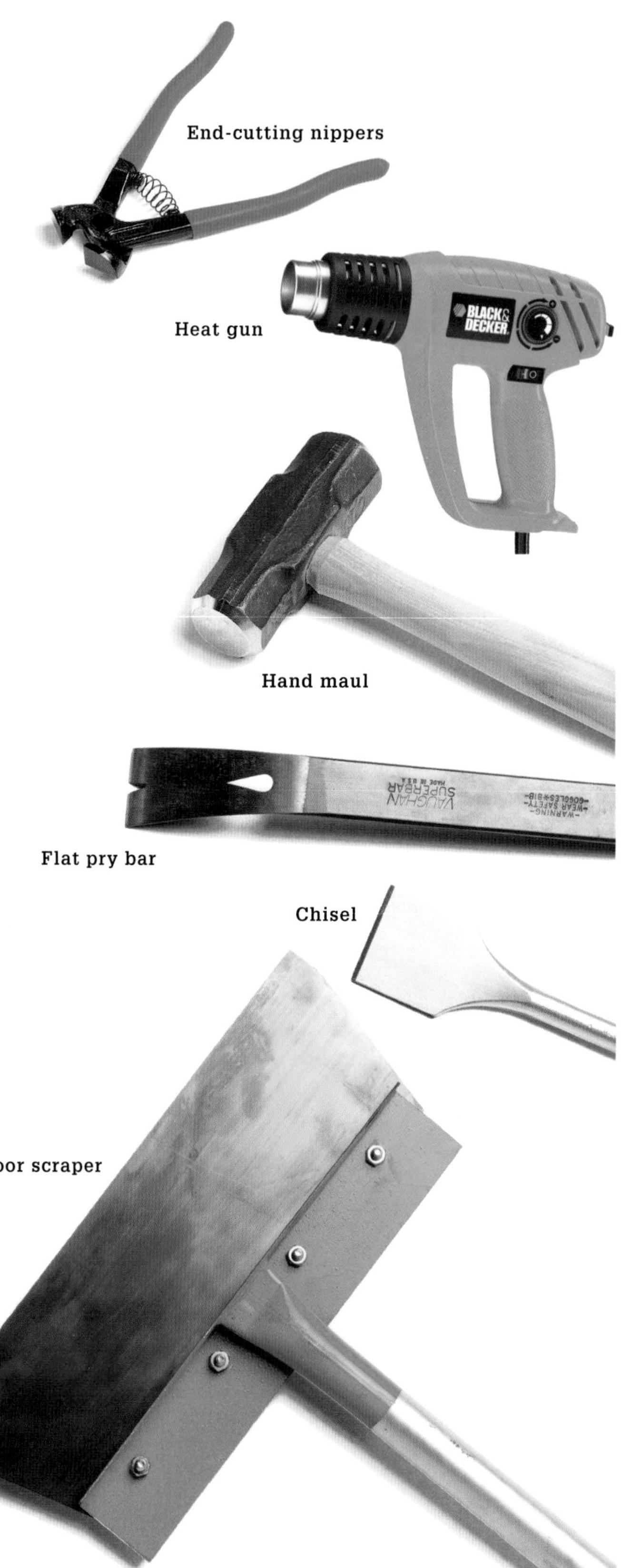

Tools for Repairing Substrates

Surfaces and substrates must be in good condition before new tile can be installed. Use the tools below to create stiff, flat surfaces that help prevent tiles from cracking and enhance the overall appearance of your finished project.

Straightedges are used to mark damaged areas of substrate for removal. They are also used to measure and mark replacement pieces for cutting.

Jigsaws are handy when cutting notches, holes, and irregular shapes in new or existing substrates. They are also used to fit new substrate pieces to existing doorways.

Portable drills secure substrates to subfloors with screws selected for the thickness and type of substrate used.

Circular saws are used to remove damaged sections of subfloor and cut replacement pieces to fit.

Straightedge

Jigsaw

Portable drill

Circular saw

Tools for Installing Substrates

Depending upon your application, you may have to cut and install a substrate of cementboard, plywood, cork, backerboard, greenboard, or moisture membrane. Whichever your tiling project demands, the tools shown here will help you measure, score, cut, and install substrate material with precision.

Drywall squares are used to measure and mark substrates, such as cementboard, fiber-cementboard, and isolation membrane. They can also be used as straightedge guides for scoring and cutting substrates with a utility knife.

Utility knives are usually adequate for scoring straight lines in wallboard, cementboard, fiber-cementboard, and for cutting isolation membrane substrates. However, because cementboard and fiber-cementboard are thick, hard substrates, utility knife blades must be replaced often for best performance.

Cementboard knives are the best choice for scoring cementboard and fiber-cementboard. The blades on these knives are stronger and wear better than utility knife blades when cutting rough surfaces.

Trowels are useful for applying leveler on existing floors and for applying thinset mortar to substrates. Trowels can also be used to scrape away ridges and high spots after levelers or mortars dry.

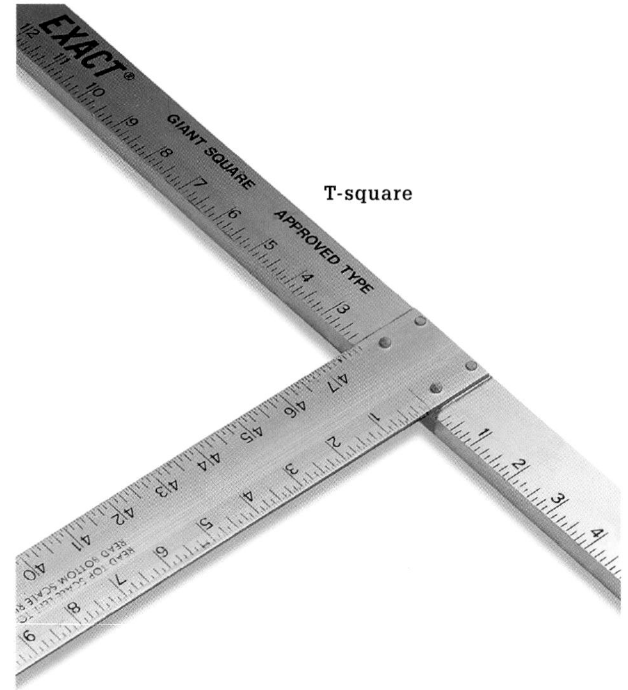

T-square

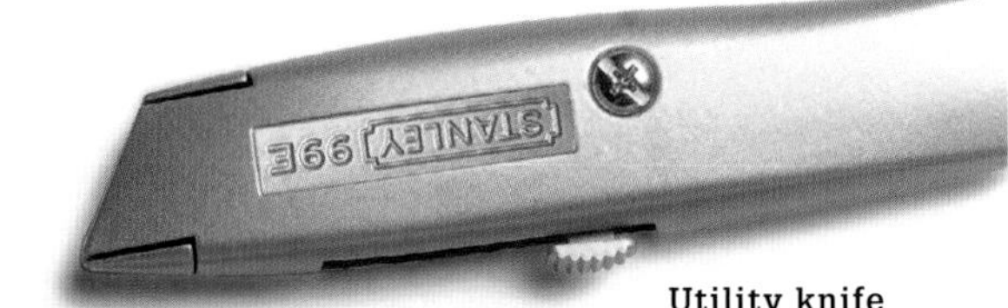

Utility knife

Cementboard knife

Notched trowel

Tools for Layout

Laying tile requires careful planning. Since tile is installed following a grid-pattern layout, marking perpendicular reference lines is essential to proper placement. Use the tools shown here to measure and mark reference lines for any type of tiling project.

Straightedges are handy for marking reference lines on small areas. They can also be used to mark cutting lines for partial tiles.

Levels are used to check walls for plumb and horizontal surfaces for level before tile is laid. Levels are also used to mark layouts for wall tile installations.

Carpenter's squares are used to establish perpendicular lines for floor tile installations.

Chalk lines are snapped to mark the reference lines for layouts.

Tape measures are essential for measuring rooms and creating layouts. They're also used to make sure that reference lines are perpendicular by using the 3-4-5 triangle method.

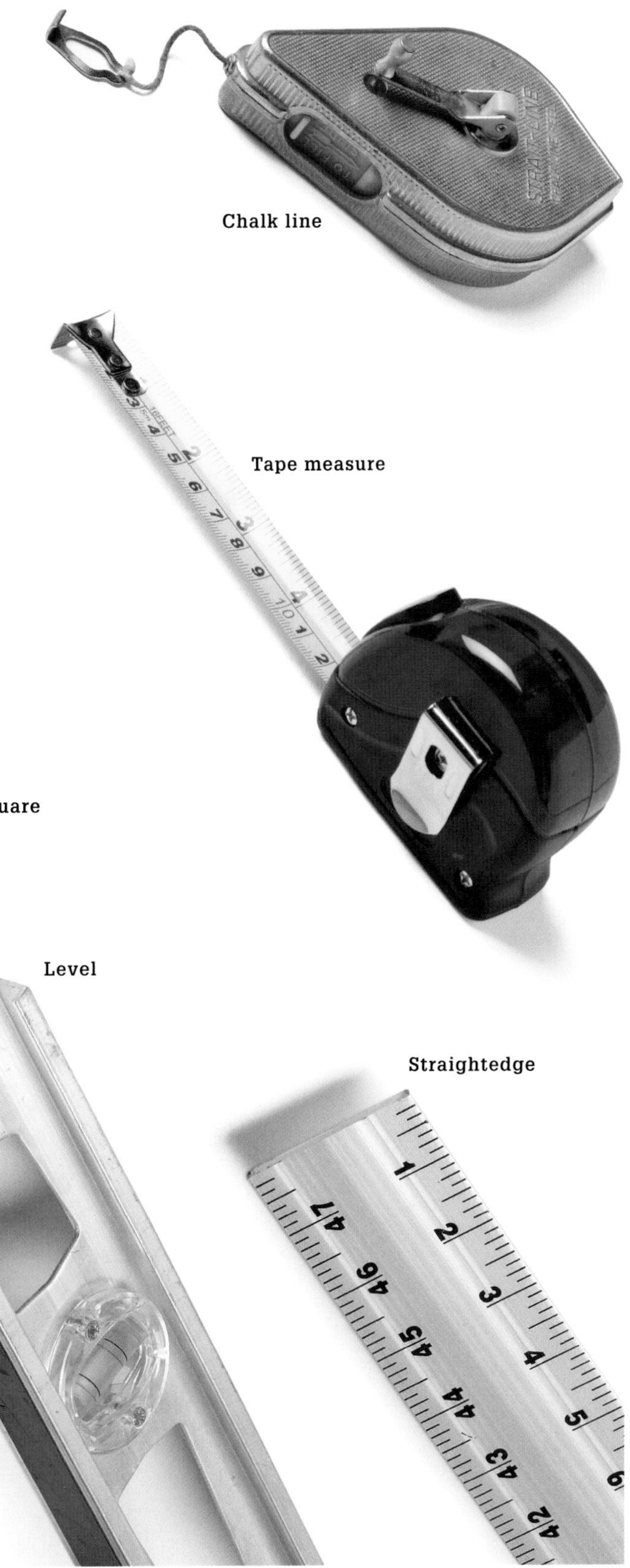

Chalk line

Tape measure

Carpenter's square

Level

Straightedge

Tools for Cutting Tile

Even though tile is a rigid material, it can be cut to fit a variety of applications. With the proper tools, tile can be trimmed, notched, and drilled. If you're planning only one tile project, consider renting the more expensive pieces of equipment.

Coping saws with rod saw blades are usually adequate for cutting soft tile, such as wall tile.

Tile nippers are used to create curves and circles. Tile is first marked with the scoring wheel of a hand-held tile cutter or a wet saw blade to create a cutting guide.

Hand-held tile cutters are used to snap tiles one at a time. They are often used for cutting mosaic tiles after they have been scored.

Tile stones file away rough edges left by tile nippers and hand-held tile cutters. Stones can also be used to shave off small amounts of tile for fitting.

Wet saws, also called "tile saws," employ water to cool both the blade and the tile during cutting. This tool is used primarily for cutting floor tile—especially natural stone tile—but it is also useful for quickly cutting large quantities of tile or notches in hard tile.

Diamond blades are used on hand-held wet saws and grinders to cut through the hardest tile materials such as pavers, marble, granite, slate, and other natural stone.

Tile cutters are quick, efficient tools for scoring and cutting straight lines in most types of light- to medium-weight tile.

Grinders come in handy for cutting granite and marble when equipped with a diamond blade. Cuts made with this hand tool will be less accurate than with a wet saw, so it is best used to cut tile for areas that will be covered with molding or fixtures.

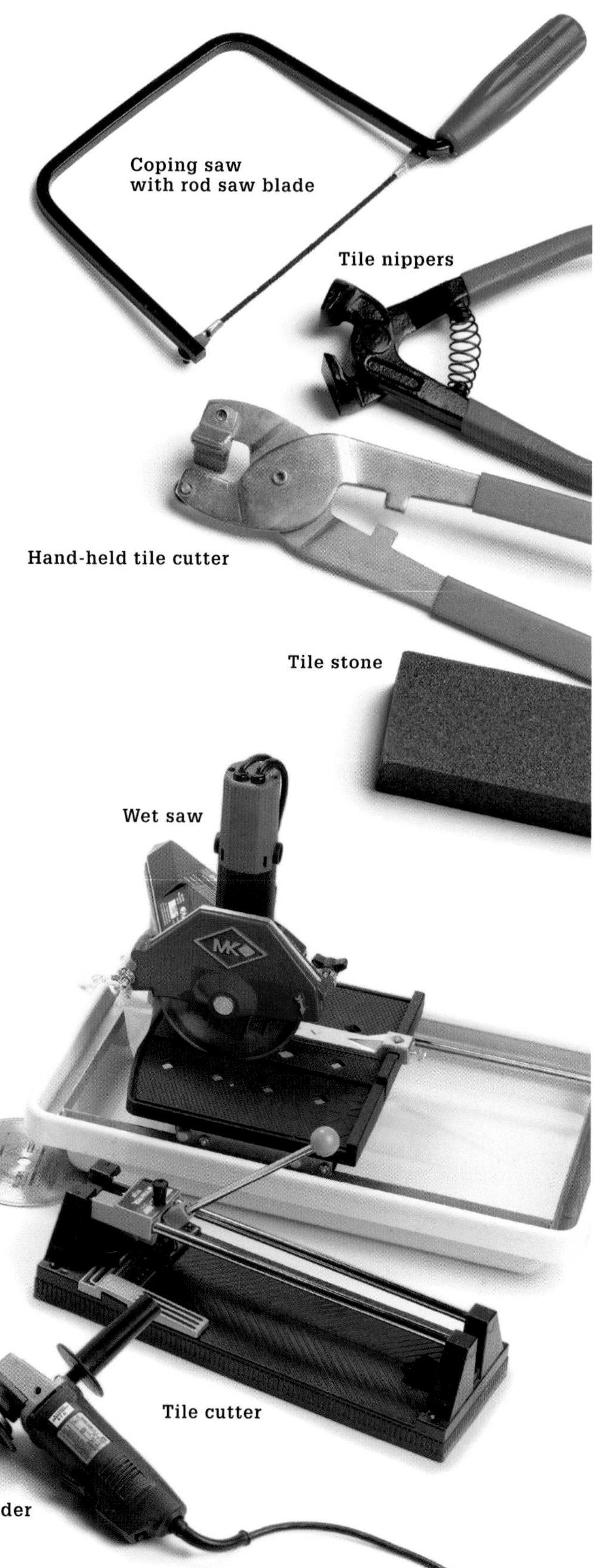

Tools for Setting & Grouting Tile

Laying tile requires quick, precise work, so it's wise to assemble the necessary supplies before you begin. You don't want to search for a tool with wet mortar already in place. Most of the tools required for setting and grouting tile are probably already in your tool box, so take an inventory before you head to the home center or hardware store.

Tile spacers are essential for achieving consistent spacing between tiles. They are set at corners of laid tile and are later removed so grout can be applied.

Grout sponges, buff rags, foam brushes, and grout sealer applicators are used after grout is applied. Grout sponges are used to wipe away grout residue, buff rags remove grout haze, and foam brushes and grout sealer applicators are for applying grout sealer.

Rubber mallets are used to gently tap tiles and set them evenly into mortar.

Needlenose pliers come in handy for removing spacers placed between tiles.

Caulk guns are used to fill expansion joints at the floor and base trim, at inside corners, and where tile meets surfaces made of other materials.

Grout floats are used to apply grout over tile and into joints. They are also used to remove excess grout from the surface of tiles after grout has been applied. For mosaic sheets, grout floats are handy for gently pressing tile into mortar.

Trowels are used to apply mortar to surfaces where tile will be laid and to apply mortar directly to the backs of cut tiles.

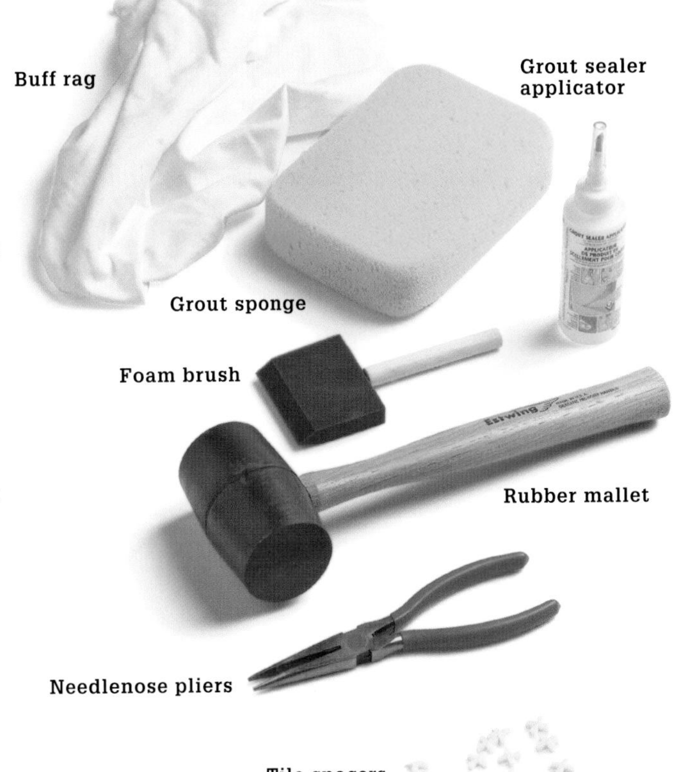

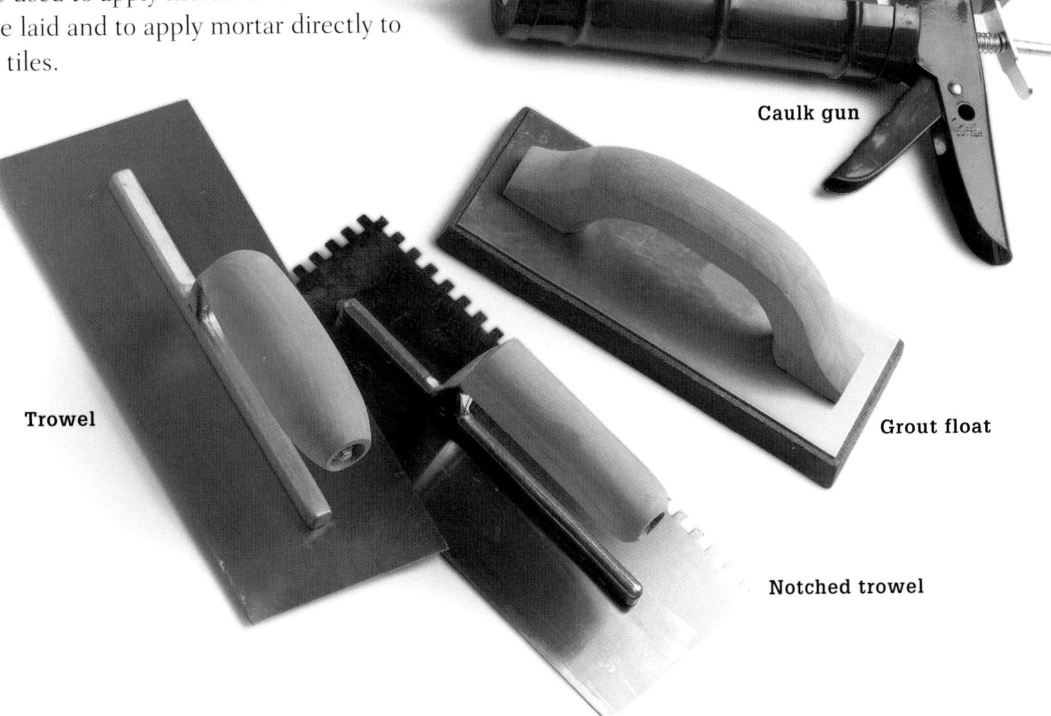

Floor Projects

The project portion of the book begins with a basic floor project, which is probably the most common tile project undertaken by homeowners. This chapter walks you through a basic installation, and then branches out to illustrate how to set a running bond tile pattern, a diagonal pattern within a border, and how to set hexagonal tile.

With these basic tile-setting techniques in hand, you'll be ready to set mosaic floor tile and even to create an original mosaic design. Finally, we present the installation of a custom-tiled shower base, an advanced but completely realistic project for a do-it-yourselfer.

A floor typically is one of the largest surfaces in a room and so plays a major role in establishing the style of the space. Neutral or dramatic, plain or elaborate, these projects present the techniques necessary for just about any design you can find or dream up.

In this chapter:

Gallery of Flooring Tile Projects

Contrasting inlays can be fashioned from contrasting tiles or from another material altogether. You can inlay within the repeat pattern of the main tile, or you may choose to custom cut field tiles to create space for the inlay.

Polished tiles with mirror finishes clean up beautifully and can make a utility room or laundry room look as spotless as an operating room. These marble tiles are installed with very narrow grout lines.

A perfectly square grid of ceramic tiles takes on the illusion of movement when it is cut with a meandering pebblestone pathway on one side and cabinet bases with curved contours on the other side.

A mélange of contrasting stone tiles creates a visually interesting floor that pulls carefully chosen colors from the other elements in this kitchen.

Rugged porcelain tile is a perfect flooring choice for a three-season porch. It is fairly resistant to temperature change as long as it is protected from direct moisture, and it is very easy to clean when it is trampled by muddy feet.

Terra cotta tile makes a dramatic visual statement indoors or outdoors. Here, the wide gray grout lines establish a strong geometric pattern that anchors a minimally appointed room.

A professionally installed granite tile floor positively gleams with reflected light. A floor like this can be a stunning design element in any room, but be forewarned that you'll see every speck of dust if you don't sweep or mop it perpetually.

Sometimes a simple layout succeeds where a fancier pattern might fail. Solid color tiles in a straightforward grid with a neutral grout color combine to form a sturdy, practical floor covering that doesn't compete with other colors and patterns in the room.

Dark, low-luster tiles with a textured surface have a visual effect similar to leather when they are laid over a large area. A contemporary room with few furnishings is the perfect showcase for this type of tile treatment.

Informal settings are perfect for tile that has random gradations in the pattern. Ceramic tiles or porcelain tiles are well-suited for casual rooms that have a light, open ambience.

Evaluating & Preparing Floors

The most important step in the success of your tile flooring project is evaluating and preparing the area. A well-done tile installation can last a lifetime, whereas poor preparation can lead to a lifetime of cracked grout and broken tile headaches.

Because of the weight of ceramic and stone tile, it is important to assess the condition of the joists, subfloor, and underlayment. Most tile installation cannot be done over existing flooring without the addition of underlayment. Check with your tile dealer for the specific requirements of the tile or stone you have chosen.

Though it may initially seem like more work, it is important to remove bathroom fixtures, vanities, and non-plumbed kitchen islands for your floor tile project. Not only will this eliminate a great deal of cutting and fitting, it will allow you more flexibility in future remodeling choices.

Start by removing any fixtures or appliances in the work area, then baseboards, then the old flooring. Shovel old flooring debris through a window and into a wheelbarrow to speed up removal work. Cover doorways with sheet plastic to contain debris and dust during the removal process. Keep the dust and dirt from blowing through your home's ductwork by covering air and heat vents with sheet plastic and masking tape.

Anatomy of Your Floor ▸

A typical wood-frame floor consists of several layers that work together to provide the required structural support and desired appearance. At the bottom of the floor are joists, the 2 × 10 or larger framing members that support the weight of the floor. Joists are typically spaced 16" apart on center. The subfloor is nailed to the joists. Most subfloors installed in the 1970s or later are made of ¾" tongue-and-groove plywood, but in older homes, the subfloor often consists of 1"-thick wood planks nailed diagonally across the floor joists. On top of the subfloor, most builders place a ½" plywood underlayment. For many types of floor coverings, adhesive or mortar is spread on the underlayment prior to installing the floor cover.

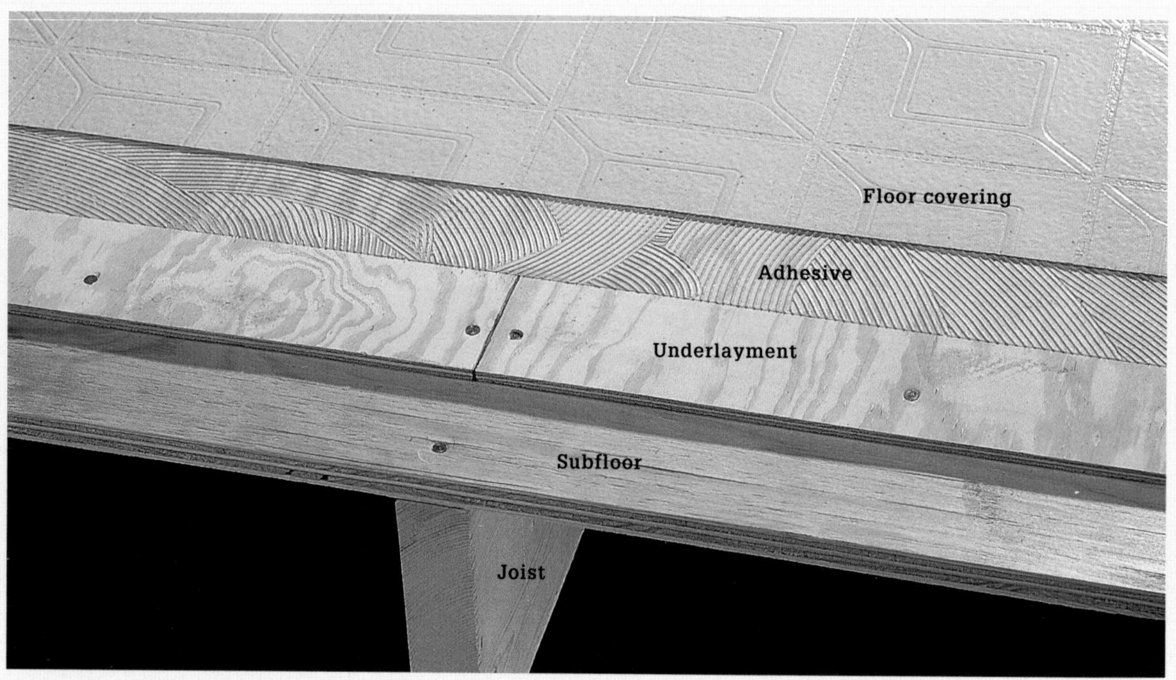

How to Evaluate & Prepare Floors

Determining the number and type of coverings already on your floor is an important first step in evaluating its condition. Ceramic and stone tile floors have specific requirements that must be met to prevent surface cracks.

Measure vertical spaces in kitchens and bathrooms to ensure the proper fit of appliances and fixtures after the installation of tile. Use a sample of the tile and any additional underlayment as spacers while measuring.

To remove baseboards, place a scrap board against the wall to avoid damaging the drywall. Remove the baseboard using a pry bar placed against the scrap board. Pry the baseboard at all nail locations. Number the baseboards as they are removed.

To prepare door jambs, measure the height of your underlayment and tile and mark the casing. Using a jamb saw, cut the casing at the mark.

To test the height of the door jamb, slide a piece of flooring under the door jamb to make sure it fits easily.

How to Remove a Toilet

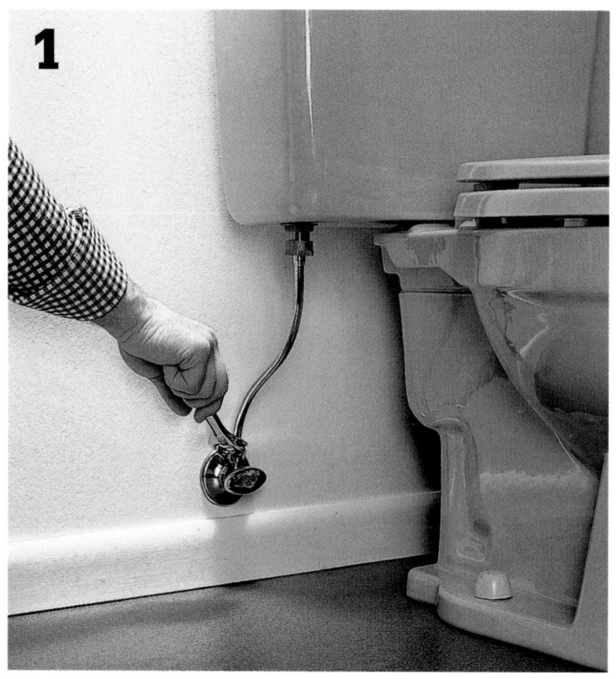

Empty the tank and disconnect. Turn off the water at the shutoff valve and flush the toilet to empty the tank. Use a sponge to soak up remaining water in the tank and bowl. Disconnect the supply tube using an adjustable wrench.

Remove the nuts from the tank bolts using a ratchet wrench. Carefully remove the tank and set it aside.

Pry off the floor bolt trim caps, then remove the nuts from the floor bolts. Rock the bowl from side to side to break the seal, then lift the toilet from the bolts and set it aside. Wear rubber gloves while cleaning up any water that spills from the toilet trap.

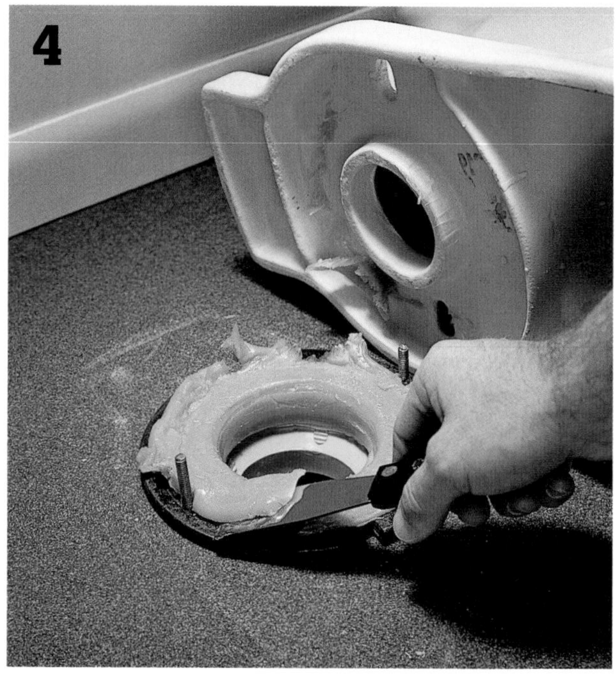

Scrape the old wax from the toilet flange, and plug the drain opening with a damp rag so sewer gas doesn't escape into the house. If you're going to reinstall the old toilet, clean the old wax and plumber's putty from around the horn and base of the toilet.

How to Remove Sinks

Self-rimming sink: Disconnect the plumbing, then slice through any caulk or sealant between the sink rim and the countertop using a utility knife. Lift the sink off the countertop.

Pedestal sink: Disconnect the plumbing. If the sink and pedestal are bolted together, disconnect them. Remove the pedestal first, supporting the sink from below with 2 × 4s. Slice through any caulk or sealant. Lift the sink off the wall brackets (inset).

How to Remove Vanities

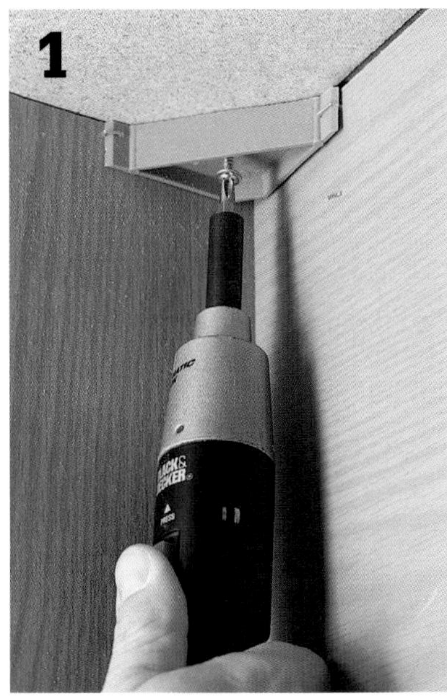

Detach any mounting hardware, located underneath the countertop inside the vanity.

Slice through any caulk or sealant between the wall and the countertop. Remove the countertop from the vanity, using a pry bar if necessary.

Remove the screws or nails (usually driven through the back rail of the cabinet) that anchor the vanity to the wall and remove cabinet.

Removing Floor Coverings

Thorough and careful removal work is essential to the quality of a new floor tile or stone installation. The difficulty of flooring removal depends on the type of floor covering and the method that was used to install it. Carpet and perimeter-bond vinyl are generally quite easy to remove, and vinyl tiles are relatively simple. Full-spread sheet vinyl can be difficult to remove, however, and removing ceramic tile is a lot of work.

With any removal project, be sure to keep your tool blades sharp and avoid damaging the underlayment if you plan to reuse it. If you'll be replacing the underlayment, it may be easier to remove the old underlayment along with the floor covering (see pages 68 to 69).

Resilient flooring installed before 1986 might contain asbestos, so consult an asbestos containment expert or have a sample tested before beginning removal. Even if asbestos is not present, wear a high quality dust mask.

Tools & Materials ▸

- Gloves
- Floor scraper
- Utility knife
- Spray bottle
- Wallboard knife
- Wet/dry vacuum
- Heat gun
- Dust mask
- Hand maul
- Masonry chisel
- Flat pry bar
- Broom
- Tape measure
- End-cutting nippers
- Liquid dishwashing detergent
- Belt sander with coarse sanding belt
- Eye and ear protection

Use a floor scraper to remove resilient flooring products and to scrape off leftover adhesives or backings. The long handle provides leverage and force, and it allows you to work in a comfortable standing position. A scraper will remove most flooring, but you may need to use other tools to finish the job.

How to Remove Sheet Vinyl

Cut strips. Remove base moldings, if necessary. Use a utility knife to cut old flooring into strips about a foot wide.

Pull up as much flooring as possible by hand, gripping the strips close to the floor to minimize tearing.

Cut stubborn sheet vinyl into strips about 5" wide. Starting at a wall, peel up as much of the floor covering as possible. If the felt backing remains, spray a solution of water and liquid dishwashing detergent under the surface layer to help separate the backing. Use a wallboard knife to scrape up particularly stubborn patches.

Scrape up the remaining sheet vinyl and backing using a floor scraper. If necessary, spray the backing again with the soap solution to loosen it. Sweep up the debris, then finish the cleanup with a wet/dry vacuum. *Tip: Fill the vacuum with about an inch of water to help contain dust.*

How to Remove Vinyl Tile

Carefully pry tiles loose. Remove base moldings, if necessary. Starting at a loose seam, use a long-handled floor scraper to remove tiles. To remove stubborn tiles, soften the adhesive with a heat gun, then use a wallboard knife to pry up the tile and scrape off the underlying adhesive.

Remove stubborn adhesive or backing by wetting the floor with a water/detergent mixture, then scraping with a floor scraper.

How to Remove Ceramic Tile

Knock tiles loose. Remove base moldings, if necessary. Knock out tile using a hand maul and masonry chisel. If possible, start in a space between tiles where the grout has loosened. Be careful when working around fragile fixtures, such as drain flanges.

If you plan to reuse the underlayment, use a floor scraper to remove any remaining adhesive. You may have to use a belt sander with a coarse sanding belt to grind off stubborn adhesive.

How to Remove Carpet

Using a utility knife, cut around metal threshold strips to free the carpet. Remove the threshold strips with a flat pry bar.

Cut the carpet into pieces small enough to be easily removed. Roll up the carpet and remove it from the room, then remove the padding. *Note: Padding is often stapled to the floor, and usually will come up in pieces as you roll it up.*

Using end-cutting nippers or pliers, remove all staples from the floor. Pry tackless strips loose with a pry bar and remove them.

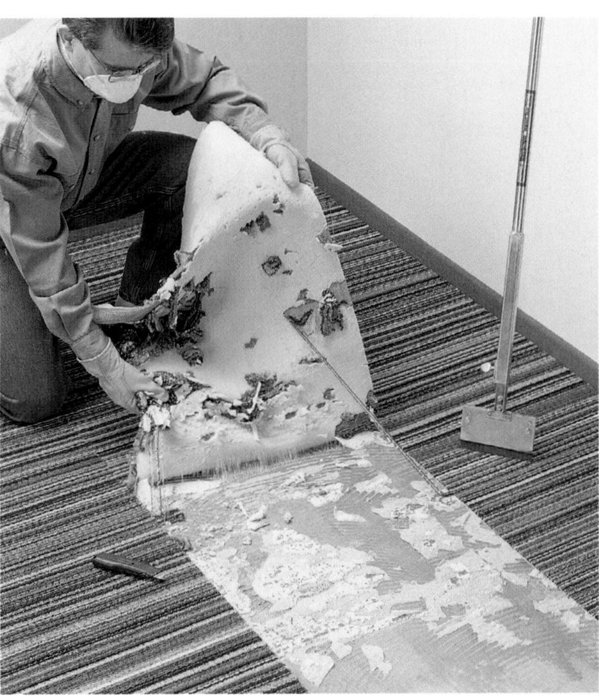

Variation: To remove glued-down carpet, first cut it into strips with a utility knife, then pull up as much material as you can. Scrape up the remaining cushion material and adhesive with a floor scraper.

Removing Underlayment

Flooring contractors routinely remove the underlayment along with the floor covering before installing new flooring. This saves time and makes it possible to install new underlayment that is ideally suited to ceramic and stone tile. Do-it-yourselfers using this technique should make sure they cut flooring into pieces that can be easily handled.

Tools & Materials ▸

- Eye and ear protection
- Gloves
- Circular saw with carbide-tipped blade
- Flat pry bar
- Reciprocating saw
- Wood chisel
- Screwdriver
- Hammer
- Hand maul
- Masonry chisel

Warning ▸

This floor removal method releases flooring particles into the air. Be sure the flooring you are removing does not contain asbestos.

Beware of Screwheads ▸

Examine fasteners to see how the underlayment is attached. Use a screwdriver to expose the heads of the fasteners. If the underlayment has been screwed down, you will need to remove the floor covering and then unscrew the underlayment.

Remove underlayment and floor covering as though they were a single layer. This is an effective removal strategy with any floor covering that is bonded to the underlayment.

How to Remove Underlayment

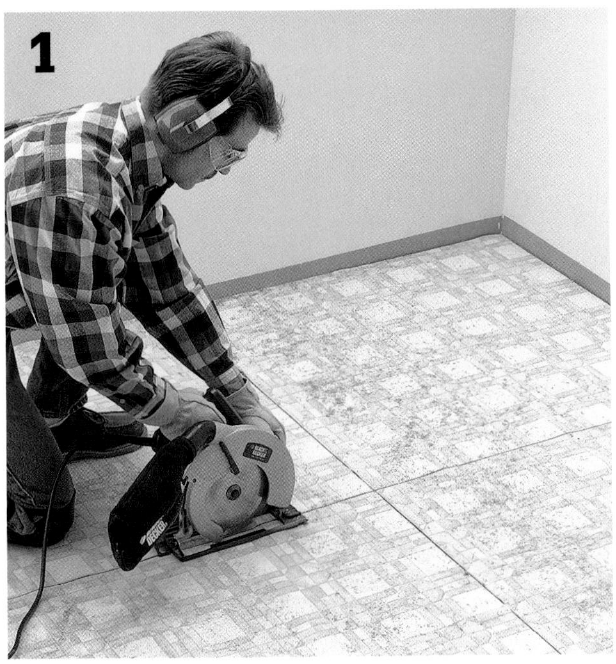

Cut the flooring and underlayment. Remove base moldings, if necessary. Adjust the cutting depth of a circular saw to equal the combined thickness of your floor covering and underlayment. Using a carbide-tipped blade, cut the floor covering and underlayment into squares measuring about 3 ft. square. Be sure to wear eye protection and gloves.

Use a reciprocating saw to extend cuts close to the edges of walls. Hold the blade at a slight angle to the floor, and try not to damage walls or cabinets. Do not cut deeper than the underlayment. Use a wood chisel to complete cuts near cabinets.

Separate the underlayment from the subfloor using a flat pry bar and hammer. Remove and discard the sections of underlayment and floor covering immediately, watching for exposed nails.

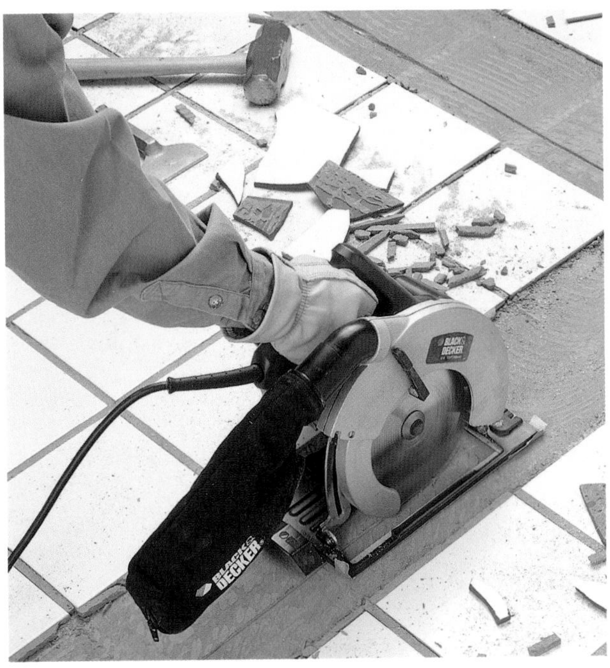

Variation: If your existing floor is ceramic tile over plywood underlayment, use a hand maul and masonry chisel to chip away the tile along the cutting lines before making the cuts.

Underlayment

Before you begin installing cementboard on a horizontal surface, the substructure will need to be examined to make sure it meets the requirements for a tile backer board installation. Wood subfloors installed over 16 inch on-center floor joists must be made of wood stock that is at least ⅝-inch thick and rated for floor sheathing. Acceptable sheathing includes exterior grade, tongue and groove, C-C plugged or better plywood, or oriented strand board (OSB) made with exterior glues. Floors that have large dips or bulges, or any areas with deflection problems, will require structural repairs or reinforcement. It is always recommended that you contact a structural engineer if you are unsure about the condition of your floor and support system.

Cabinet countertops require a minimum overlay of ¾-inch thick sheathing. The application of ¼-inch thick cementboard is optional for installation over countertops, as well as for floor joists spaced 16 inches on center (if the substructure is overlaid with ¾-inch thick sheathing). Unless otherwise allowed by the manufacturer, use ½-inch thick cementboard for all other applications.

Tools & Materials ▸

- 6" joint knife
- Eye and ear protection
- 2" fiberglass mesh tape
- 1¼" cementboard screws
- ¼" square notched trowel
- Floor-patching compound
- Latex or acrylic additive
- Heavy flooring roller
- Work gloves
- Drill
- Straightedge
- Tape measure
- Utility knife
- Thinset mortar
- Cementboard
- 1" deck screws
- Circular saw
- Power sander
- Dust mask

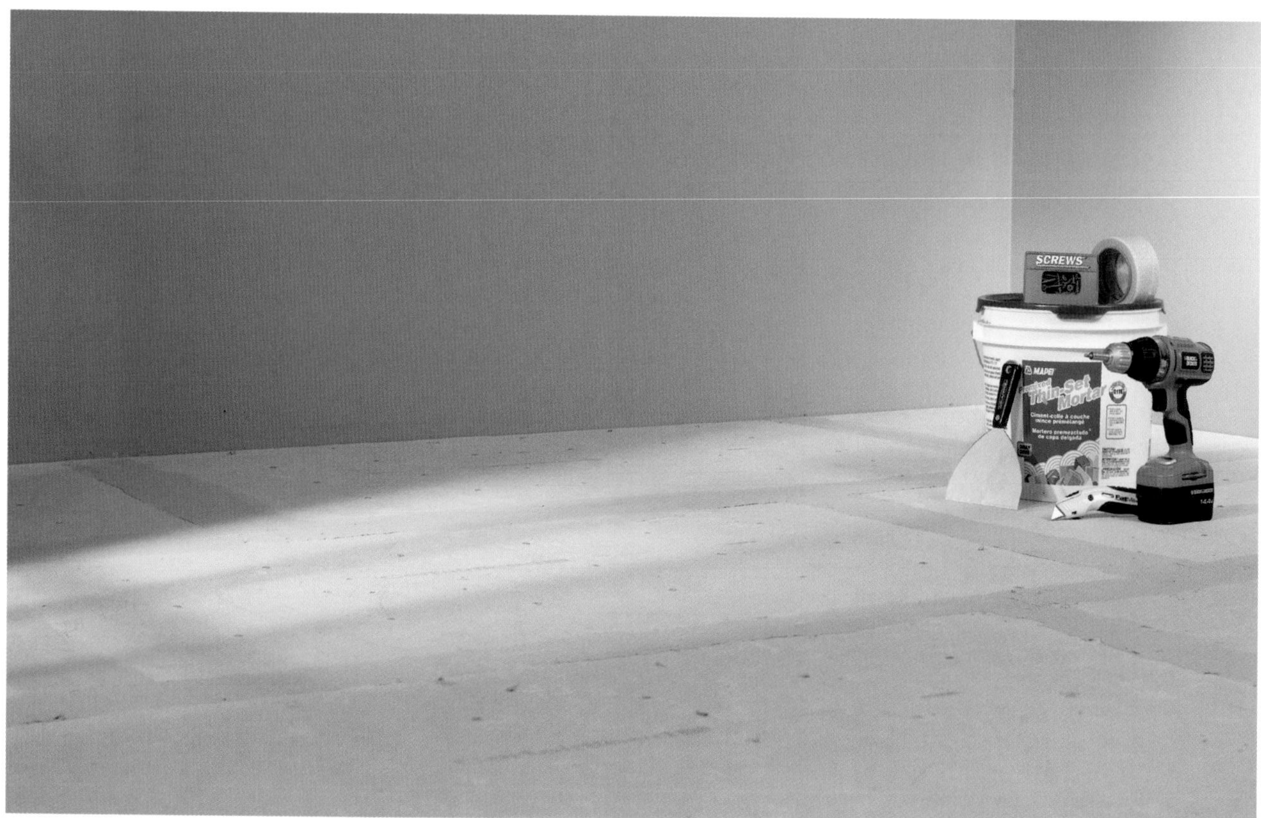

Cementboard is the preferred underlayment material for a ceramic tile floor. When installed correctly it forms a highly stable subbase that resists cracking of the tiles or grout lines.

How to Install Cementboard Underlayment

In most cases, cementboard should be set into a bed or layer of thinset mortar. Use a ¼" square notched trowel to spread the setting bed of dry-set or modified thinset mortar. Apply only enough thinset for each panel and then set the panel into position according to your layout lines. Set the panels with the rougher-textured side facing up.

Fasten panels to the subfloor with 1¼" self-piloting cementboard screws. Fasten screws every 6 to 8" in the field, keeping fasteners 2" away from each corner but no less than ⅜" from the panel edges. Properly fastened, the head of each screw will sit flush with or just slightly below the surface of the panel.

Add new panels, staggering the seams at adjoining panels to prevent any four corners from converging at one point. Install the cementboard perpendicular to floor joists, but avoid aligning them with existing plywood joints on the sub-floor.

Maintain ⅛"-wide gaps between panels. Fill these gaps with a modified thinset mortar, overlapping at least 2 to 3" on each side of the juncture. Center and embed 2"-wide alkaline-resistant fiberglass tape over the joint and tightly skim thinset over the length of the abutment using a joint knife. Scrape off excess mortar to ensure an even transition between panel edges.

How to Install Plywood Underlayment

Begin by installing a full sheet of plywood along the longest wall, making sure the underlayment seams will not be aligned with the subfloor seams. Fasten the plywood to the subfloor, using 1" deck screws driven every 6" along the edges and at 8" intervals in the field of the sheet.

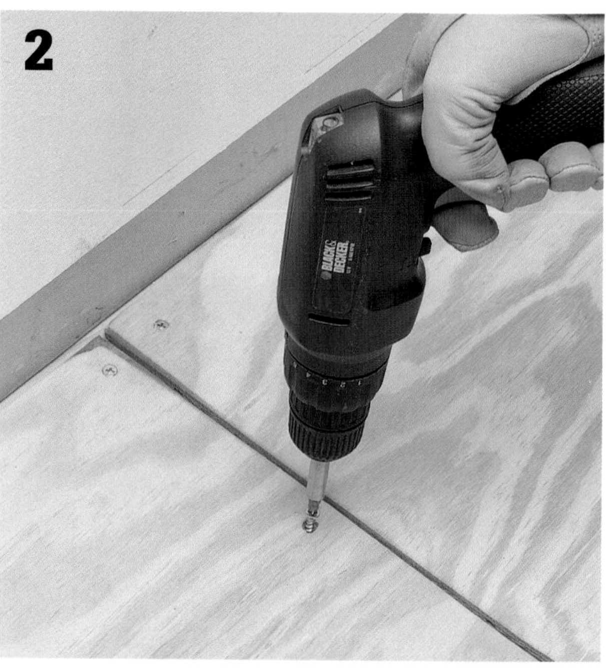

Continue fastening sheets of plywood to the subfloor, driving the screw heads slightly below the underlayment surface. Leave ¼" expansion gaps at the walls and between sheets. Offset seams in subsequent rows.

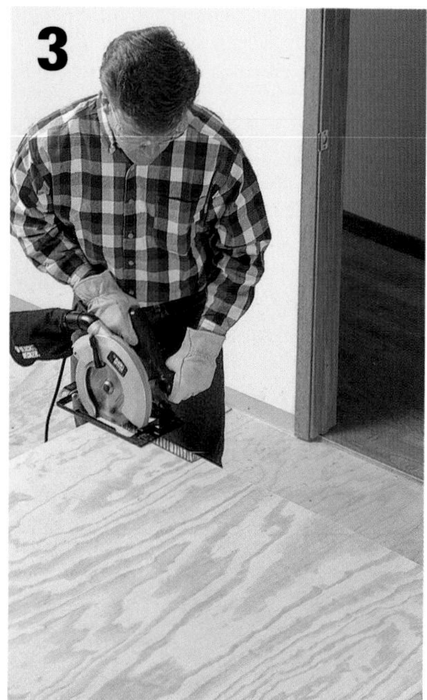

Using a circular saw or jigsaw, notch plywood to meet existing flooring in doorways, then fasten the notched sheets to the subfloor.

Mix floor-patching compound and latex or acrylic additive according to the manufacturer's directions. Spread it over seams and screw heads with a joint knife.

Let the patching compound dry, then sand the patched areas using a power sander.

How to Install Isolation Membrane

Thoroughly clean the subfloor, then apply thinset mortar with a notched trowel. Start spreading the mortar along a wall in a section as wide as the membrane and 8 to 10 ft. long. *Note: For some membranes, you must use a bonding material other than mortar. Read and follow label directions.*

Roll out the membrane over the mortar. Cut the membrane to fit tightly against the walls using a straightedge and utility knife.

Starting in the center of the membrane, use a heavy flooring roller (available at rental centers) to smooth out the surface toward the edges. This frees trapped air and presses out excess bonding material.

Repeat steps 1 through 3, cutting the membrane as necessary at the walls and obstacles, until the floor is completely covered with membrane. Do not overlap the seams, but make sure they are tight. Allow the mortar to cure for two days before installing the tile.

Radiant Floor

Floor-warming systems require very little energy to run and are designed to heat ceramic tile floors only; they are not generally used as sole heat sources for rooms.

A typical floor-warming system consists of one or more thin mats containing electric resistance wires that heat up when energized like an electric blanket. The mats are installed beneath the tile and are hardwired to a 120-volt GFCI circuit. A thermostat controls the temperature, and a timer turns the system off automatically.

The system shown in this project includes two plastic mesh mats, each with its own power lead that is wired directly to the thermostat. Radiant mats may be installed over a plywood subfloor, but if you plan to install floor tile you should put down a base of cementboard first, and then install the mats on top of the cementboard.

A crucial part of installing this system is to use a multimeter to perform several resistance checks to make sure the heating wires have not been damaged during shipping or installation.

Electrical service required for a floor-warming system is based on size. A smaller system may connect to an existing GFCI circuit, but a larger one will need a dedicated circuit; follow the manufacturer's requirements.

To order a floor-warming system, contact the manufacturer or dealer (see Resources, page 249). In most cases, you can send plans to the manufacturer and they'll custom-fit a system for your project area.

Tools & Materials ▸

Vacuum cleaner
Multimeter
Tape measure
Scissors
Router/rotary tool
Marker
Electric wire fault indicator (optional)
Hot glue gun
Radiant floor mats
12/2 NM cable
Trowel or rubber float
Conduit
Thinset mortar
Thermostat with sensor
Junction box(es)
Tile or stone floorcovering
Drill
Double-sided carpet tape
Cable clamps

A radiant floor-warming system employs electric heating mats that are covered with floor tile to create a floor that's cozy underfoot.

Installation Tips

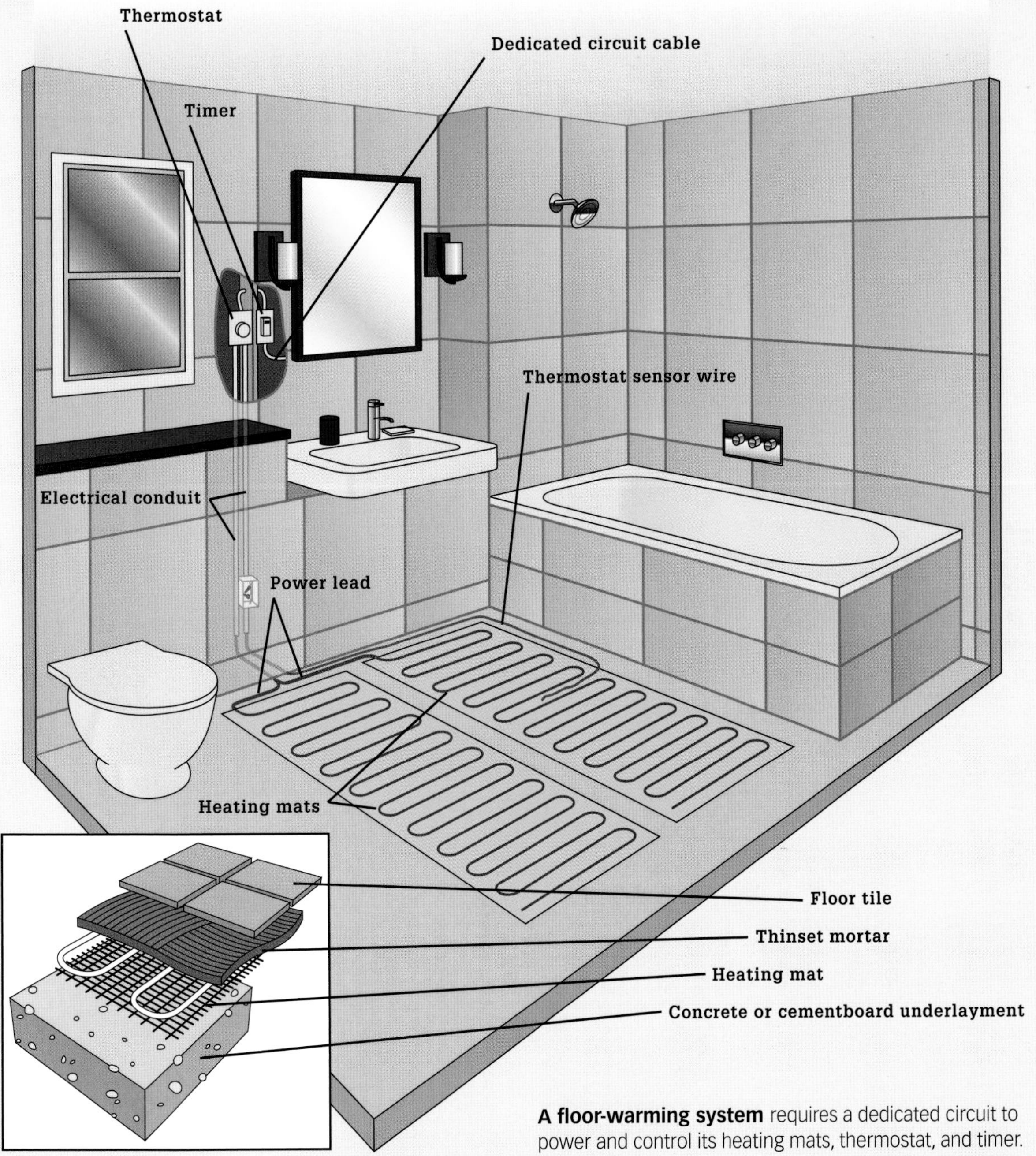

A floor-warming system requires a dedicated circuit to power and control its heating mats, thermostat, and timer.

- Each radiant mat must have a direct connection to the power lead from the thermostat, with the connection made in a junction box in the wall cavity. Do not install mats in series.
- Do not install radiant floor mats under shower areas.
- Do not overlap mats or let them touch.
- Do not cut heating wire or damage heating wire insulation.
- The distance between wires in adjoining mats should equal the distance between wire loops measured center to center.

Installing a Radiant Floor-Warming System

Floor-warming systems must be installed on a circuit with adequate amperage and a GFCI breaker. Smaller systems may tie into an existing circuit, but larger ones need a dedicated circuit. Follow local building and electrical codes that apply to your project.

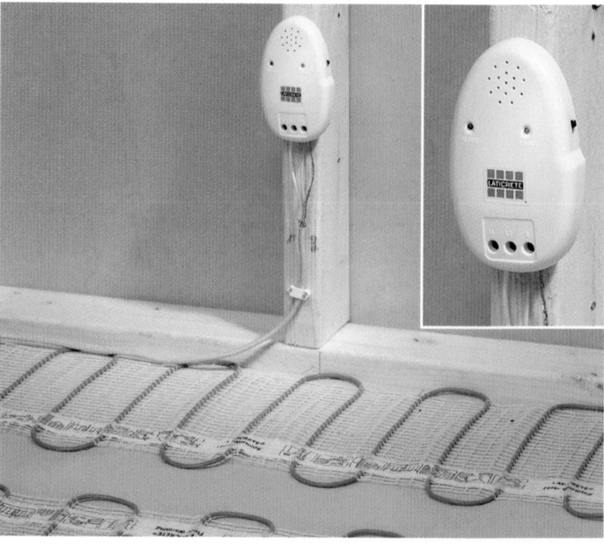

An electric wire fault indicator monitors each floor mat for continuity during the installation process. If there is a break in continuity (for example, if a wire is cut), an alarm sounds. If you choose not to use an installation tool to monitor the mat, test for continuity frequently using a multimeter.

How To Install a Radiant Floor-Warming System

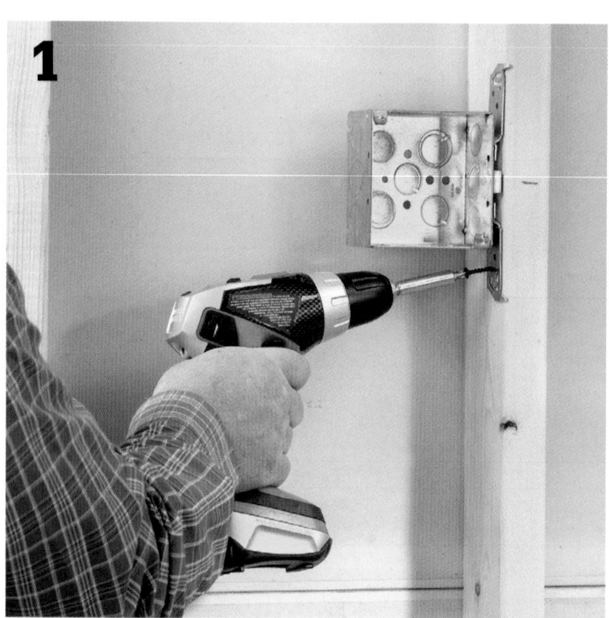

Install electrical boxes to house the thermostat and timer. In most cases, the box should be located 60" above floor level. Use a 4"-deep × 4"-wide double-gang box for the thermostat/timer control if your kit has an integral model. If your timer and thermostat are separate, install a separate single box for the timer.

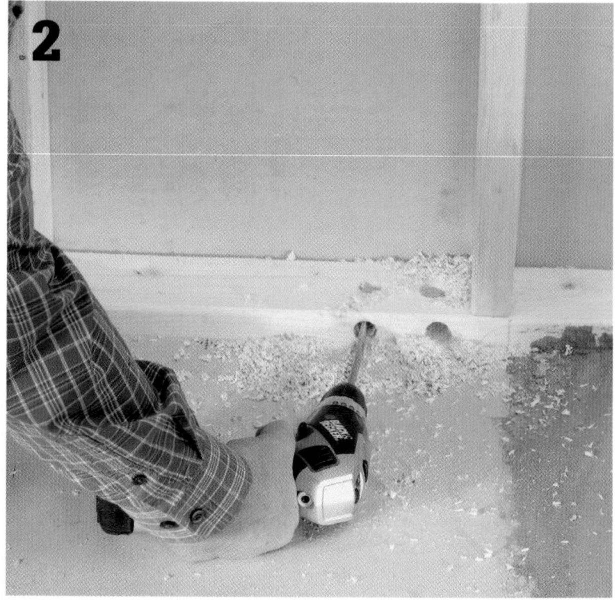

Drill access holes in the sole plate for the power leads that are preattached to the mats (they should be over 10 ft. long). The leads should be connected to a supply wire from the thermostat in a junction box located in a wall near the floor and below the thermostat box. The access hole for each mat should be located directly beneath the knockout for that cable in the thermostat box. Drill through the sill plate vertically and horizontally so the holes meet in an L-shape.

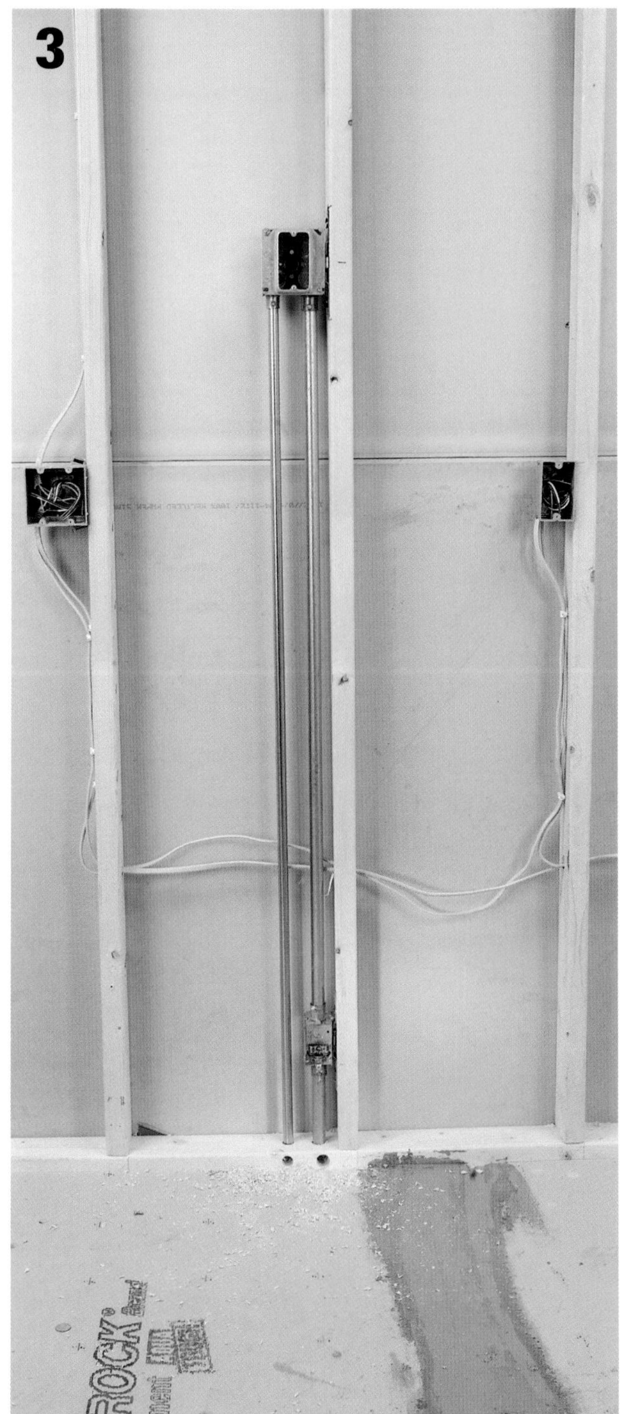

Run conduit from the electrical boxes to the sill plate. The line for the supply cable should be ¾" conduit. If you are installing multiple mats, the supply conduit should feed into a junction box about 6" above the sill plate and then continue into the ¾" hole you drilled for the supply leads. The sensor wire needs only ½" conduit that runs straight from the thermostat box via the thermostat. The mats should be powered by a dedicated 20-amp GFCI circuit of 12/2 NM cable run from your main service panel to the electrical box (this is for 120-volt mats—check your instruction manual for specific circuit recommendations).

Clean the floor surface thoroughly to get rid of any debris that could potentially damage the wire mats. A vacuum cleaner generally does a more effective job than a broom.

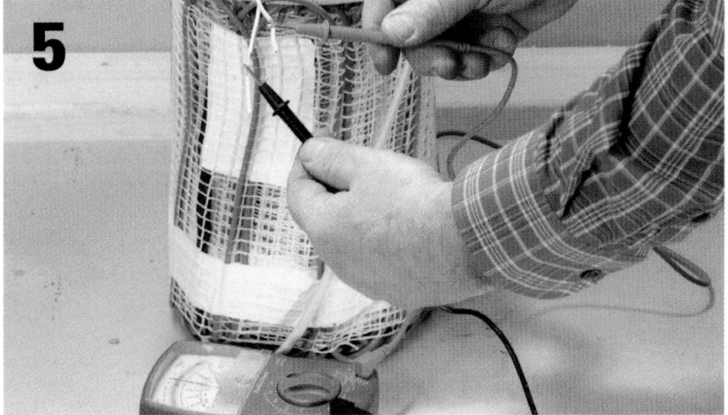

Test for resistance using a multimeter set to measure ohms. This is a test you should make frequently during the installation, along with checking for continuity. If the resistance is off by more than 10% from the theoretical resistance listing (see manufacturer's chart in installation instructions), contact a technical support operator for the kit manufacturer. For example, the theoretical resistance for the 1 × 50 ft. mat seen here is 19, so the ohms reading should be between 17 and 21.

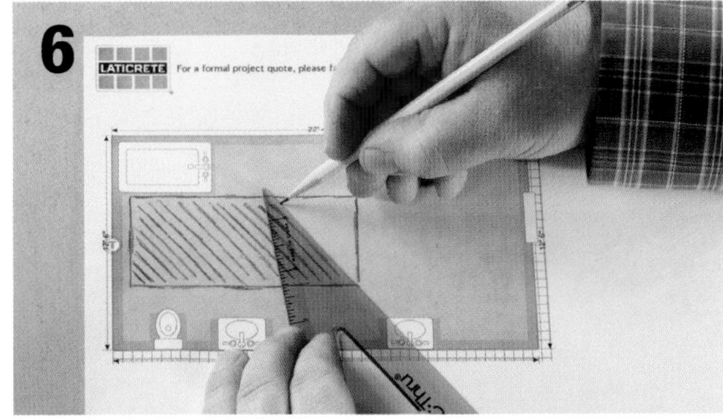

Finalize your mat layout plan. Most radiant floor warming mat manufacturers will provide a layout plan for you at the time of purchase, or they will give you access to an online design tool so you can come up with your own plan. This is an important step to the success of your project, and the assistance is free.

(continued)

Unroll the radiant mat or mats and allow them to settle. Arrange the mat or mats according to the plan you created. It's okay to cut the plastic mesh so you can make curves or switchbacks, but do not cut the heating wire under any circumstances, even to shorten it.

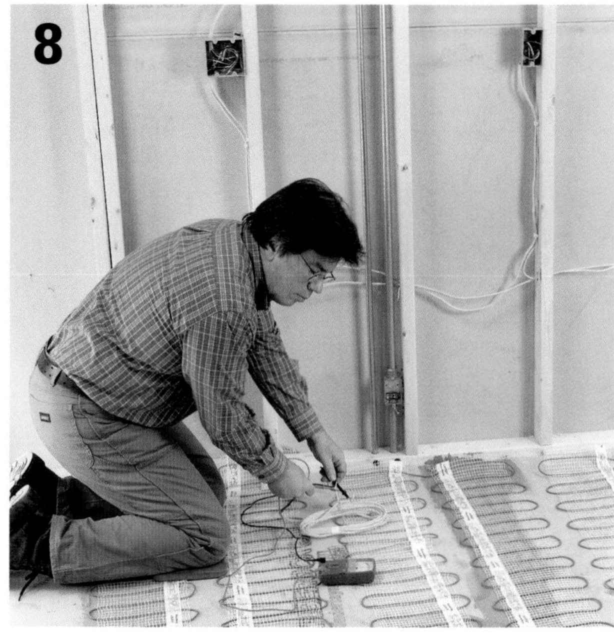

Finalize the mat layout and then test the resistance again using a multimeter. Also check for continuity in several different spots. If there is a problem with any of the mats, you should identify it and correct it before proceeding with the mortar installation.

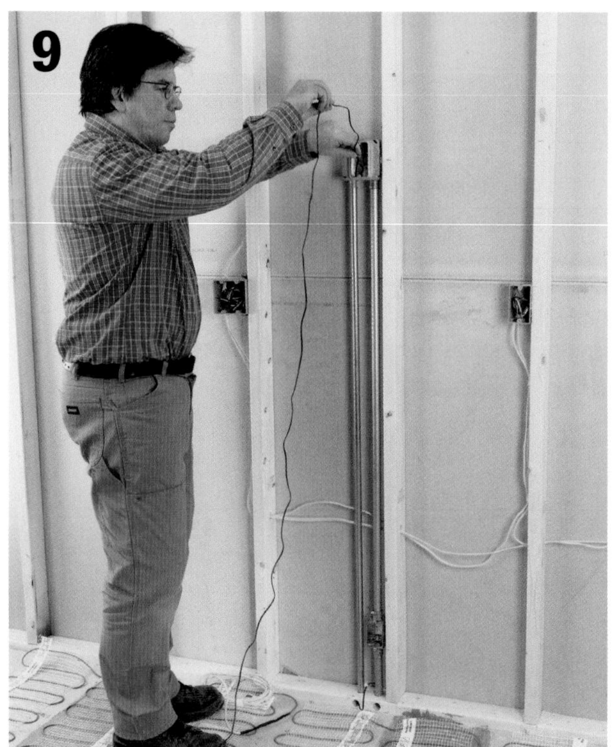

Run the thermostat sensor wire from the electrical box down the ½" conduit raceway and out the access hole in the sill plate. Select the best location for the thermostat sensor and mark the location onto the flooring. Also mark the locations of the wires that connect to and lead from the sensor.

Variation: If your local codes require it, roll the mats out of the way and cut a channel for the sensor and the sensor wires into the floor or floor underlayment. For most floor materials, a spiral cutting tool does a quick and neat job of this task. Remove any debris.

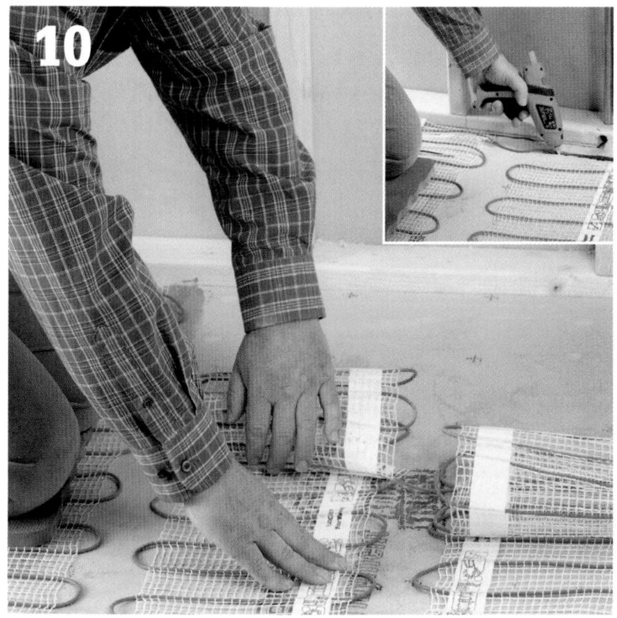

Bond the mats to the floor. If the mats in your system have adhesive strips, peel off the adhesive backing and roll out the mats in the correct position, pressing them against the floor to set the adhesive. If your mats have no adhesive, bind them with strips of double-sided carpet tape. The thermostat sensor and the power supply leads should be attached with hot glue (inset photo) and run up into their respective holes in the sill plate if you have not done this already. Test all mats for resistance and continuity.

Cover the floor installation areas with a layer of thinset mortar that is thick enough to fully encapsulate all the wires and mats (usually around ¼" in thickness). Check the wires for continuity and resistance regularly and stop working immediately if there is a drop in resistance or a failure of continuity. Allow the mortar to dry overnight.

Connect the power supply leads from the mat or mats to the NM cable coming from the thermostat inside the junction box near the sill. Power must be turned off. The power leads should be cut so about 8" of wire feeds into the box. Be sure to use cable clamps to protect the wires.

Connect the sensor wire and the power supply lead (from the junction box) to the thermostat/timer according to the manufacturer's directions. Attach the device to the electrical box, restore power, and test the system to make sure it works. Once you are convinced that it is operating properly, install floor tiles and repair the wall surfaces.

Ceramic Floor Tile

To begin a ceramic tile installation, snap perpendicular reference lines and dry-fit tiles to ensure the best placement.

When setting tiles, work in small sections so the mortar doesn't dry before the tiles are set. Use spacers between tiles to ensure consistent spacing. Plan an installation sequence to avoid kneeling on set tiles. Be careful not to kneel or walk on tiles until the designated drying period is over.

Tools & Materials ▸

¼" square-notched trowel
Rubber mallet
Tile cutter
Tile nippers
Hand-held tile cutter
Needlenose pliers
Grout float
Grout sponge
Soft cloth
Thinset mortar
Tile
Tile spacers
Grout
Latex grout additive
Wall adhesive
2 × 4 lumber
Grout sealer
Tile caulk
Sponge brush
Cementboard
Chalk line
Tape measure
Drill
Caulk gun
1¼" cementboard screws
Fiberglass-mesh wallboard tape
Utility knife or grout knife
Threshold material
Jigsaw or circular saw with a tungsten-carbide blade
Rounded bullnose tile
Eye protection and gloves

Floor tile can be laid in many decorative patterns, but for your first effort, it may be best to stick to a basic grid. In most cases, floor tile is combined with profiled base tile (installed after flooring).

How to Install Ceramic Floor Tile

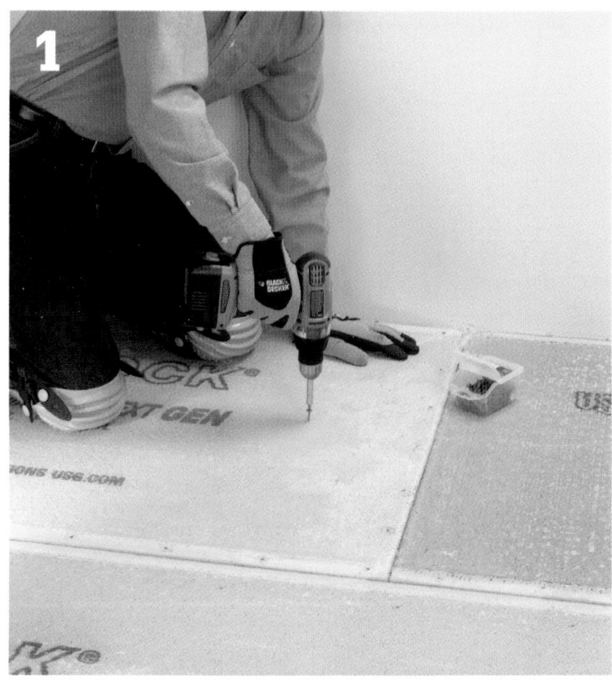

Fasten cementboard in place with 1¼" cementboard screws. Place fiberglass-mesh wallboard tape over the seams. Cover the remainder of the floor, following the steps on page 71.

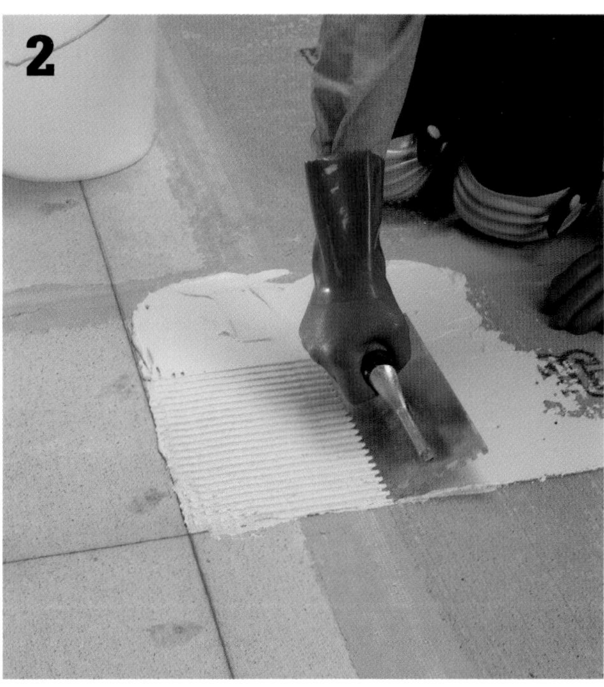

Draw reference lines and establish the tile layout. Mix a batch of thinset mortar, then spread the mortar evenly against both reference lines of one quadrant, using a ¼" square-notched trowel. Use the notched edge of the trowel to create furrows in the mortar bed.

Option: Build a grid system of chalk lines based on the actual dimensions of your tiles, including the grout lines. A grid system ensures that you will stay on track and it helps you divide the project into small sections so you can apply the correct amount of thinset without guessing.

Set the first tile in the corner of the quadrant where the reference lines intersect. When setting tiles that are 8" square or larger, twist each tile slightly as you set it into position.

(continued)

Using a soft rubber mallet, gently tap the central area of each tile a few times to set it evenly into the mortar.

Variation: For large tiles or uneven stone, use a larger trowel with notches that are at least ½" deep.

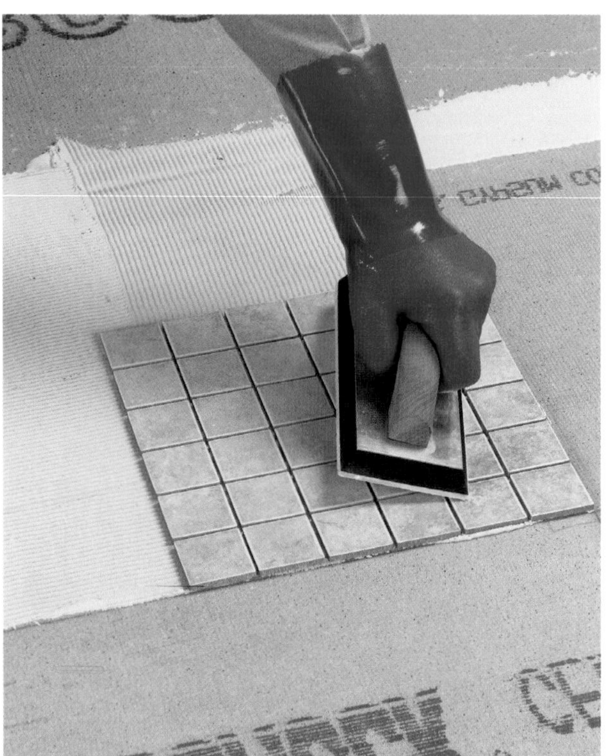

Variation: For mosaic sheets, use a $\frac{3}{16}$" V-notched trowel to spread the mortar and a grout float to press the sheets into the mortar. Apply pressure gently to avoid creating an uneven surface.

To ensure consistent spacing between tiles, place plastic tile spacers at the corners of the set tile. With mosaic sheets, use spacers equal to the gaps between tiles.

Position and set adjacent tiles into the mortar along the reference lines. Make sure the tiles fit neatly against the spacers.

To make sure the tiles are level with one another, place a straight piece of 2 × 4 across several tiles, then tap the board with a mallet.

Lay tile in the remaining area covered with mortar. Repeat steps 2 to 8, continuing to work in small sections, until you reach walls or fixtures.

Measure and mark tiles to fit against walls and into corners. Cut the tiles to fit leaving an expansion joint of about 1". Apply thinset mortar directly to the back of the cut tiles, instead of the floor, using the notched edge of the trowel to furrow the mortar.

(continued)

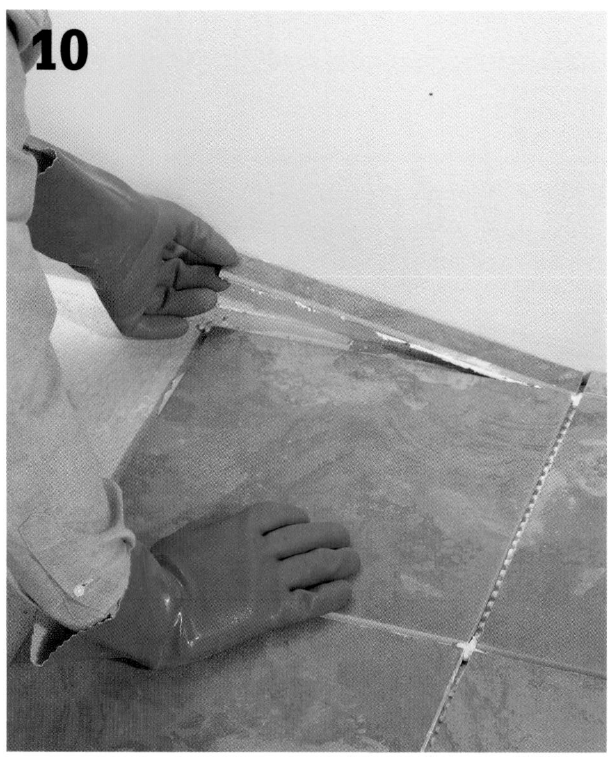

Set the cut pieces of tile into position. Press down on the tile until each piece is level with adjacent tiles.

Measure, cut, and install tiles that require notches or curves to fit around obstacles, such as exposed pipes or toilet drains.

Carefully remove the spacers with needlenose pliers before the mortar hardens.

Apply mortar and set tiles in the remaining quadrants, completing one quadrant before starting the next. Inspect all tile joints and use a utility knife or grout knife to remove any high spots of mortar that could show through the grout.

Install threshold material in doorways. If the threshold is too long for the doorway, cut it to fit with a jigsaw or circular saw and a tungsten-carbide blade. Set the threshold in thinset mortar so the top is even with the tile. Keep the same amount of space between the threshold as between tiles. Let the mortar set for at least 24 hours.

Prepare a small batch of floor grout to fill the tile joints. When mixing grout for porous tile, such as quarry or natural stone, use an additive with a release agent to prevent grout from bonding to the tile surfaces.

Starting in a corner, pour the grout over the tile. Use a rubber grout float to spread the grout outward from the corner, pressing firmly on the float to completely fill the joints. For best results, tilt the float at a 60° angle to the floor and use a figure eight motion.

Use the grout float to remove excess grout from the surface of the tile. Wipe diagonally across the joints, holding the float in a near-vertical position. Continue applying grout and wiping off excess until about 25 sq. ft. of the floor has been grouted.

(continued)

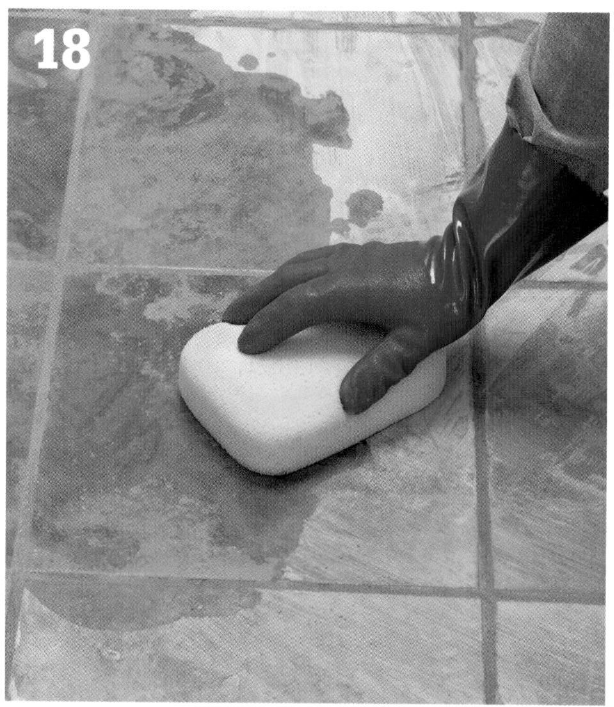

Wipe a damp grout sponge diagonally over about 2 sq. ft. of the floor at a time. Rinse the sponge in cool water between wipes. Wipe each area only once, since repeated wiping can pull grout back out of joints. Repeat steps 15 to 18 to apply grout to the rest of the floor.

Allow the grout to dry for about 4 hours, then use a soft cloth to buff the tile surface and remove any remaining grout film.

Apply grout sealer to the grout lines using a small sponge brush. Avoid brushing sealer onto the tile surfaces. Wipe up any excess sealer immediately.

Option: Use a tile sealer to seal porous tile, such as quarry tile or unglazed tile. Following the manufacturer's instructions, roll a thin coat of sealer over the tile and grout joints using a paint roller and extension handle.

How to Install Bullnose Base Trim

Dry-fit the tiles to determine the best spacing. Grout lines in base tile do not always align with grout lines in the floor tile. Use rounded bullnose tiles at outside corners, and mark tiles for cutting as needed.

Leaving a ⅛" expansion gap between tiles at corners, mark any contour cuts necessary to allow the coved edges to fit together. Use a jigsaw with a tungsten-carbide blade to make curved cuts.

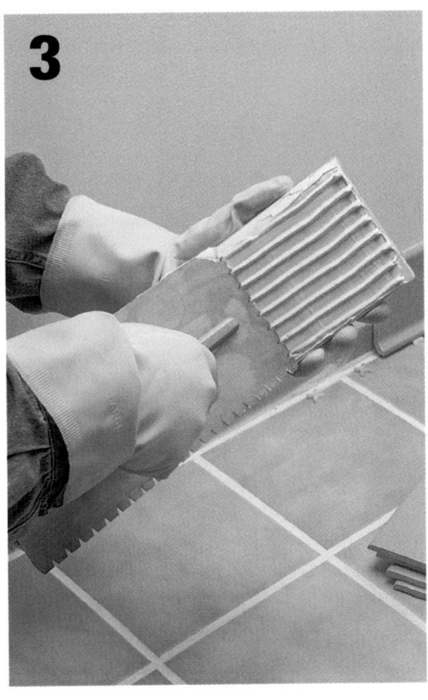

Begin installing base-trim tiles at an inside corner. Use a notched trowel to apply wall adhesive to the back of the tile. Place ⅛" spacers on the floor under each tile to create an expansion joint.

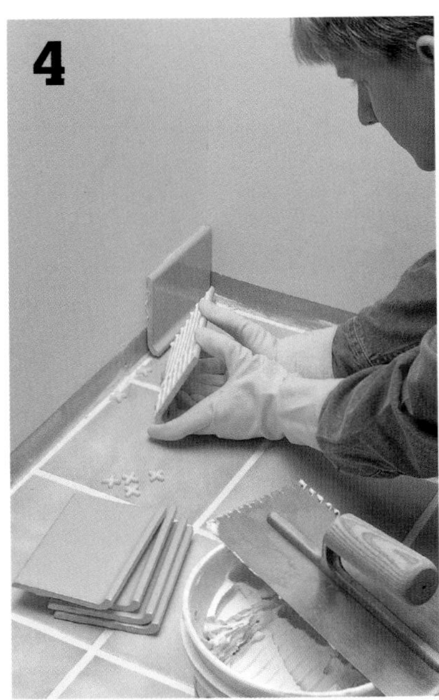

Press the tile onto the wall. Continue setting tiles, using spacers to maintain ⅛" gaps between the tiles and ⅛" expansion joints between the tiles and floor.

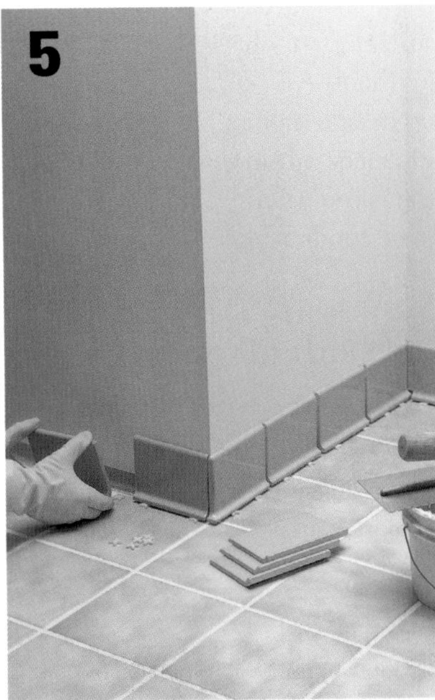

Use a double-bullnose tile on one side of outside corners to cover the edge of the adjoining tile.

After the adhesive dries, grout the vertical joints between tiles and apply grout along the tops of the tiles to make a continuous grout line. Once the grout hardens, fill the expansion joint between the tiles and floor with caulk.

Installing Ceramic Tile on a Basement Floor

Setting tile or flagstone on a concrete floor is a simple project. Its success depends on proper preparation of the concrete, a good layout, and attention to detail during the setting process. It's important to fill dips, cracks, and holes in the concrete with concrete patch or floor leveler before setting tile. If the surface is too uneven, the tile will crack under the pressure of foot traffic.

Choose tile or stone with enough texture to be a safe surface despite the moist conditions of a basement. After you've chosen the tile or stone, ask your retailer about the appropriate mortar and grout for your application.

Before establishing reference lines for your project, think about where to start tiling. The goal is to continue working without having to step on previously laid tile.

Ceramic, porcelain, or stone tile is impervious to water and therefore makes an excellent flooring choice for basements.

Tools & Materials ▸

- Sponge
- Rubber mallet
- Paint roller
- Chalk line
- Framing square
- ¼" notched square trowel
- Needlenose pliers
- Rubber grout float
- Trisodium phosphate
- Rubber gloves
- Concrete patching compound
- Concrete sealer
- Grout sealer
- Ceramic or stone tile
- Thinset or other mortar
- Grout
- Spacers
- Paintbrush

How to Install Tile on a Basement Floor

Scrub the floor with a solution of trisodium phosphate (TSP) and water, let it dry completely, and then check the clean concrete for cracks, holes, and other damage. Fill cracks and holes with concrete patching compound. Apply concrete sealer to the clean, patched, and dry concrete. Use a paintbrush for the edges and the corners and a paint roller for the remaining areas.

Test the layout by dry-setting one vertical and one horizontal row of tile all the way to the walls in both directions. If the layout results in uneven or awkward cuts at the edges, adjust the reference lines to produce a better layout.

Mix a batch of reinforced thinset mortar and spread it onto the floor with a ¼" square-notched trowel. Hold the trowel at a 30° angle and avoid obscuring your reference lines.

Set a tile into the mortar bed so it aligns with your reference lines. Rap the tile very gently with a rubber mallet to seat it in the mortar bed. Make sure it remains aligned properly. Spread mortar for the next tile, or as many as you think you can install in about 20 minutes. If your tiles do not have cast-in nibs that set the spacing automatically, use plastic tile spacers between tiles to create consistent grout gaps.

"Butter" smaller tiles that are cut to fill out the ends of runs by applying thinset mortar directly to the tile back, using a ¼" square-notched trowel. Set remaining tiles and let the mortar set up and dry for at least 24 hours before walking on the tiles.

Mix sanded grout according to the manufacturers directions and fill the gaps between tiles with the grout. Use a grout gloat to apply the grout. Remove excess grout with a sponge and clean water after the grout film on the tile surfaces dries to a haze. Don't get too aggressive here.

Seal the grout lines with penetrating grout sealer after the material has cured for at least a week (see manufacturer's directions). Use a sponge brush or a corner paint roller to apply the sealant.

Stone & Mosaic Tile Floor

The project that follows combines 4 × 4 tumbled stone tile with a stone mosaic medallion and border to produce a decorative effect in an entryway. This idea could be adapted for many rooms. You could border a seating area or create the effect of a rug in front of a fireplace, for example. To lay out a similar design, refer to pages 92 and 93, then center the medallion within the border.

The techniques for setting natural stone are the same as those used with ceramic tile. There are several special considerations, however.

First, stone tile cracks more easily than ceramic. It's extremely important to provide a firm, flat substrate for stone tile projects, especially when you're using large tiles. The larger the tile, the more susceptible it is to stress fractures if the floor structure doesn't support it adequately. See pages 70 to 73 for information on installing underlayment.

Natural stone is subject to greater variation from one tile to the next than manufactured materials. Cartons of some stone tile, especially larger polished stone varieties, may include warped tiles. Be sure to buy enough tile that any severely warped tiles can be sorted out and returned.

Some stone should be sealed before it's set because grout tends to stain it. Ask your dealer for specific recommendations.

Tools & Materials ▸

- Chalk line
- ¼" square-notched trowel
- Rubber mallet
- Tile-cutting tools
- Needlenose pliers
- Utility knife
- Grout float
- Grout sponge
- Buff rag
- Foam brush
- 4 × 4" stone tile
- Mosaic tile
- Mosaic medallion
- Thinset mortar
- Tile spacers
- Threshold material
- Grout
- Latex additive (mortar and grout)
- Grout sealer
- Cementboard
- Fiberglass-mesh tape
- Wallboard knife
- Eye protection
- Hammer
- Baseboards or base-trim tile

Setting Stone Tile Floors ▸

Make sure the subfloor is flat and firm. If problems exist, resolve them before beginning the tile project. This is important for any stone tile floor but critical for a polished stone tile floor.

Check for warped tiles. Lay polished stone tiles next to one another and check carefully. Mark tiles that are slightly warped and build up thinset mortar to level them during installation. Return significantly warped tile to the dealer.

Dry-lay polished stone tile floors with 1⁄16" spacers. Plan to use unsanded grout. Use larger spacers (and sanded grout) for informal stone floors.

Use white thinset mortar for light-colored marble, travertine, and other natural stones, which are somewhat translucent. Take extra care to create a very even surface when combing the mortar.

Seal tiles before installation to help keep contrasting grout from staining the stone. Check manufacturer's recommendations or consult your tile retailer for suggestions. This is particularly important when dealing with porous or rough-surfaced stone.

Keep grout from staining stone tile by wiping the tiles early and often using a clean, damp cloth.

How to Set a Stone & Mosaic Tile Floor

Measure the area and make a scaled diagram of the space. Measure the mosaic medallion and determine the size and placement of the bordered area.

Install and tape cementboard in the project area. (See pages 70 to 71 for full details.)

Snap perpendicular reference lines. Check the lines for squareness using the 3-4-5 triangle method.

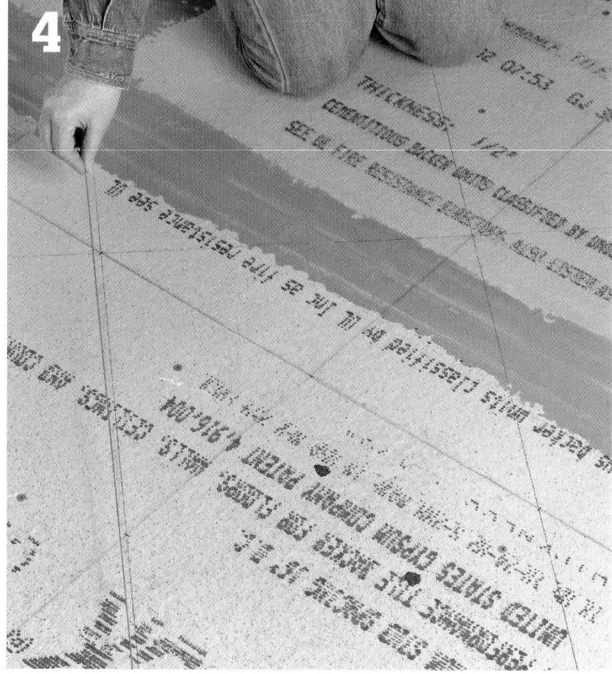

On each line, mark a point equally distant from the center. If your mosaic medallion is a 12" square, mark the points at 12"; if it's a 24" square, mark the points at 24", and so on. Snap chalk lines to connect the points, establishing lines at a 45° angle.

Following the layout created in step 1, measure and mark placement lines for the border. (Make sure these lines are aligned with the first set of reference lines.) Cut mosaic tiles into strips and dry-fit the border.

Dry-fit the tiles at the outside corners of the border arrangement, aligning the tile with the diagonal reference lines. Use spacers and adjust as necessary. When the layout of the tiles is set, trace the edges of the outside tiles.

Set the field tile, cutting tile as necessary. Remove the spacers. Let the mortar cure according to manufacturer's instructions. Set the border tile.

Place the medallion in the center of the bordered area, aligning it with the diagonal reference lines. Dry-fit the field tiles within the border using spacers and aligning the tile with the perpendicular reference lines.

(continued)

For tricky cuts, make paper templates to match the tile size. Use the templates to mark tiles for cutting.

Determine placement of accent tiles within field tile. Measure the field accent tile and mark cutting lines on field tile to accommodate them.

Set medallion, then the field tile within the border. (Avoid placing your weight on newly set tiles.) Remove the spacers and let the mortar dry overnight or according to manufacturer's instructions.

Distribute Your Weight ▸

If it is absolutely necessary to work from newly set tile, kneel on a wide board to distribute your weight.

Install threshold material in doorways. Set the threshold in thinset mortar so the top is even with the tile. Use the same spacing used for the tiles. Let the mortar cure for at least 24 hours.

Prepare a small batch of grout and fill the tile joints (see page 85 for details on grouting tile). When the grout has cured, seal the grout lines using a small sponge brush or sash brush.

Add wood baseboards or base-trim tiles at the edges of the room.

Glass Mosaic Tile Floor

Throughout history, mosaic tile has been more than a floor or wall covering—it's an art form. In fact, the Latin origins of the word mosaic refer to art "worthy of the muses." Mosaic tile is beautiful and durable, and working with it is easier than ever today. Modern mosaic floor tile is available in squares that are held together by an underlayer of fabric mesh. These squares are set in much the same way as larger tile, but their flexibility makes them slightly more difficult to hold, place, and move. The instructions given with this project simplify the handling of these squares.

The colors of mosaic tile shift just as much as any other tile, so make sure all the boxes you buy are from the same lot and batch. Colors often vary from one box to another, too, so it's a good idea to mix tile between boxes to make any shifts less noticeable.

It's also important to know that adhesive made for other tile may not work with glass or specialty mosaic tile. Consult your tile retailer for advice on the right mortar or mastic for your project. Before you start, clean and prepare the floor. Measure the room and draw reference lines. Lay out sheets of tile along both the vertical and horizontal reference lines. If these lines will produce small or difficult cuts at the edges, shift them until you're satisfied with the layout.

Tools & Materials ▸

- Tape measure
- Chalk line
- ¼" notched trowel
- Grout float
- Grout sponge
- Buff rag
- Sponge applicator
- Needlenose pliers
- 2 × 4 wrapped in carpet
- Mosaic tile
- Tile adhesive
- Tile spacers
- Grout
- Grout sealer
- Tile nippers
- Rubber mallet
- Tile cutter
- Straightedge
- Eye protection

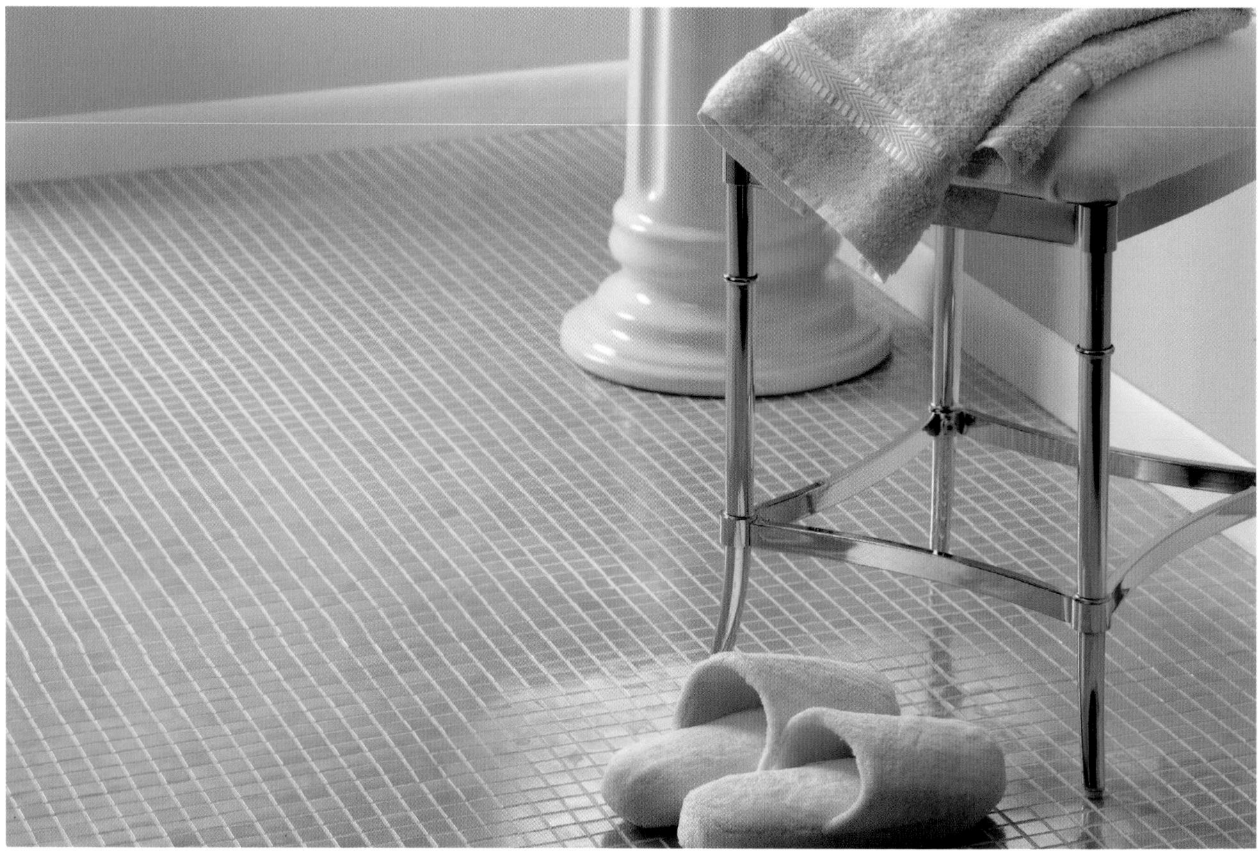

How to Install a Glass Mosaic Floor

Beginning at the intersection of the horizontal and vertical lines, apply the recommended adhesive in one quadrant. Spread it outward evenly with a notched trowel. Lay down only as much adhesive as you can cover in 10 to 15 minutes.

Stabilize a sheet of tile by randomly inserting three or four plastic spacers into the open joints.

Pick up diagonally opposite corners of the square and move it to the intersection of the horizontal and vertical references lines. Align the sides with the reference lines and gently press one corner into place on the adhesive. Slowly lower the opposite corner, making sure the sides remain square with the reference lines. Massage the sheet into the adhesive, being careful not to press too hard or twist the sheet out of position. Continue setting tile, filling in one square area after another.

(continued)

When two or three sheets are in place, lay a scrap of 2 × 4 wrapped in carpet across them and tap it with a rubber mallet to set the fabric mesh into the adhesive and force out any trapped air.

When you've tiled up close to the wall or another boundary, lay a full mosaic sheet into position and mark it for trimming. If you've planned well and are installing small-tile mosaics, you can often avoid cutting tiles.

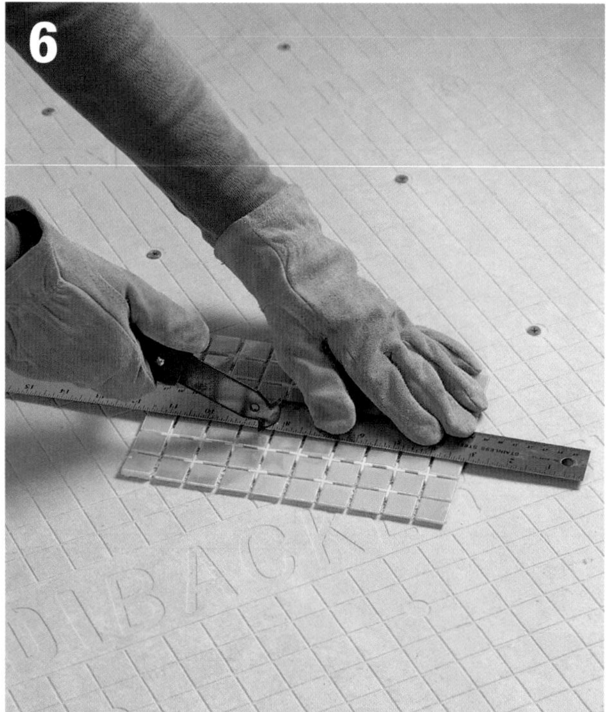

If you do need to cut tiles in the mosaic sheet, and not just the backing, score the tiles with a tile cutter. Be sure the tiles are still attached to the backing. Add spacers between the individual tiles to prevent them from shifting as you score.

After you've scored the tiles, cut them each individually with a pair of tile nippers.

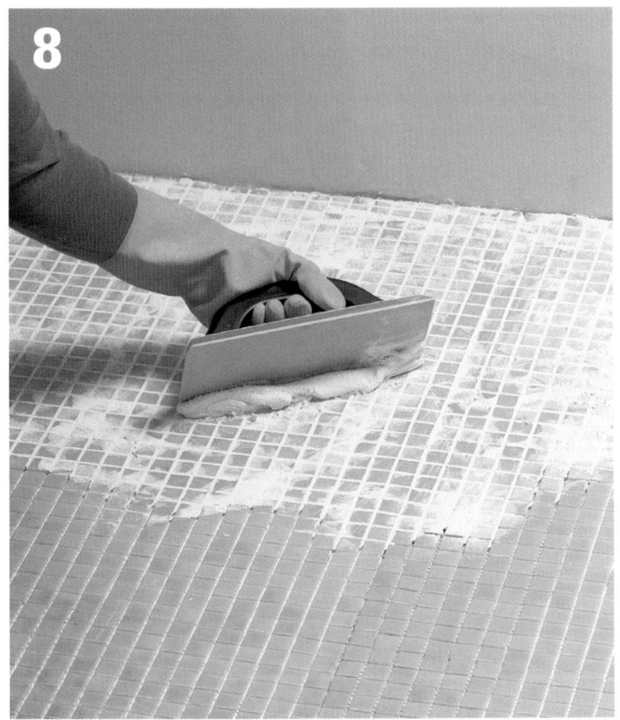

Set tile in the remaining quadrants. Let the adhesive cure according to the manufacturer's instructions. Remove spacers with a needlenose pliers. Mix a batch of grout and fill the joints. Allow the grout to dry, according to manufacturer's instructions.

Mosaic tile has a much higher ratio of grout to tile than larger tiles do, so it is especially important to seal the grout with a quality sealer after it has cured.

Working Around Obstacles ▸

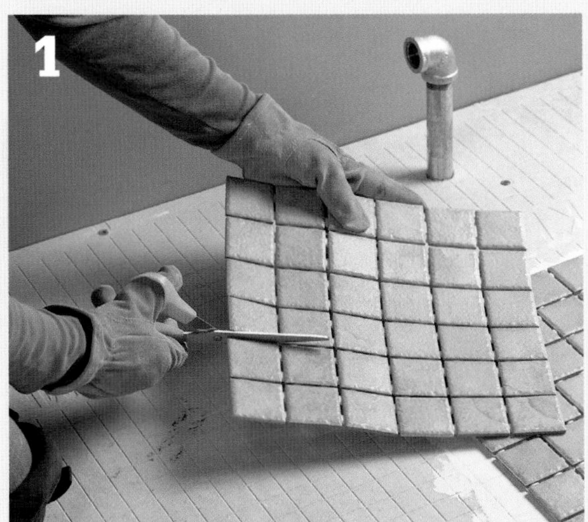

To work around pipes and other obstructions, cut through the backing to create an access point for the sheet. Then, remove the tiles within the mosaic sheet to clear a space large enough for the pipe or other obstruction.

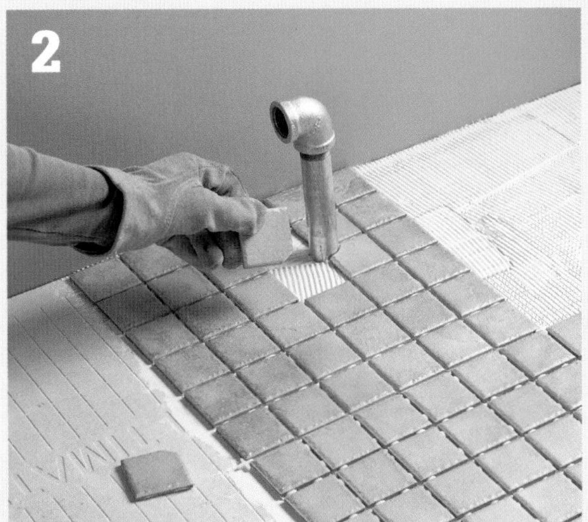

Set the cut sheet into an adhesive bed, and then cut small pieces of tile and fit them into the layout as necessary.

DIY Mosaic Design

Years ago, a mosaic was created slowly and painstakingly by an artist. Some still create mosaics this way, but today you don't have to be an accomplished artist to complete this project. With the help of technology and the right supplies, practically anyone can create and set an original mosaic.

You can create a mosaic pattern with colored pencils and graph paper, or you can use a digital image and a color printer. Basic desktop publishing programs, and even some word processing programs, allow you to size and crop an image, overlay a scaled grid, and print it out. Or, you can actually build an electronic grid of photo boxes and assign a color to each box individually as a layout reference. If you'd rather not take such a hands-on approach to creating your own pattern, there are several websites online that can adapt any image to a mosaic pattern for a nominal charge.

The appearance of your final project depends largely on available tile sizes and colors at the mosaic tile supplies retailer. When making your tile purchase, add at least 10 percent for cutting and breakage.

Tools & Materials ▸

Computer and printer
Chalk line
¼" notched trowel
Rubber mallet
Tile-cutting tools
Grout float
Grout sponge
Buff rag
Tile grids
Floor tile
Needlenose pliers
Grout
Thinset mortar
Tile spacers
Mosaic mounting media
Photograph or other image
Latex additive (mortar and grout)
¾" mosaic floor tiles

How to Install an Original Mosaic Design

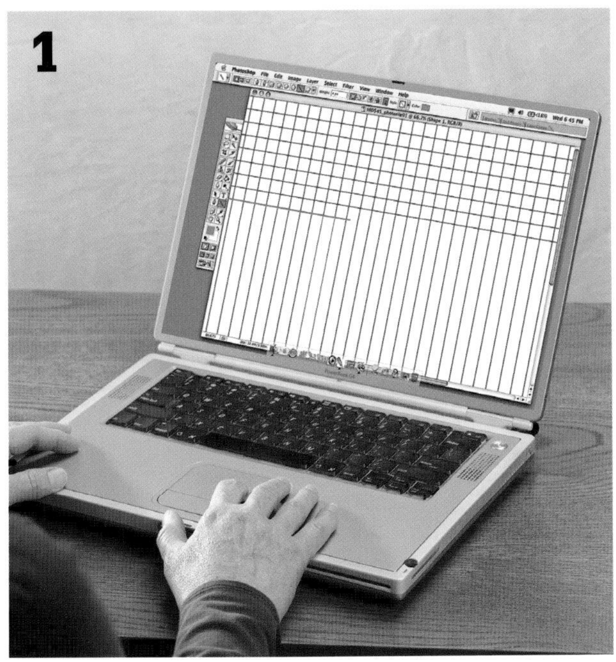

Choose a tile size (we used ¾ × ¾") and create a scaled grid that represents the whole project layout. You can use a computer program to do this, or draw your own grid, or even use graph paper.

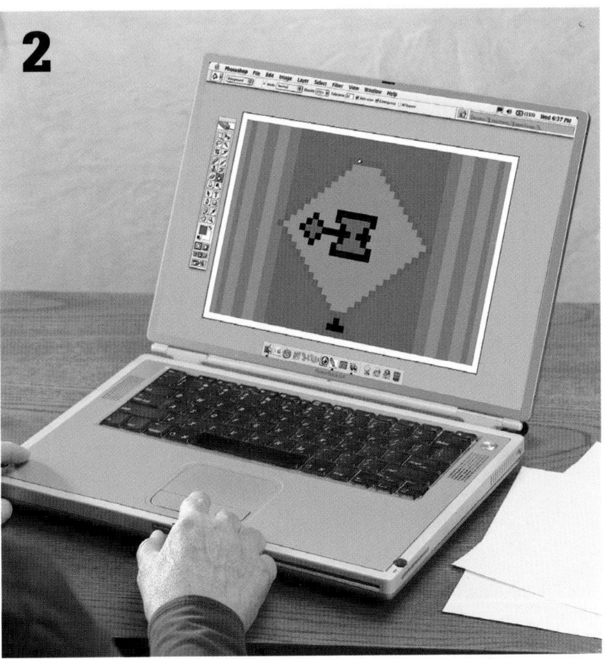

Browse through some images for ideas and inspiration, focusing especially on simple, geometric forms. Using your reference images as a general guide, fill in the boxes with color to replicate the pattern you like. Because this involves a lot of trial and error to get the best results, you're much better off using the computer program for this part.

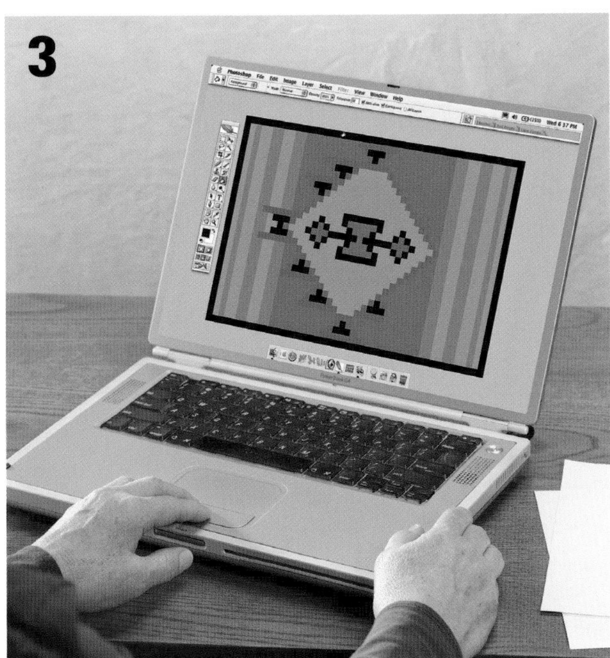

Leave a couple of squares all around for a border. Once you've arrived at the pattern you like, add the border. Borders can be a solid color or multicolored, but they should contrast with the adjoining tiles if possible.

Print the pattern to actual size. Lay it on the floor and view it from several angles—you may find that it looks very different than it did on the computer. Make any adjustments you feel improve the pattern.

(continued)

Using the pattern as a guide, assemble the mosaic tiles into tile grids. Start at the intersection of the horizontal and vertical reference lines and mark off each square on the printout as the corresponding square is filled in the grid.

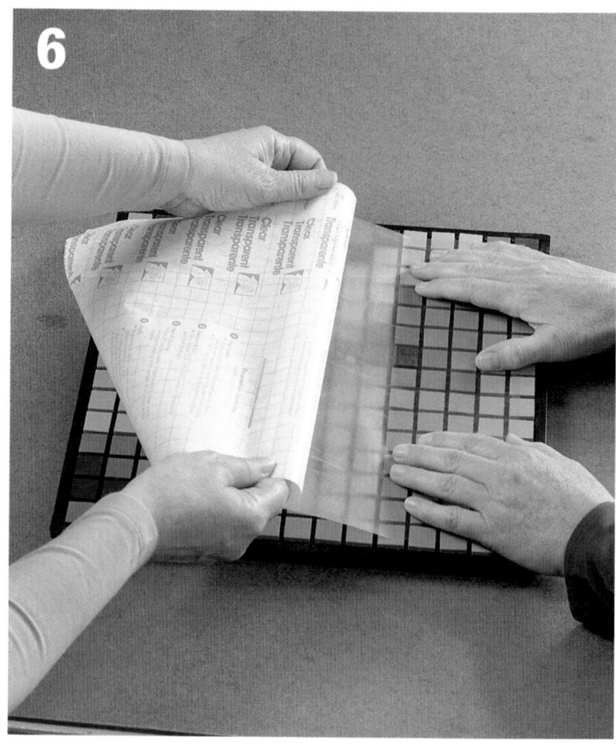

As each frame is completed, cover it with mosaic mounting media. Peel the backing off the media and press it over the tile grid. Rub the media to make sure it sticks to each tile. (This may be easier with a helper.)

Hold the mounting media at the corners, and lift the tile from the grid. (Handle the media carefully to make sure the tile stays in place.) Set the section aside.

Remove any old flooring and prepare the floor (see pages 60 to 73). Measure the area and snap reference lines.

Spread thinset mortar in a grid-sized section at the intersection of the horizontal and vertical reference lines. Position the mosaic at the exact intersection of the lines and press it into position.

Use a grout float to seat the tile in the mortar. Slide the grout float over the surface of the mounting media, pressing down gently.

Reach under the mounting media to set a spacer at each corner of the section and one in the middle of each side.

Continue filling tile grids and adding them to the mosaic in an orderly fashion.

(continued)

Allow the mortar to cure, according to manufacturer's instructions. When the mortar is dry, carefully peel the mounting media away from each section of tile.

Dry-lay the field tile around the custom mosaic, and cut tiles as necessary. Then apply thinset mortar in small sections and place field tile until the entire floor is tiled.

Mix a batch of grout, spread it over the tile, and press it into the joints using a grout float.

Wipe away excess grout with a damp sponge. Continue gently wiping the surface until it's as clear as possible. Rinse the sponge frequently and change the water as necessary. Allow the area to dry. Polish off remaining grout residue with a clean, dry cloth.

Tips for Working with Mosaics ▸

To use computer programs to generate your design, you need specialized software, access to a scanner, and a photograph or piece of artwork to scan. After you import the image file, the program reads the file, assigns tile colors to it, and creates a pattern—some even produce a precise shopping list for the project. The process is fairly easy and the results can be spectacular. Following a computer-generated chart, place tiles in grids and use mosaic mounting media to transfer them to the project area (see pages 101 to 104).

Use bright white grout around small mosaic tiles, especially glass mosaic tiles. A white-tinted thinset mortar is also used with most glass tiles—standard thinset will read through the tile and dull the appearance.

Cross-stitch and needlepoint patterns are designed to create patterns from small squares of color. Simpler patterns can be used as mosaic designs, too. Assign tile colors for the various thread colors indicated on the pattern. Set the tile as described on page 102.

Combination Tile Floor

This hybrid product combines the classic, refined look of ceramic tile with the easy installation of resilient flooring. Made to resemble a range of hard materials, from slate to quarry tile to marble, combination tiles feel warmer and more comfortable underfoot than ordinary ceramic tile.

Designs vary from brand to brand, but most major manufacturers of resilient tile now offer combination products as well. You can install them like resilient tile, with each tile placed tightly against the next, or you can leave spaces between the squares and add grout to replicate the look and feel of ceramic tile.

With or without grout, combination tile—also known as compound resilient tile—is easy to maintain. Some manufacturers offer generous warranties, promising that the tiles will not fade, stain, crack, or show wear for many years. This confidence translates to peace of mind for you.

Tools & Materials ▸

- Tape measure
- Chalk line
- 1/16" notched trowel
- Combination tile
- Flooring adhesive
- Weighted roller
- Joint sealer
- Cleaning supplies
- Coping saw (or cutting tool recommended by manufacturer)
- Grout (optional)
- Eye protection

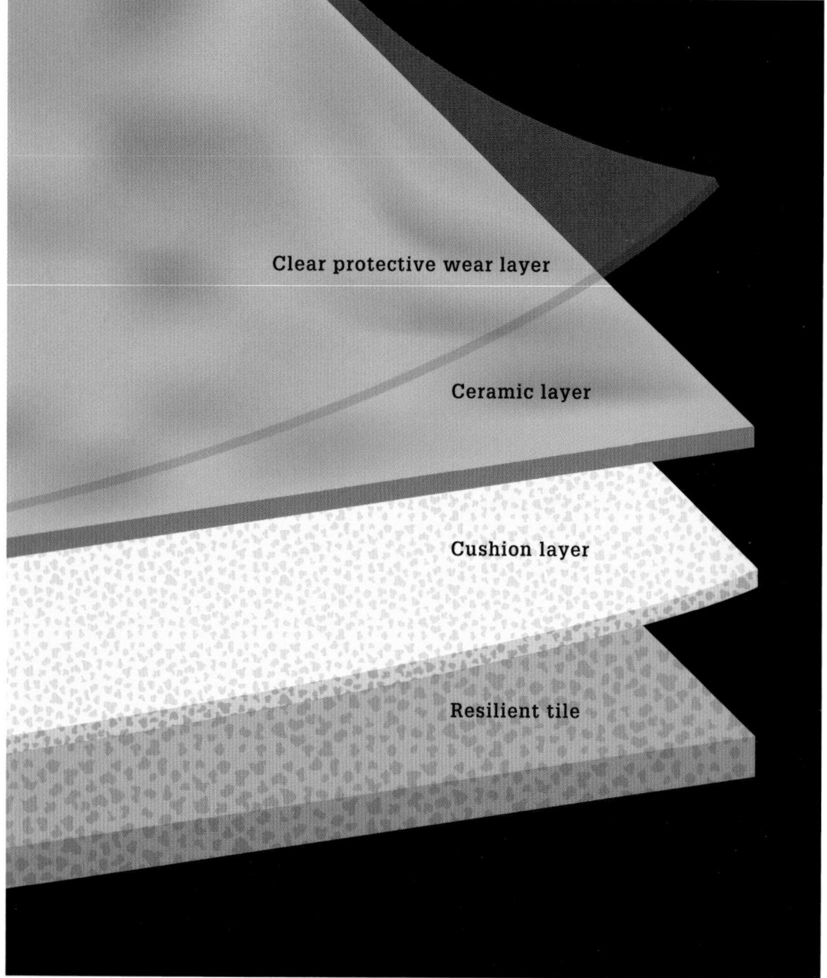

In kitchens and bathrooms, floor coverings need to withstand heavy traffic, frequent cleaning, and lots of moisture. Ceramic tile meets these needs, but it can be difficult to install, feels cold underfoot, and is not forgiving with dropped dishes. Vinyl, in sheets or tiles, makes a softer, warmer surface that is inexpensive and relatively easy to install. But vinyl is vulnerable to scrapes and gouges and doesn't last as long as ceramic tile. In recent years, manufacturers have found ways of using the best properties of both materials in combination tiles. These vinyl tiles are covered with a thin layer of ceramic composite. They can be installed like regular vinyl tiles, with their edges pushed together, or with spaces left for grout.

Combination tile cultivates the beauty and durability of stone or ceramic tile and adds the comfort and warmth of vinyl flooring. The resulting material is truly the best of both worlds.

How to Install Combination Tile

Combination tiles can be installed on a variety of surfaces. Check the manufacturer's instructions to make sure your underlayment is recommended. It should be clean, dry, and free of dust, dirt, grease, and wax. Sweep, vacuum, and damp-mop the surface before you begin.

Measure the outside edges of the room. Find the middle point on opposite walls and snap chalk lines between them. The intersection of the lines should be in the middle of the room.

Starting at the central intersection, dry-lay a row of tiles to one wall. If the last tile will be less than ¼ the width of a full tile, you may want to move the center point.

Re-mark your layout lines to match your adjusted center point from step 3. Check the central intersecting lines for square using the 3-4-5 method.

Avoid positioning tile joints directly over underlayment joints or seams in existing flooring. If this happens, reposition the chalk lines to offset joints by at least 3" or half the width of one tile. Repeat the dry-laying test, adjusting the lines as needed, until you have a definite starting point.

Apply the recommended adhesive to one quadrant of the center intersection with a notched trowel. Let adhesive set for the time specified by the manufacturer and then lay tiles along the layout lines. Use only as much adhesive as you can cover during the working time allowed. Continue to work from the center outward in each quadrant.

To work around obstacles, place the tile up against the obstacle and mark cut lines. Follow manufacturer instructions for cutting tile.

Within an hour after the tiles are set, roll the floor with a weighted roller. Work in both directions, taking care not to push any tiles out of place. Re-roll the floor before grouting the tiles or applying a joint sealer.

Porcelain Snap-lock Tile

Porcelain snap-lock tile flooring is a relatively new innovation that combines the easy installation of laminate floors with the durability and feel of ceramic tile. Each square porcelain tile is placed on a plastic tray with interlocking tabs on top of a rubberized non-skid base. This construction allows the tiles to be assembled into a floating floor that requires no adhesive and creates a remarkably similar feel to a conventional tile floor.

This type of tile floor is much quicker to lay, less expensive, and it can be replaced with far less hassle than a floor installed in a bed of adhesive. The floor can also be installed over any clean and stable existing surface as long as variations in the floor surface don't exceed ¼-inch over a 10-foot span. You can also choose from 12-inch or four-inch square tiles. Once sealed with the flexible grout supplied by the manufacturer, the floor is as resistant to moisture as any tile floor.

The one drawback to the snap-lock porcelain tile currently on the market is the palette of colors, which is currently limited to a family of earth-tone beiges and browns. These colors do blend with a wide range of décor schemes, however. The mottled satin finish is also easy to clean and doesn't show dirt between cleanings. And, as the technology catches on, more and more colors will likely become available.

Tools & Materials ▸

- Snap-lock tiles (See Resources, page 249)
- Carpenter's square
- Rubber tapping block
- Rubber coated pull bar
- Eye and ear protection
- Trowel
- Wet saw
- Angle grinder
- Utility knife
- Mallet
- Flexible grout
- Grout float
- Sponge
- Tape measure
- Gloves

The look and feel of traditional ceramic tile is replicated with these snap-together tiles made up of a porcelain ceramic surface over a substrate that has interlocking tabs (inset). Flexible grout is the key to this system's workability.

How to Install a Snap-Lock Tile Floor

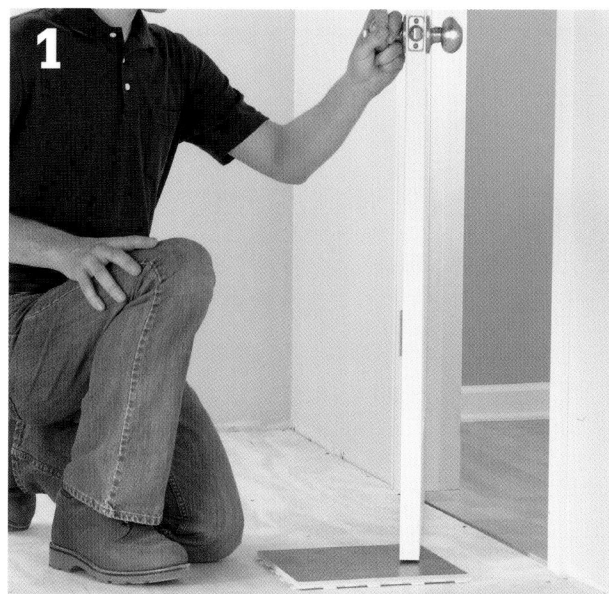

Check the door swing for all doors in the room to make sure they will clear the new tile floor. If the door won't clear, or if the gap between the door and the floor is less than ¼", remove and shorten the door. Flush-cut the door casings to allow for tile clearance, and remove shoe molding and all appliances and fixtures that block access to the floor.

Check that walls are square using a carpenter's square or the 3-4-5 measurement method. If walls are out of square, decide how you will adjust rows to compensate. Also measure floor width and decide if you want to place the first row in the center of the floor or begin at a wall.

Lay the first two tiles after removing the lock tabs on the wall-facing side or sides using a sharp utility knife. Start placing tiles in the corner and leave a ¼" expansion gap between the tiles and the walls. Although the locking tabs project out ¼" from the tiles and thus would function as ¼" spacers, the fact that they are integral parts of the tiles makes this gap ineffective as an expansion gap. Use traditional removable spacers. Attach each new tile by aligning the tiles, connecting at the corner and then pressing together until the tiles lock.

Use a rubber tapping block if you have difficulty engaging the locking tabs by simply pressing them together. Align the tiles, then hold the block against the side of the tile—not the plastic tray or grid. Gently tap the block until the tiles lock together.

(continued)

Continue to lay tiles, paying careful attention to layout patterns and directional veining in the tile surfaces. If you make a mistake and need to remove and adjust a tile, you can disconnect the joints with a rubber coated pull bar or any other prying tool with a protective surface coating. Place the tool edge between the two tiles and gently pry them apart.

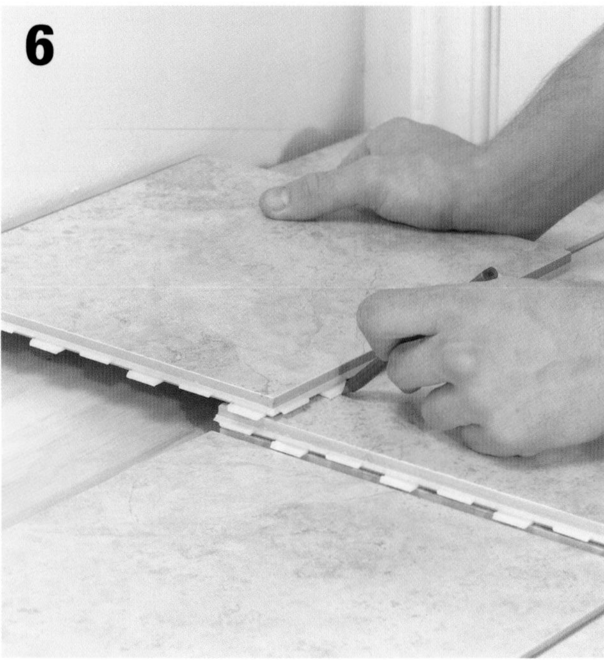

Mark tiles to fit around obstacles or for the final row by laying one tile on top and aligning with the previous row. Then lay a tile on top of that one, and align within ¼" of the wall or obstacle. Mark a cutline on the middle tile using the space between the tabs of the top tile as guidance.

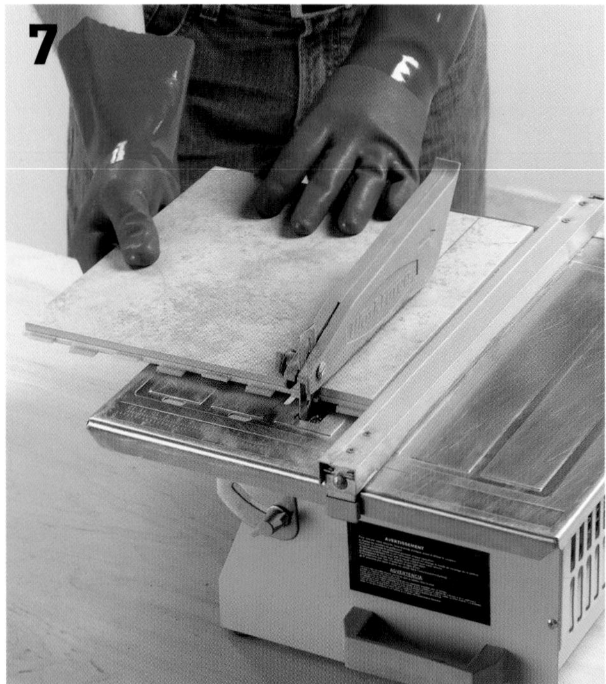

Cut tiles using a wet saw with a blade meant for cutting ceramic and porcelain tiles. Cut on the waste side of the marked line, and change water in the basin frequently to ensure clean cuts. Porcelain takes a long time to cut. Be patient and do not force the tile into the saw blade.

Cutting Curves ▸

To cut curves and other irregular shapes, use an angle grinder that's fitted with a diamond-tipped cutting wheel. Cut all the way through the tile, including the plastic base layer. This will take several passes. *Note: The tiles seen here have very aggressive anti-skid ribs on the bottom and do not require securing to the worksurface as a typical workpiece would.*

8

Set final tiles into position and then pull them back into the preceding rows using a rubberized pull bar. When the floor is completed, open the pail of flexible grout and mix thoroughly with a trowel according to the manufacturer's instructions.

9

Apply grout in the tile gaps with a firm rubber grout float. Spread grout diagonally to the tile joints, working the grout firmly into the joints. Remove excess grout from the tiles with the edge of the float and touch up voids or low areas in the grout joints.

10

Clean off excess grout. Fill a 5 gal. bucket with clean water and use a sponge to clean the surfaces of the tiles. Wipe off grout residue and use sponge to smooth grout lines. *Important: Rinse the sponge thoroughly with clean water after each pass.*

Replacing a Damaged Tile ▸

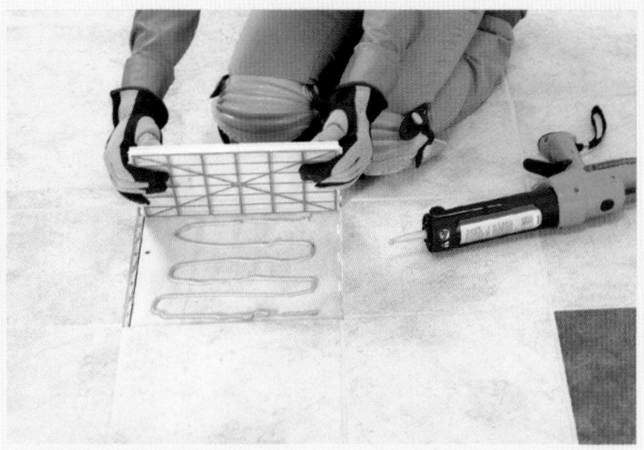

To replace a porcelain snap-lock tile that has been cracked or damaged, remove the grout all around the tile. Use a grout cutter or simply chip out the grout with an awl or fine chisel. In either case, be careful not to chip the surrounding tiles. Then cut the downward-facing tabs on three sides of the tile with a utility knife. Pry up the broken tile and pull away from the uncut side. Remove downward tabs on three sides of the new tile and lay a bed of general construction adhesive under the new tile. Slide the new tile into place and lock the uncut side to the adjacent tile. Let adhesive dry and grout with flexible grout.

Shower Base

Building a custom-tiled shower base lets you choose the shape and size of your shower rather than having its dimensions dictated by available products. Building the base is quite simple, though it does require time and some knowledge of basic masonry techniques because the base is formed primarily using mortar. What you get for your time and trouble can be spectacular.

Before designing a shower base, contact your local building department regarding code restrictions and to secure the necessary permits. Most codes require water controls to be accessible from outside the shower and describe acceptable door positions and operation. Requirements like these influence the size and position of the base.

Choosing the tile before finalizing the design lets you size the base to require mostly full tile. Showers are among the most frequently used amenities in the average home, so it really makes sense to build one that is comfortable and pleasing to your senses. Consider using small tile and gradate the color from top to bottom or in a sweep across the walls. Or, use trim tile and listellos on the walls to create an interesting focal point.

Whatever tile you choose, remember to seal the grout in your new shower and to maintain it carefully over the years. Water-resistant grout protects the structure of the shower and prolongs its useful life.

Tools & Materials ▸

- Tape measure
- Circular saw
- Hammer
- Utility knife
- Stapler
- 2-ft. level
- Mortar mixing box
- Trowel
- Wood float
- Felt-tip marker
- Ratchet wrench
- Tin snips
- Torpedo level
- Tools for installing tile
- Framing lumber (1×, 2 × 4, 2 × 10)
- 16d galvanized common nails
- 15# building paper
- Staples
- 3-piece shower drain
- PVC cement
- Galvanized metal lath
- Thick-bed floor mortar ("deck mud")
- Latex mortar additive
- Thinset mortar
- CPE waterproof membrane & preformed dam corners
- CPE membrane solvent glue
- CPE membrane sealant
- Cementboard and materials for installing cementboard
- Materials for installing tile
- Builder's sand
- Portland cement
- Masonry hoe
- Gloves
- Dust mask or respirator
- Straightedge
- ¼" wood shims
- Mortar
- Tile spacers
- Balloon tester
- Silicon caulk
- Caulk gun

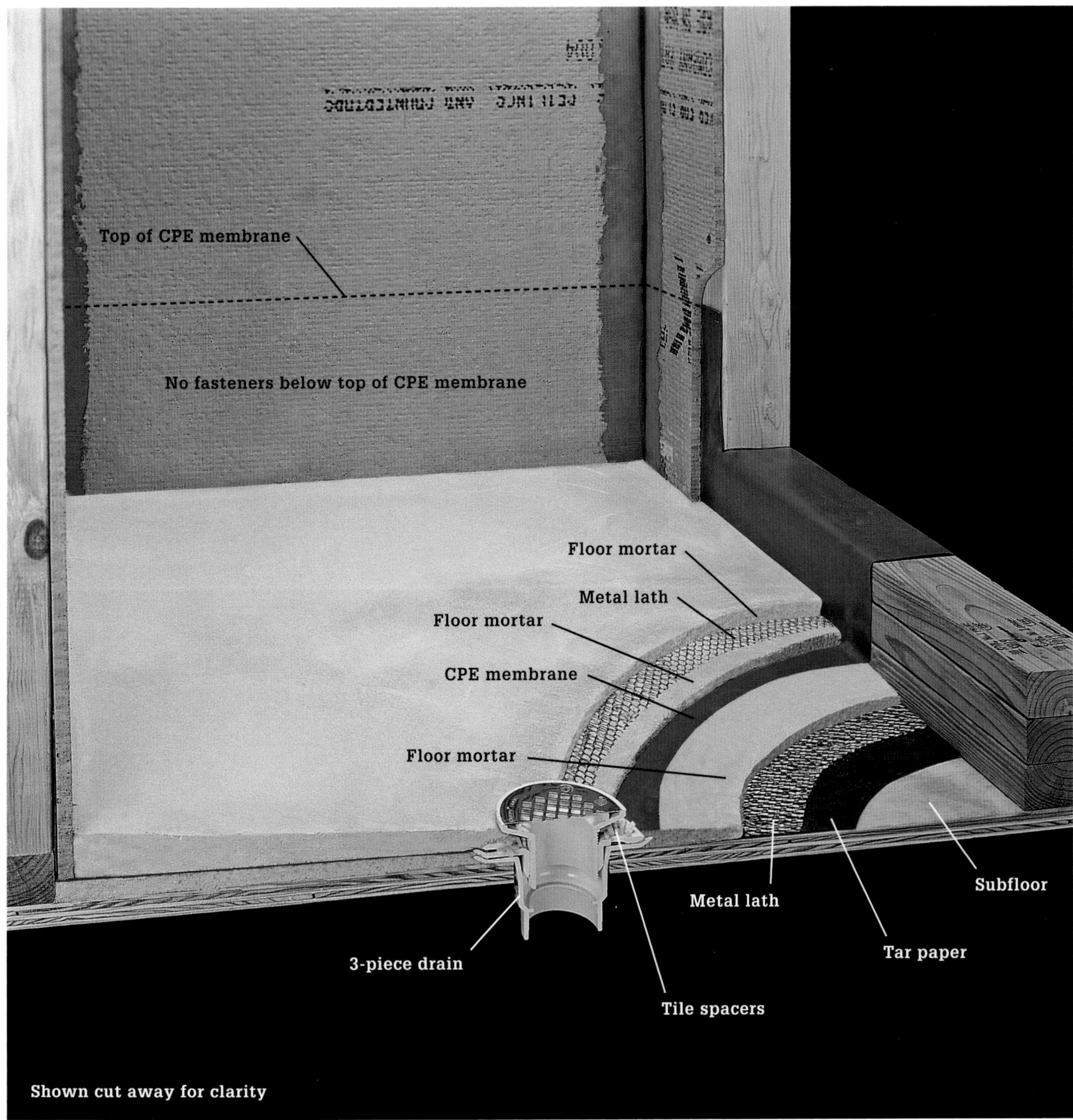

Tips for Building a Custom Shower Base ▸

A custom-tiled shower base is built in three layers to ensure proper water drainage: the pre-pan, the shower pan, and the shower floor. A mortar pre-pan is first built on top of the subfloor, establishing a slope toward the drain of ¼" for every 12" of shower floor. Next, a waterproof chlorinated polyethylene (CPE) membrane forms the shower pan, providing a watertight seal for the shower base. Finally, a second mortar bed reinforced with wire mesh is installed for the shower floor, providing a surface for tile installation. If water penetrates the tiled shower floor, the shower pan and sloped pre-pan will direct it to the weep holes of the 3-piece drain.

One of the most important steps in building a custom-tiled shower base is testing the shower pan after installation (step 13). This allows you to locate and fix any leaks to prevent costly damage.

Mixing Deck Mud ▸

Mortar beds for laying tile are made from deck mud, a simple mortar consisting of a proportioned mixture of builders sand and Portland cement, with a little water added to bind the particles together. Sometimes referred to as dry pack mortar or floor mud, it can be purchased in prepackaged blends or you can easily make it yourself. It can be set in thicker layers than ordinary thinset mortar.

Deck mud is made using a recipe consisting of a ratio of four to six parts of builders sand to one part of Portland cement. The higher the proportion of Portland cement in the mixture, the richer it is considered to be. Leaner mortars contain a lower proportion of Portland cement. A mortar bed 1¼" thick (a common thickness for a shower receptor base) requires approximately 12 pounds of dry sand per square foot of application. Add an additional three pounds of sand per square foot for each additional ¼" of mortar thickness desired. The amount of Portland cement required will depend on the mixing ratio and the total volume of sand required to complete the job. A richer blend that uses a four to one ratio is suitable for small areas like shower pan mortar beds.

The ingredients for making your own mortar bed "mud" are minimal. You'll need sharp sand (also called builders sand), Portland cement, and water. The proportions vary by application.

How to Mix Deck Mud

Add the dry ingredients (builders sand and Portland cement) to a mortar box in the correct ratios. For general purposes, four parts sand to one part mortar mix (by volume) works. Don't mix more mud than you can use in a half hour or so.

Add small amounts of clean, potable water to the dry mixture and blend to an evenly moist consistency using a masonry hoe. Be sure to wear gloves and a dust mask or respirator.

A squeezed clump of deck mud should hold its shape without sagging or falling apart.

How to Build a Custom-tiled Shower Base

Remove building materials to expose subfloor and stud walls. Cut three 2 × 4s for the curb and fasten them to the floor joists and the studs at the shower threshold with 16d galvanized common nails. Also cut 2 × 10 lumber to size and install in the stud bays around the perimeter of the shower base.

Staple 15# building paper to the subfloor of the shower base. Disassemble the 3-piece shower drain and glue the bottom piece to the drain pipe with PVC cement. Partially screw the drain bolts into the drain piece, and stuff a rag into the drain pipe to prevent mortar from falling into the drain.

Mark the height of the bottom drain piece on the wall farthest from the center of the drain. Measure from the center of the drain straight across to that wall, then raise the height mark ¼" for every 12" of shower floor to slope the pre-pan toward the drain. Trace a reference line at the height mark around the perimeter of the entire alcove using a level.

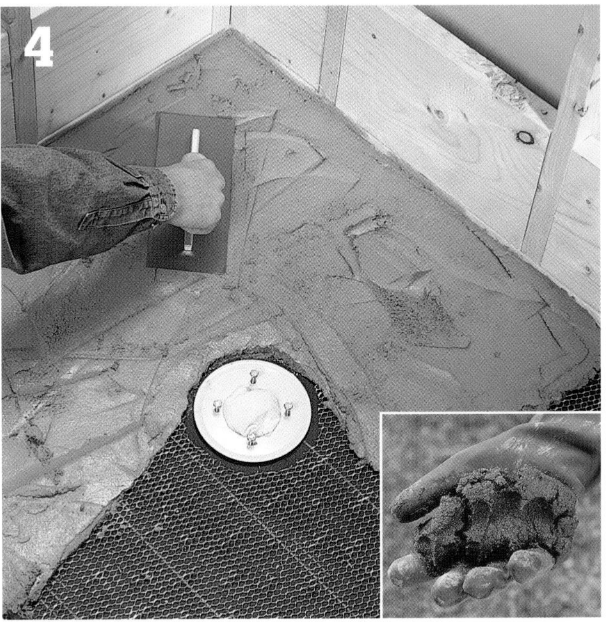

Staple galvanized metal lath over the building paper; cut a hole in the lath ½" from the drain. Mix floor mortar (or "deck mud") to a fairly dry consistency using a latex additive for strength; mortar should hold its shape when squeezed (inset). Trowel the mortar onto the subfloor, building the pre-pan from the flange of the drain piece to the height line on the perimeter of the walls.

(continued)

Continue using the trowel to form the pre pan, checking the slope using a level and filling any low spots with mortar. Finish the surface of the pre-pan with a wood float until it is even and smooth. Allow the mortar to cure overnight.

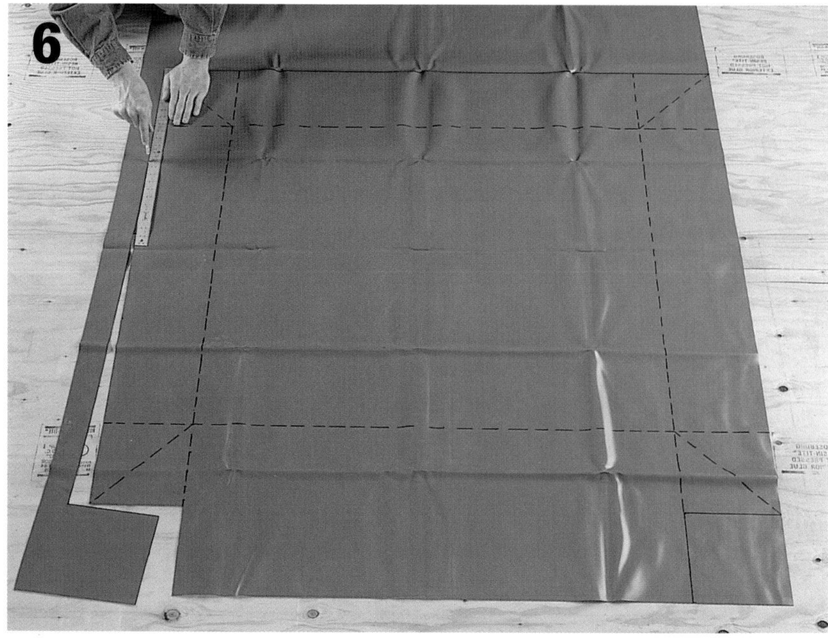

Measure the dimensions of the shower floor, and mark it out on a sheet of CPE waterproof membrane using a felt-tipped marker. From the floor outline, measure out and mark an additional 8" for each wall and 16" for the curb end. Cut the membrane to size using a utility knife and straightedge. Be careful to cut on a clean, smooth surface to prevent puncturing the membrane. Lay the membrane onto the shower pan.

Measure to find the exact location of the drain and mark it on the membrane, outlining the outer diameter of the drain flange. Cut a circular piece of CPE membrane roughly 2" larger than the drain flange, then use CPE membrane solvent glue to weld it into place and reinforce the seal at the drain.

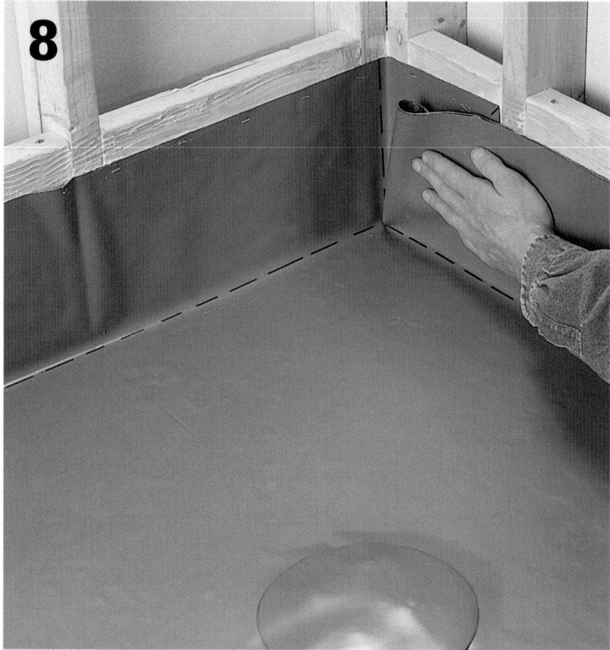

Apply CPE sealant around the drain. Fold the membrane along the floor outline. Set the membrane over the pre-pan so the reinforced drain seal is centered over the drain bolts. Working from the drain to the walls, carefully tuck the membrane tight into each corner, folding the extra material into triangular flaps.

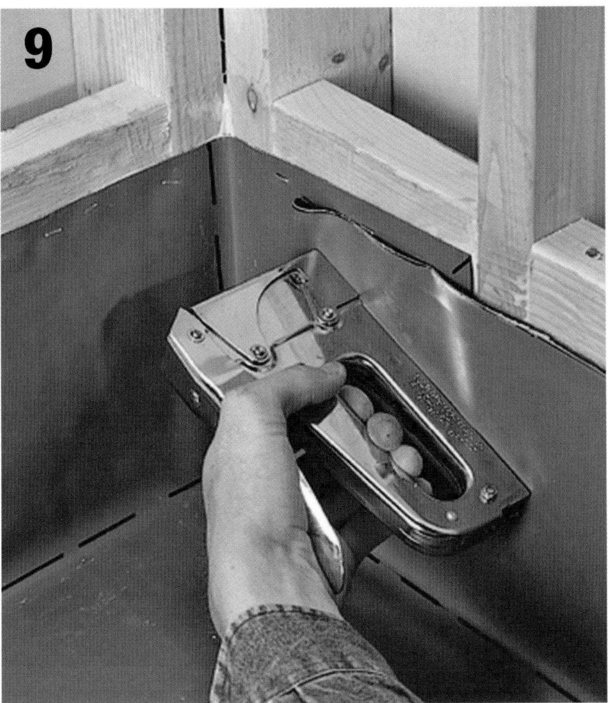

Apply CPE solvent glue to one side, press the flap flat, then staple it in place. Staple only the top edge of the membrane to the blocking; do not staple below the top of the curb, or on the curb itself.

At the shower curb, cut the membrane along the studs so it can be folded over the curb. Solvent-glue a dam corner at each inside corner of the curb. Do not fasten the dam corners with staples.

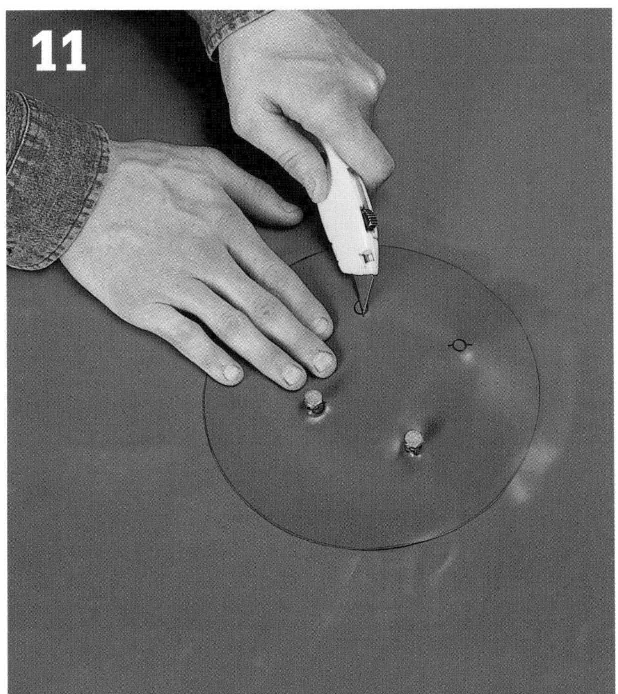

At the reinforced drain seal on the membrane, locate and mark the drain bolts. Press the membrane down around the bolts, then use a utility knife to carefully cut a slit just large enough for the bolts to poke through. Push the membrane down over the bolts.

Use a utility knife to carefully cut away only enough of the membrane to expose the drain and allow the middle drain piece to fit in place. Remove the drain bolts, then position the middle drain piece over the bolt holes. Reinstall the bolts, tightening them evenly and firmly to create a watertight seal.

(continued)

Test the shower pan for leaks overnight. Place a balloon tester in the drain below the weep holes, and fill the pan with water, to 1" below the top of the curb. Mark the water level and let the water sit overnight. If the water level remains the same, the pan holds water. If the level is lower, locate and fix leaks in the pan using patches of membrane and CPE solvent.

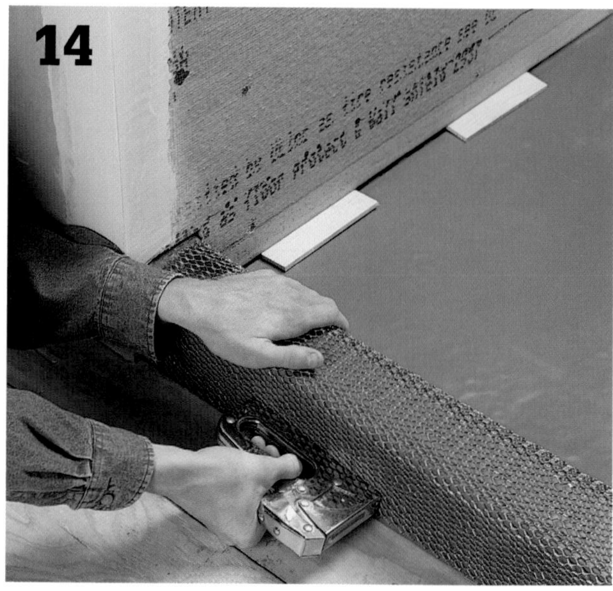

Install cementboard on the alcove walls, using ¼" wood shims to lift the bottom edge off the CPE membrane. To prevent puncturing the membrane, do not use fasteners in the lower 8" of the cementboard. Cut a piece of metal lath to fit around the three sides of the curb. Bend the lath so it tightly conforms to the curb. Pressing the lath against the top of the curb, staple it to the outside face of the curb. Mix enough mortar for the two sides of the curb.

Overhang the front edge of the curb with a straight 1× board, so it is flush with the outer wall material. Apply mortar to the mesh with a trowel, building to the edge of the board. Clear away excess mortar, then use a torpedo level to check for plumb, making adjustments as needed. Repeat for the inside face of the curb. Allow the mortar to cure overnight. *Note: The top of the curb will be finished after tile is installed (step 19).*

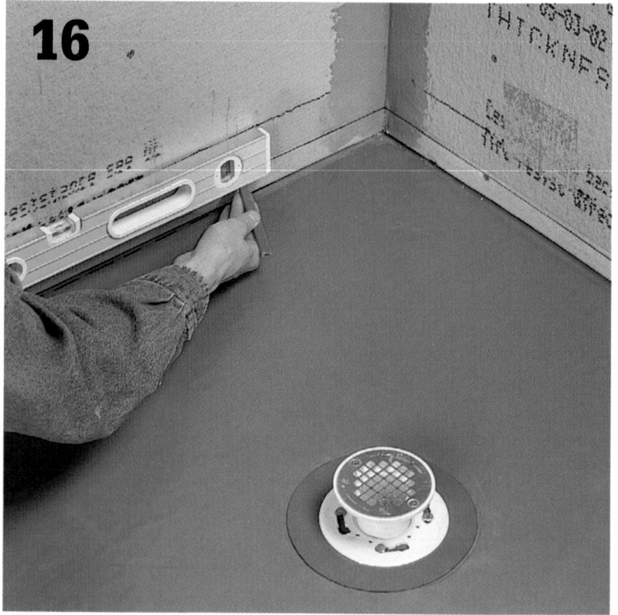

Attach the drain strainer piece to the drain, adjusting it to a minimum of 1½" above the shower pan. On one wall, mark 1½" up from the shower pan, then use a level to draw a reference line around the perimeter of the shower base. Because the pre-pan establishes the ¼" per foot slope, this measurement will maintain that slope.

Spread tile spacers over the weep holes of the drain to prevent mortar from plugging the holes. Mix the floor mortar, then build up the shower floor to roughly half the thickness of the base. Cut metal lath to cover the mortar bed, keeping it ½" from the drain (see photo in step 18).

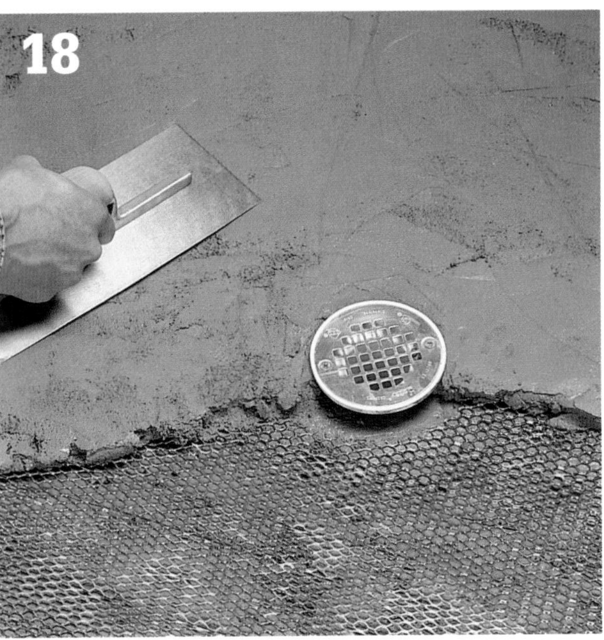

Continue to add mortar, building the floor to the reference line on the walls. Use a level to check the slope, and pack mortar into low spots with a trowel. Leave space at the drain for the thickness of the tile. Float the surface using a wood float until it is smooth and slopes evenly to the drain. When finished, allow the mortar to cure overnight before installing the tiles.

After the floor has cured, draw reference lines and establish the tile layout, then mix a batch of thinset mortar and install the floor tile. At the curb, cut the tiles for the inside to protrude ½" above the unfinished top of the curb, and the tiles for the outside to protrude ⅝" above the top, establishing a ⅛" slope so water drains back into the shower. Use a level to check the tops of the tiles for level as you work.

Mix enough floor mortar to cover the unfinished top of the curb, then pack it in place between the tiles using a trowel. Screed off the excess mortar flush with the tops of the side tiles. Allow the mortar to cure, then install bullnose cap tile. Install the wall tile, then grout, clean, and seal all the tile. After the grout has cured fully, run a bead of silicone caulk around all inside corners to create control joints.

Wall Projects

This chapter starts with a very basic wall project that can be adapted for many different applications. Then, we go over how to tile a tub alcove, another tile project that's frequently undertaken by do-it-yourselfers.

From these beginnings, it's a small step to learn how to embellish an existing tile wall with a medallion or decorative tile, or tile a fireplace surround or kitchen backsplash. With the confidence developed in those projects, you'll be ready to tile a tub deck or build a wall niche, if the opportunity arises.

The projects in this chapter introduce you to several new and interesting techniques. The tub deck project shows you how to set several types of trim tile and the wall niche project illustrates how to set irregularly shaped, groutless tile. The medallion project walks you through how to embellish an otherwise plain tiled wall without re-tiling the entire surface.

Use these projects as jumping off points, as places from which to let your imagination soar. Study the techniques and information presented here, then throw in some accent tiles or get creative and add splashes of color—make a project your own.

In this chapter:

Gallery of Wall Tile Projects

Subway tile has a horizontal orientation that many designers find appealing. Although most subway tile installations feature white or primary colors, the earth tone tiles seen here have a mellow, natural appearance.

Larger tiles make sense in a shower because the relatively low number of grout lines means the likelihood of a leak is smaller. The large areas also make cleaning easier.

Mirrored glass and polished tiles are a natural pairing with a cool, clean look. Glass shelving intensifies the effect.

Using the same tile style on the walls and floors can be a tricky design maneuver, but if handled with some expertise the effect can be highly dramatic.

Mosaic wall tile works best when it is installed with some discretion. Featuring it only on one wall is a tested strategy that usually succeeds. Choose a wall with some interesting features, such as a lavatory sink, a mirror, or a built-in shelf or cabinet.

Bold colors and a contrasting installation scheme combine for an attention-getting statement. This may be very successful in a small bath, but the effect can be dizzying if it is not restrained somewhat.

High-tech, contemporary furnishings look great in a room with bright glass tile walls.

Checkered mosaic accents not only make a tiled room more interesting, they help define space according to its function.

You can use every tile shape and style in the book if you stick to a consistent color scheme.

Etched tiles can be created for you by custom tile suppliers. The large tub surround tile with its etched form functions very much as wall art in this installation.

Wall tile can be installed as wainscot for a traditional look that makes a small room seem larger. Raising the top height of the wainscot above the typical 36" creates an even more old-fashioned effect that is often found in Victorian-style rooms.

Colorful tiles are fun to look at and they can be used to effectively complement unconventional design choices, such as the green glass valve handle on this lavatory.

Evaluating & Preparing Walls

The substrate for wall tiles must be stable; that is, it must not expand and contract in response to changes in temperature or humidity. For this reason, it will be necessary to strip all wallpaper before tiling, even if the paper has been painted. Similarly, remove any type of wood paneling before tiling a wall. Even painted walls need some preparation. For example, paint that's likely to peel needs to be sanded thoroughly before the project starts.

Smooth concrete walls can be tiled, but the concrete has to be prepared. Scrub it with a concrete cleaner, then apply a concrete bonding agent. Use a grinder to smooth any unevenness. Install an isolation membrane (see page 42) to keep the tile from cracking if the walls crack, which is a common problem.

Brick or block walls are a good substrate for tiling, but the surface is not smooth enough to be tiled without additional preparation. Mix extra Portland cement into brick mortar, apply a smooth, even skim coat to the walls, and let it dry thoroughly before beginning the tile project.

Existing tile can be tiled over as long as the glaze has been roughened enough for the adhesive to adhere properly. Remember, though, that the new tile will protrude quite a way from the wall. You'll need to accommodate for this on the edges and around receptacles, switches, windows or doors, and other obstacles.

In some cases, you'll find that it's easiest to remove the old substrate and install new (see pages 130 to 131). Even if you're working with an appropriate substrate in good condition, you will need to evaluate the wall to make sure it is plumb and flat, and fix surface flaws before you begin your wall tiling project.

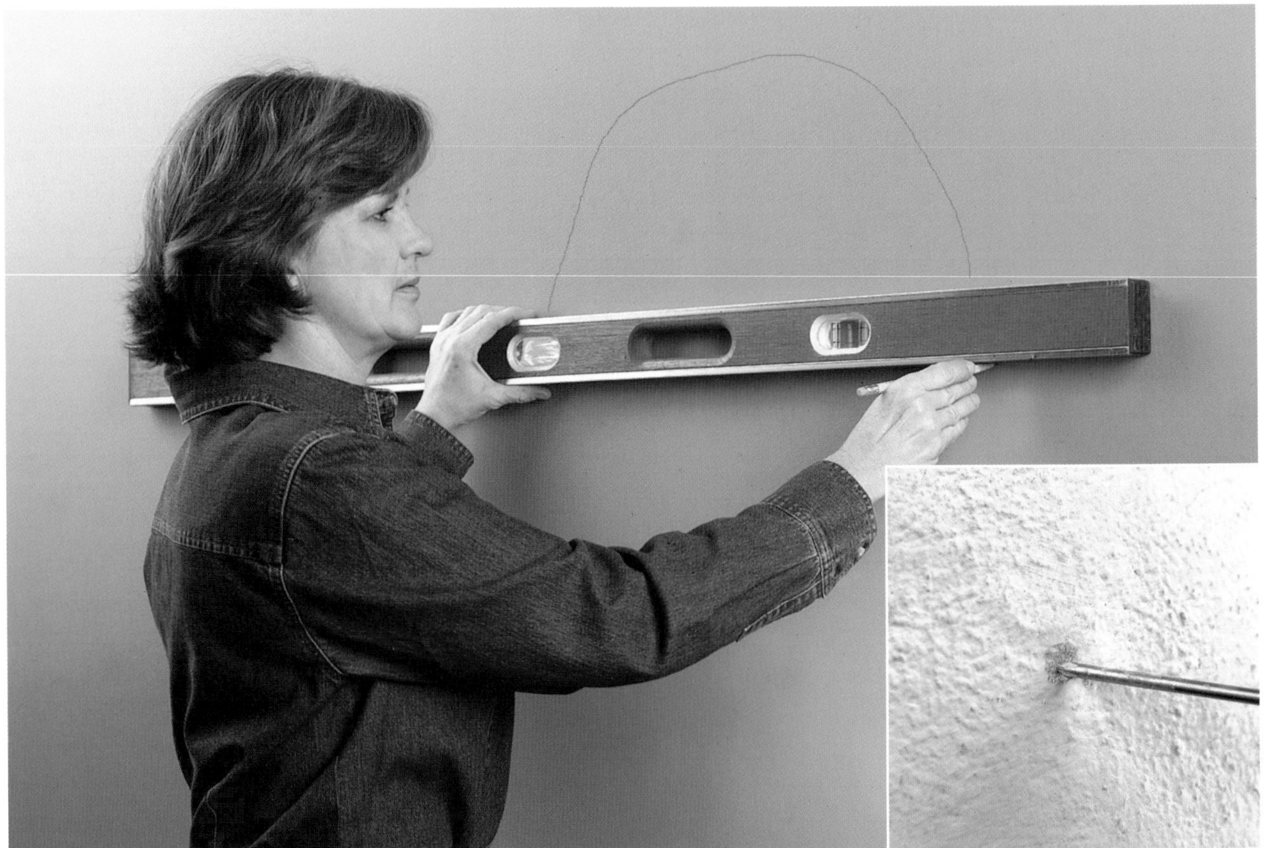

Run a straightedge up and down and side-to-side along wall surfaces and outline the valleys. Any difference of ¼" or more must be filled with joint compound using a 12" taping knife. You may need to apply a number of thin layers for best results. Some plaster surfaces are softer than others. High lime content plaster (inset) is too soft to serve as a backing surface for tile.

How to Patch Holes

Patching small holes: Fill smooth holes with spackle, then sand smooth. Cover ragged holes with a repair patch, then apply two coats of spackle or wallboard compound. Use a damp sponge or wet sander to smooth the repair area, then sand when dry, if necessary.

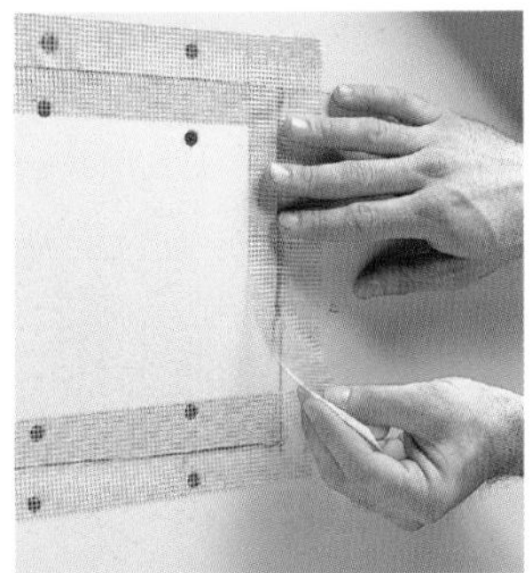

Patching large holes: Draw cutting lines around the hole, then cut away the damaged area using a wallboard saw. Place plywood strips behind the opening and drive wallboard screws to hold them in place. Drive screws through the wallboard patch and into the backers. Cover the joints with wallboard tape and finish with compound.

Checking & Correcting Out-of-Plumb Walls

Use a plumb bob to determine if corners are plumb. A wall more than ½" out of plumb should be corrected before tiling.

If the wall is out of plumb, use a long level to mark a plumb line the entire height of the wall. Remove the wall covering from the out-of-plumb wall.

Cut and install shims on all the studs to create a new, plumb surface for attaching backing materials. Draw arrows at the shim highpoints to mark for wallboard screw placement.

Removing Wall Surfaces

You may have to remove and replace interior wall surfaces before starting your tiling project. Most often, the material you'll be removing is wallboard, but you may be removing plaster or ceramic tile. Removing wall surfaces is a messy job, but it is not difficult. Before you begin, shut off the power and inspect the wall for wiring and plumbing.

Make sure you wear appropriate safety gear—glasses and dust masks—since you will be generating dust and small pieces of debris. Use plastic sheeting to close off doorways and air vents to prevent dust from spreading throughout the house. Protect floor surfaces and the bathtub with rosin paper securely taped down. Dust and debris will find their way under drop cloths and will quickly scratch your floor or tub surfaces.

Tools & Materials ▸

- Utility knife
- Pry bar
- Circular saw with demolition blade
- Straightedge
- Maul
- Masonry chisel
- Heavy tarp
- Reciprocating saw with bimetal blade
- Hammer
- Protective eyewear
- Dust mask
- 2 × 4 lumber

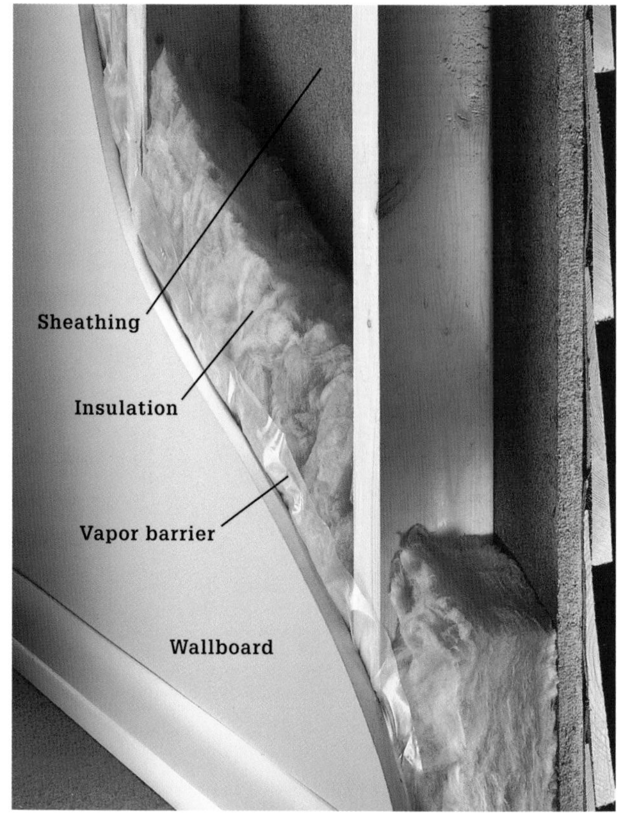

Be aware of how your wall is built before you start tearing off surfaces. If it is an exterior wall take extra care not to disturb insulation. You should plan on replacing the vapor barrier before installing new wallcoverings.

How to Remove Wallboard

Remove baseboards and other trim and prepare the work area. Make a ½"-deep cut from floor to ceiling using a circular saw. Use a utility knife to finish the cuts at the top and bottom and to cut through the taped horizontal seam where the wall meets the ceiling surface.

Insert the end of a pry bar into the cut near one corner of the opening. Pull the pry bar until the wallboard breaks, then tear away the broken pieces. Take care to avoid damaging the wallboard outside the project area.

How to Remove Plaster

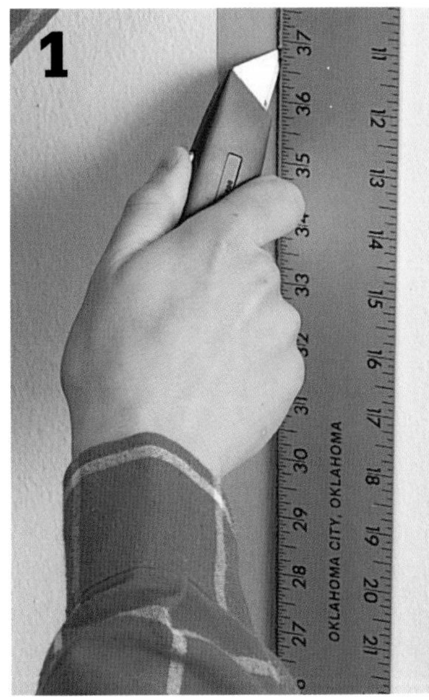

Remove baseboards and other trim and prepare the work area. Score the cutting line several times with a utility knife using a straightedge as a guide. The line should be at least ⅛" deep.

Break the plaster along the edge by holding a scrap piece of 2 × 4 on edge just inside the scored line, and rapping it with a hammer. Use a pry bar to remove the remaining plaster.

Cut through the lath along the edges of the plaster using a reciprocating saw or jigsaw. Remove the lath from the studs using a pry bar.

How to Remove Ceramic Wall Tile

Cover the floor with a heavy tarp, and shut off the electricity and water. Knock a small starter hole into the bottom of the wall using a maul and masonry chisel.

Begin cutting out small sections of the wall by inserting a reciprocating saw with a bimetal blade into the hole, and cutting along grout lines. Be careful when sawing near pipes and wiring.

Cut the entire wall surface into small sections, removing each section as it is cut. Be careful not to cut through studs.

Installing & Finishing Wallboard

Regular wallboard is an appropriate backer for ceramic tile in dry locations. Greenboard, a moisture-resistent form of wallboard, is good for kitchens and the dry areas of bathrooms. Tub and shower surrounds and kitchen backsplashes should have a cementboard backer.

Wallboard panels are available in 4 × 8-foot or 4 × 10-foot sheets, and in ⅜-, ½-, and ⅝-inch thicknesses. For new walls, ½-inch thick is standard.

Install wallboard panels so that seams fall over the center of framing members, not at sides. Use all-purpose wallboard compound and paper joint tape to finish seams.

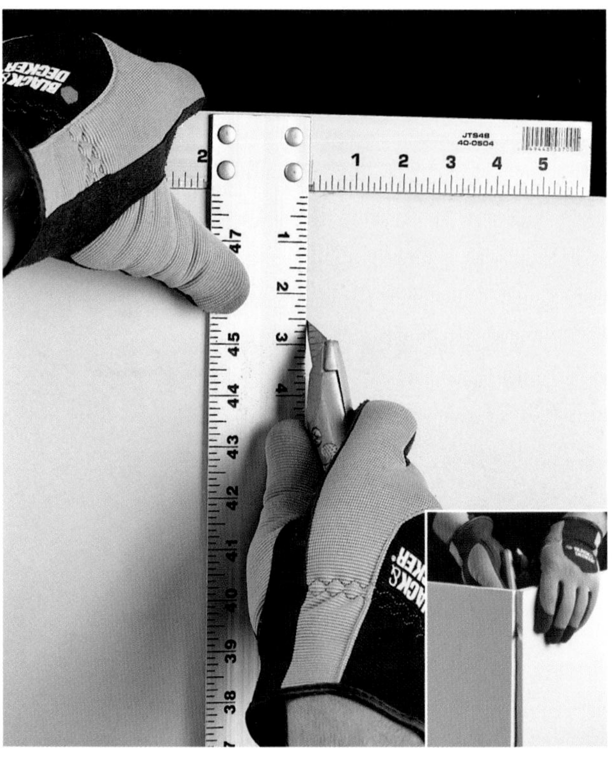

Score wallboard face paper with a utility knife using a drywall T-square as a guide. Bend the panel away from the scored line until the core breaks, then cut through the back paper (inset) with a utility knife, and separate the pieces.

Tools & Materials ▸

- Tape measure
- Utility knife
- T-square
- 6" and 12" taping knives
- 150-grit sanding sponge
- Screw gun
- Wallboard
- Wallboard tape
- 1¼" coarse-thread wallboard screws
- Wallboard compound
- Metal inside corner bead

How to Install and Finish Wallboard

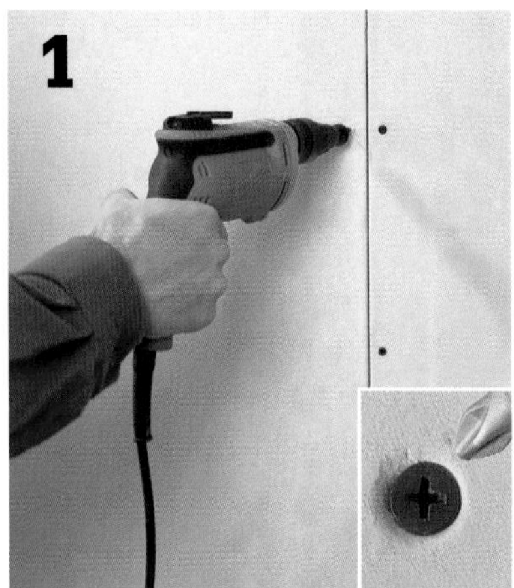

Install panels with their tapered edges butted together. Fasten with 1¼" wallboard screws, driven every 8" along the edges, and every 12" in the field. Drive screws deep enough to dimple surface without ripping face paper (inset).

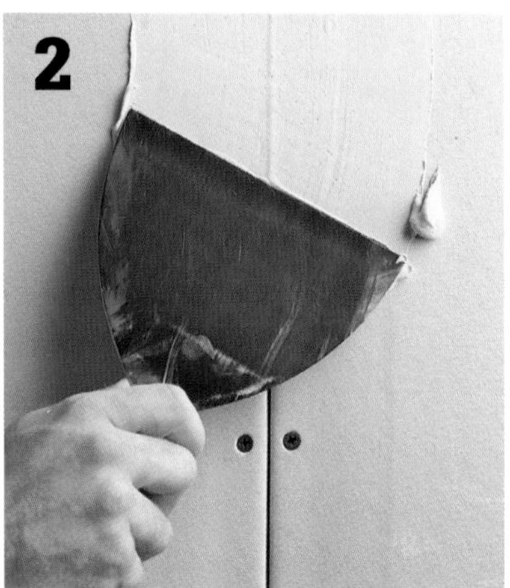

Finish the seams by applying an even bed layer of wallboard compound over the seam, about ⅛" thick using a 6" taping knife.

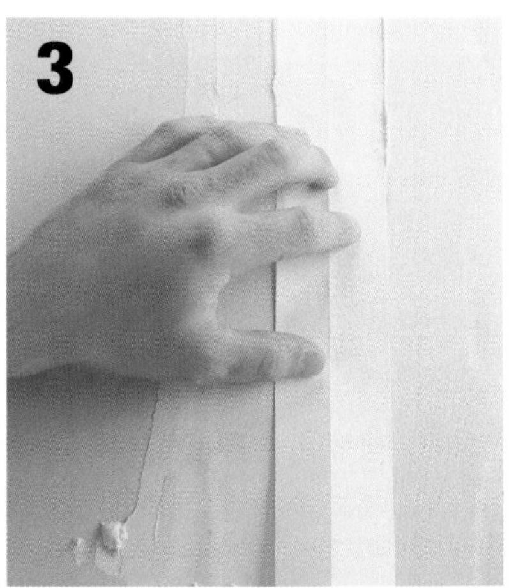

Center the wallboard tape over the seam and lightly embed it into the compound, making sure it's smooth and straight.

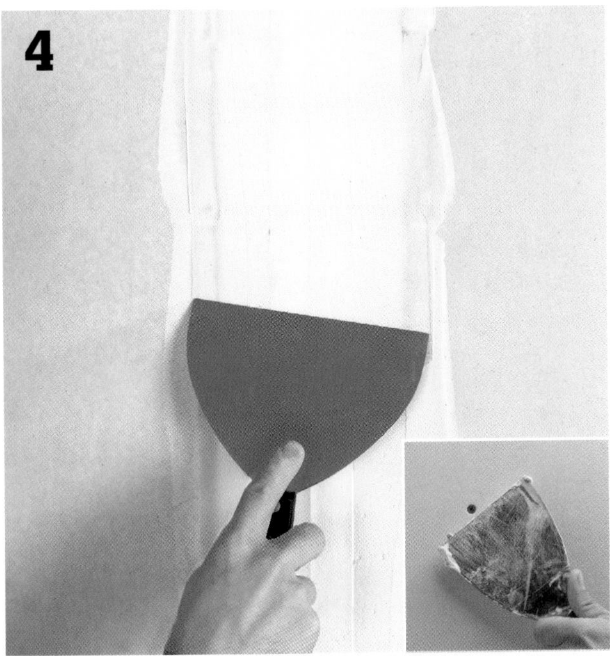

Smooth the tape with the taping knife. Apply enough pressure to force compound from underneath the tape, leaving the tape flat and with a thin layer underneath. Cover all exposed screw heads with the first of three coats of compound (inset). Let compound dry overnight.

Second-coat the seams with a thin, even layer of compound using a 12" knife. Feather the sides of the compound first, holding the blade almost flat and applying pressure to the outside of the blade so the blade just skims over the center of the seam.

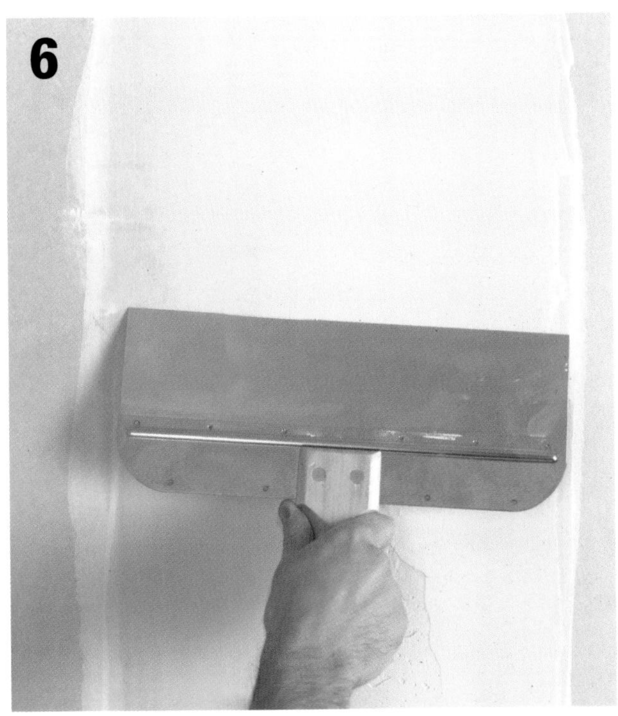

After feathering both sides, make a pass down the center of the seam, leaving the seam smooth and even, the edges feathered out even with the wallboard surface. Completely cover the joint tape. Let the second coat dry, then apply a third coat using the 12" knife. After the third coat dries completely, sand the compound lightly with a wallboard sander or a 150-grit sanding sponge.

Inside Corner Bead ▸

Finish any inside corners using paper-faced metal inside corner bead to produce straight, durable corners with little fuss. Embed the bead into a thin layer of compound, then smooth the paper with a taping knife. Apply two finish coats to the corner, then sand the compound smooth.

Installing Cementboard on Walls

Before you begin working, the wall and ceiling framing will need to be examined to make sure it meets the structural requirements for a backer board installation. Studs, joists, and rafters, often referred to as framing members, should be spaced a maximum of 16 inches on center for wall applications.

In wet areas, the application of a moisture barrier, 15 pound roofing felt or polyethylene film, is required to protect the wall cavity from moisture intrusion. This is fastened directly to the framing members using staples or roofing nails. Polyethylene sheeting is commonly found in rolls that are wide enough to cover an entire wall in one piece. Asphalt roofing felt (also called building paper) is installed in lapped rows, starting from the bottom of the wall assembly. Subsequent rows should overlap the subjacent row a minimum of two inches for horizontal seams and six inches for vertical seams and corners.

Tools & Materials ▸

- Eye and ear protection
- Screw fastening bit
- Stapler and staples
- Modified thinset mortar
- 4-mil clear poly sheeting
- 2" fiberglass mesh tape
- 1¼" cementboard screws
- 15# roofing felt
- ½" cementboard
- Work gloves
- Drill
- Tape measure
- 6" joint knife

Attach ½"-thick cementboard to the framing members horizontally with the rough side facing out. Use 1¼" cementboard screws. Fasten screws every 6" on-center for ceiling applications and every 8" on-center for wall applications. Keep fasteners 2" away from each corner and no less than ⅜" from the panel edges.

Preparing the Wall

A moisture barrier consisting of 4-mil clear polyethylene sheeting can be stapled to framing members in wet areas before installing the cementboard.

Asphalt roofing felt (15# building paper) can also be used as a moisture barrier behind cementboard panels in wet areas.

How to Hang Cementboard on Walls

Fasten panels to the wall framing members using 1¼" cementbord screws. Properly fastened, the head of each screw will sit flush with the surface of the panel. Make sure all seams fall at stud locations and install the bottom course so the panels are around ¼" off the ground.

Fill the joints using a modified thinset mortar and then embed fiberglass mesh tape into the mortar. Skim off excess mortar from the joint using a joint knife.

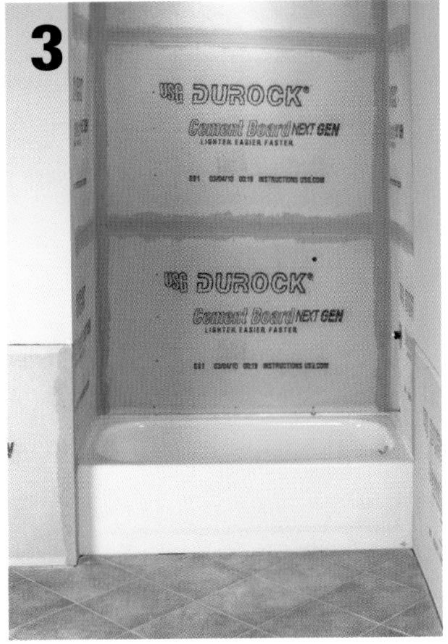

Complete the cementboard installation by applying thinset mortar over the tape and feathering out the edges. If you will be applying a waterproofing membrane over the cementboard surfaces, allow 24 hrs. for the thinset in the seams to dry.

Wall Tile Layouts

Establishing perpendicular reference lines is a critical part of every tile project, including wall projects. To create these lines, measure and mark the midpoint at the top and bottom of the wall, and then again along each side. Snap chalk lines between opposite marks to create your vertical and horizontal centerlines. Use the 3-4-5 triangle method to make sure the lines are drawn correctly. Adjust the lines until they are exactly perpendicular.

Next, do a dry run of your proposed layout, starting at the center of the wall and working toward an adjoining wall. If the gap between the last full tile and the wall is too narrow, adjust your starting point. Continue to dry-fit tile along the walls, paying special attention to any windows, doors, or permanent fixtures in the wall. If you end up with very narrow tiles anywhere, adjust the reference lines (and your layout) to avoid them. It's best not to cut tiles by more than half.

If your wall has an outside corner, start your dry run there. Place bullnose tiles over the edges of the adjoining field tiles. If this results in a narrow gap at the opposite wall, install trimmed tile next to the bullnose edge to even out or avoid the gap.

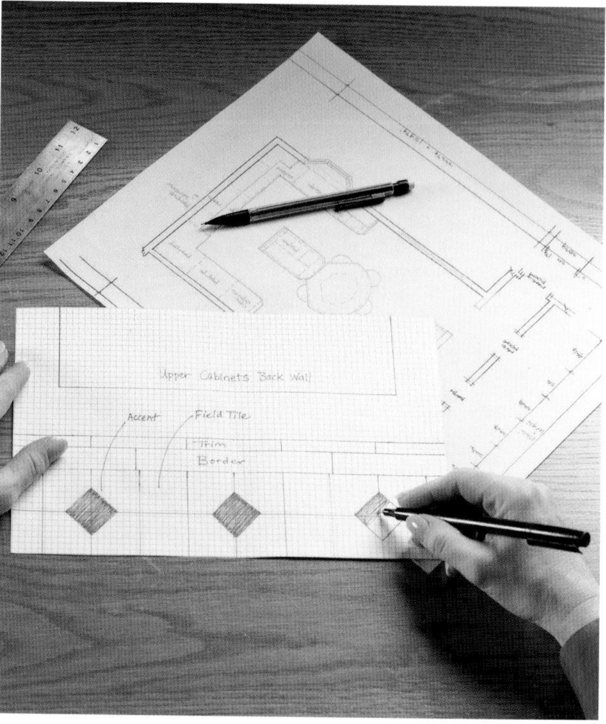

Draw your tile layout to scale on the wall drawing to establish your reference lines.

Check the Walls

Check the walls and corners to see if they're plumb. Make any necessary adjustments before beginning your tile project.

Measure the walls, paying particular attention to the placement of windows, doors, and permanent fixtures. Use these measurements to create a scale drawing of each wall to be tiled.

How to Test a Wall Layout

Attach a batten to the wall along your horizontal reference line using screws. Dry-fit tiles on the batten, aligning the middle tile with the vertical centerline.

If you end up with too narrow a gap along the wall in step 1, move over half the width of a tile by centering the middle tile over the vertical centerline.

Use a story stick to determine whether your planned layout works vertically. If necessary, adjust the size of the first row of tile.

Dry-fit the first row of tile, then hold a story stick along the horizontal guideline with one grout line matched to the vertical reference line. Mark the grout lines, which will correspond with the grout lines of the first row and can be used as reference points.

Installing Wall Tile

Tile is an ideal covering for walls, particularly in bathrooms. Beautiful, practical, and easy to clean and maintain, tile walls are well suited to bathrooms, kitchens, mudrooms, and other hard-working spaces in your home.

When shopping for tile, keep in mind that tiles that are at least 6 × 6 inches are easier to install than small tiles, because they require less cutting and cover more surface area. Larger tiles also have fewer grout lines that must be cleaned and maintained. Check out the selection of trim and specialty tiles and ceramic accessories that are available to help you customize your project.

Most wall tile is designed to have narrow grout lines (less than ⅛-inch wide) filled with unsanded grout. Grout lines wider than ⅛-inch should be filled with sanded floor-tile grout. Either type will last longer if it contains, or is mixed with, a latex additive. To prevent staining, it's a good idea to seal your grout after it fully cures, then once a year thereafter.

You can use standard drywall or water-resistant drywall (called "greenboard") as a backer for walls in dry areas. In wet areas, install tile over cementboard. Made from cement and fiberglass, cementboard cannot be damaged by water, though moisture can pass through it. To protect the framing, install a waterproof membrane, such as roofing felt or polyethylene sheeting, between the framing members and the cementboard. Be sure to tape and finish the seams between cementboard panels before laying the tile.

Tools & Materials ▸

Tile-cutting tools
Marker
Notched trowel
Mallet
Grout float
Grout sponge
Soft cloth
Small paintbrush or foam brush
Caulk gun
Scrap 2 × 4
Carpet
Thinset tile mortar with latex additive
Ceramic wall tile
Ceramic trim tile (as needed)
Tile grout with latex additive
Tub & tile caulk
Alkaline grout sealer
Tile spacers
⅛" shims
Eye protection

Tile is a practical, easy-to-maintain choice for bathroom walls. The variety of colors, shapes, and sizes available ensures there's a tile out there for every design and application. Keep in mind that larger tiles are easier to install, maintain, and clean than smaller tiles.

How to Set Wall Tile

Design the layout and mark the reference lines. Begin installation with the second row of tiles above the floor. If the layout requires cut tiles for this row, mark and cut the tiles for the entire row at one time.

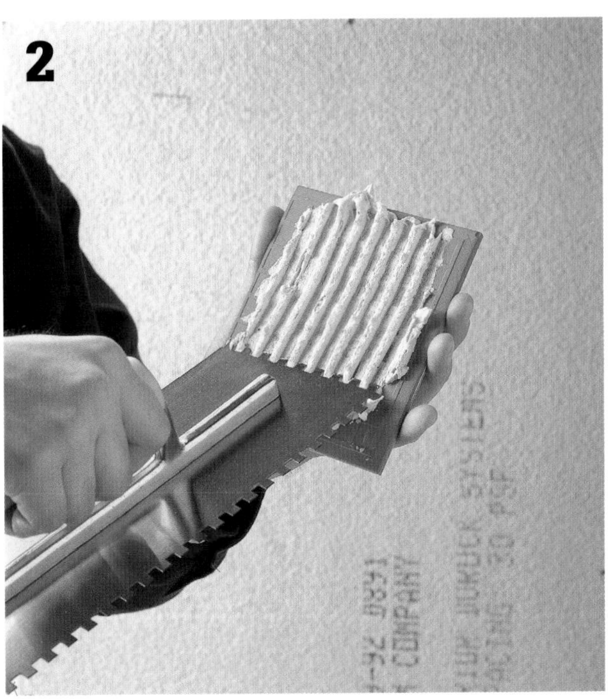

Mix a small batch of thinset mortar containing a latex additive. (Some mortar has additive mixed in by the manufacturer and some must have additive mixed in separately.) Cover the back of the first tile with adhesive, using a ¼" notched trowel.

Variation: Spread adhesive on a small section of the wall, then set the tiles into the adhesive. Thinset adhesive sets fast, so work quickly if you choose this installation method.

Beginning near the center of the wall, apply the tile to the wall with a slight twisting motion, aligning it exactly with the horizontal and vertical reference lines. When placing cut tiles, position the cut edges where they will be least visible.

(continued)

Continue installing tiles, working from the center to the sides in a pyramid pattern. Keep the tiles aligned with the reference lines. If the tiles are not self-spacing, use plastic spacers inserted in the corner joints to maintain even grout lines. The base row should be the last row of full tiles installed. Cut tile as necessary.

As small sections of tile are completed, set the tile by laying a scrap of 2 × 4 wrapped with carpet onto the tile and rapping it lightly with a mallet. This embeds the tile solidly in the adhesive and creates a flat, even surface.

To mark bottom and edge row tiles for straight cuts, begin by taping ⅛" spacers against the surfaces below and to the side of the tile. Position a tile directly over the last full tile installed, then place a third tile so the edge butts against the spacers. Trace the edge of the top tile onto the middle tile to mark it for cutting.

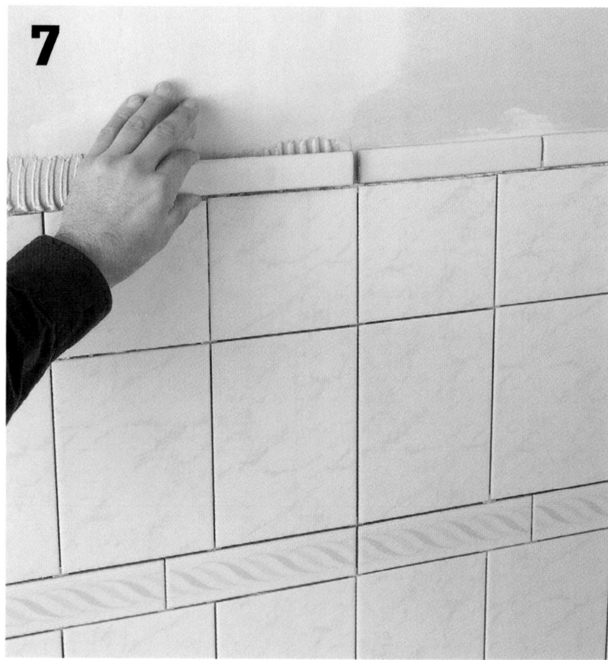

Install any trim tiles, such as the bullnose edge tiles shown above, at border areas. Wipe away excess mortar along the top edges of the edge tiles. Use bullnose and corner bullnose (with two adjacent bullnose edges) tiles at outside corners to cover the rough edges of the adjoining tiles.

Let mortar dry completely (12 to 24 hrs.), then mix a batch of grout containing latex additive. Apply the grout with a rubber grout float, using a sweeping motion to force it deep into the joints. Do not grout joints adjoining bathtubs, floors, or room corners. These will serve as expansion joints and will be caulked later.

Wipe a damp grout sponge diagonally over the tile, rinsing the sponge in cool water between wipes. Wipe each area only once; repeated wiping can pull grout from the joints. Allow the grout to dry for about 4 hrs., then use a soft cloth to buff the tile surface and remove any remaining grout film.

When the grout has cured completely, use a small foam brush to apply grout sealer to the joints, following the manufacturer's directions. Avoid brushing sealer on the tile surfaces, and wipe up excess sealer immediately.

Seal expansion joints at the floor and corners with silicone caulk. After the caulk dries, buff the tile with a soft, dry cloth.

Installing a Tub Tile Surround

With a nearly limitless selection of styles, colors, and sizes of tile to choose from, a tub tile surround replacement is an ideal home improvement project. It can transform your bathroom into a luxurious retreat, while increasing the value of your home.

Tub tile surrounds can be broken down to three basic components. The back wall is always tiled first. The towel bar wall contains the optional posts and rod used for hanging bath towels. Lastly, the manifold wall contains the valve stems, shower head, and tub spout. Some tub surrounds are topped off with a low hanging ceiling. If this is the case for your project, install the cementboard on the ceiling first and tile the ceiling after the walls have been tiled. Ceiling tile is often installed on a diagonal pattern to avoid alignment issues with the wall tile joints.

With proper care and maintenance, nearly any type of wall or floor tile can be used for a surround. Tiles that are rated vitrified or impervious, however, absorb less moisture and are better suited for wet areas. Unglazed tiles such as the tile installed in this project may be used, but be sure to seal them well with at least two coats of tile sealant.

While field tile is estimated and purchased by the total number of square feet, trim tile such as bullnose or cap tile is quantified in linear feet. If the tile you select isn't available with matching trim tile, consider making your own using a wet tile saw fitted with a bevel profile wheel. Through-body porcelain tile is an excellent choice for making custom trim because the surface color is uniform throughout the body of the tile. Most tiled surrounds include bath accessories such as a soap dish and towel bar fixtures. Some tile families offer these accessories in the same patterns and colors. In other cases, you'll have to choose a similar—or perhaps contrasting—style or color. Make sure the thickness of the base for these accessories matches the tile thickness.

To introduce a splash of color to an otherwise plain tile surround, consider adding one or more bands of contrasting tile into the installation. Some tile product lines are available in a variety of solid colors, allowing the installer to incorporate colored rows of similarly sized tiles into the installation without having to make special adjustments to the layout. For added effect, you can even match the trim color to the colored bands of tile or sprinkle some decorative accent tiles throughout the tile installation.

Tools & Materials ▸

- 1 × 2 furring strips
- 1¼" cementboard screws
- ½" cementboard
- 2" fiberglass mesh tape
- 4-ft. level
- 4-mil polyethylene sheeting
- 6" joint knife
- Cardboard
- Caulk gun
- Drill
- Eye and ear protection
- Square notched trowel
- Modified thinset mortar
- Stapler and staples
- Carbide scoring tool
- Carbide hole saw bit
- Grout release agent
- Grout float
- Grout
- Grout sponge
- Keyhole saw
- Latex tile caulk
- Tape measure
- Tarps
- Tile
- Tile-cutting tools
- Trim tile
- Work gloves
- Utility knife
- Screwdriver
- Hammer
- Wood blocking
- Tile spacers
- Small roller
- Caulk gun

A perfectly functional alcove bathtub surround (above) can be utterly transformed with tile (page opposite).

After

How to Install a Tiled Tub Surround

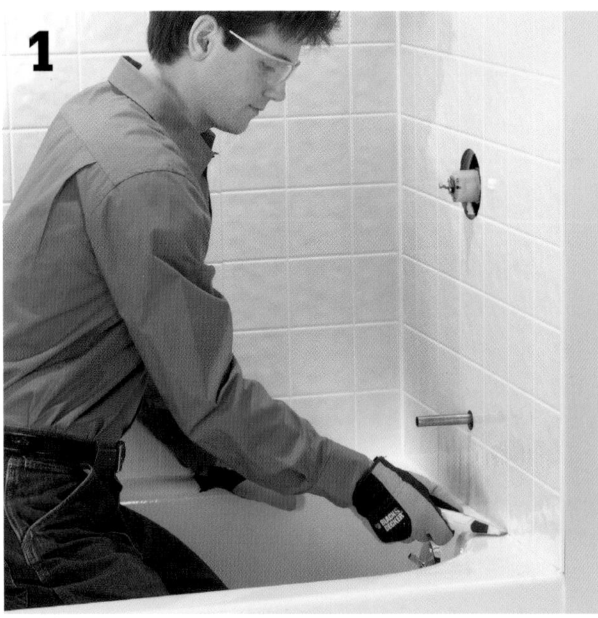

Remove the old fittings. To begin, remove the tub spout, faucet handles, and shower head. Then, slice and remove the caulk from the corner joints. Existing ceramic fittings such as soap dishes should also be removed to prevent them from falling later and damaging the tub. Use a utility knife to remove old caulk, grout, and adhesive from around the lip of the tub. Finally, lay protective cardboard over the exposed surfaces of the tub and drape tarps over cabinets and toilets.

Cut out old surround panels or tiles. A keyhole or drywall saw can be used to safely cut through the drywall at the junction where it meets the surround. Use the edge of the tile or panel as a guide, taking care to feel for and avoid plumbing or other unseen obstacles hidden within the wall cavity.

Remove any drywall in the new tile installation area. This will need to be replaced with cementboard. Remove all nails and debris from the framing members. If necessary, install additional wood blocking to accommodate the cementboard installation.

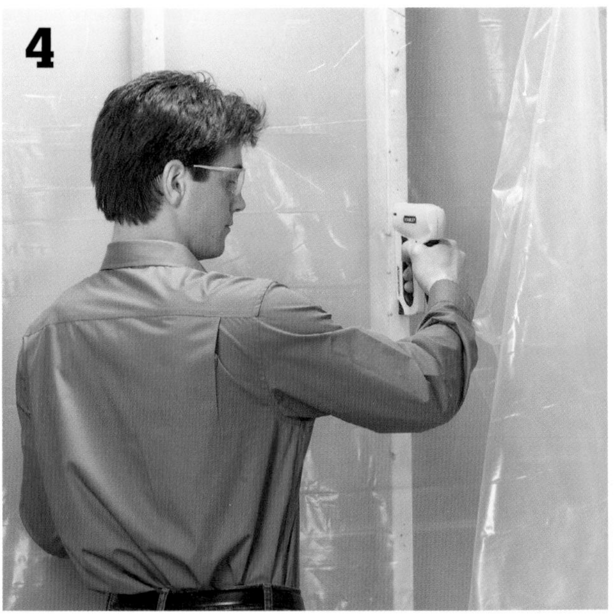

Install a moisture barrier. Fasten 4-mil clear polyethylene sheeting to the studs using staples. This step may be omitted if a waterproofing membrane will be applied over the surface of the cementboard later.

Install ½"-thick cementboard horizontally on the back wall first, and then on the side walls. Fasten the panels to the studs using 1¼" cementboard screws. To make straight cuts, score the panel using a carbide scoring tool, then snap the panel along the scored line. To make hole cuts for plumbing protrusions, use a drill fitted with a carbide hole saw bit.

Fill the gaps between cementboard panels with thinset mortar, overlapping at least 2 to 3" on each side of the joint. Center and embed 2"-wide alkaline-resistant fiberglass tape over the joint and lightly skim thinset over the joint.

Dry-lay tile for your surround on a flat surface, inserting ⅛" spacers between the tiles to set the gap. Lay out enough for roughly half the surround height and then measure the length of the dry-laid row to find the actual height of the tiles on the wall.

Draw horizontal reference lines on the wall using a 4-ft. level to make sure the lines are level. Extend these reference lines to each side wall. Measure down from the horizontal lines to the tub at several points on all walls to make sure the tub deck and the lines are parallel. If they aren't, re-measure from the point where the tub deck is highest and transfer level lines all around from that point.

(continued)

Draw a vertical reference line down the center of the back wall. To temporarily support the weight of the tile that will be installed above, align and fasten 1 × 2 furring strips just below the horizontal reference lines located in the midsection of the tub surround.

Set the first tiles. Mix a small batch of thinset mortar. Apply the thinset using a ¼" square-notched trowel held at a 45° angle. Spread the adhesive within the guidelines on the wall, aligning the ridges of the setting bed in a horizontal direction. Install tile on the back wall first, keeping tile aligned to the centered guide line.

Install two or three rows of tiles—here, a row of decorative accent tiles is installed as well.

To mark tiles for straight cuts, place a full tile directly on top of the field tile that is installed adjacent to the void. Position another full tile over the void, abutting the overhanging edge of the tile against a ⅛" spacer. Trace the edge of this tile to mark the underlying tile for cutting.

Complete the upper sections. After the top portion of the back wall is tiled, fill in the upper portions of each side wall. Leave out tiles as needed to accommodate tiled-in accessories such as a soap dish or towel rod.

Mark and cut tiles to fit around the valve stems and water pipes as required to install your tub spout, diverter, and shower head (often, shower heads are installed above the tiles). Finish tiling the lower portions of the tile installation, then allow to dry for 24 hrs. *Tip: Tape tiles together to prevent slippage while they dry.*

Coat the tile surfaces with a sealer or other grout-release agent if they are not glazed by the manufacturer. This treatment will prevent grout from getting into places where it should not go.

Grout the tiles (see page 141). To apply grout, hold the grout float at an angle and force the mortar into the joints, skimming excess grout from the tile surface with each pass. Wipe tile clean using a damp grout sponge. After grouting, buff tile surfaces with a soft cloth to remove haze. Install fittings and hardware, and caulk around the tub deck.

Tiled Tub Apron

The aprons that are cast into alcove bathtubs simplify the tub installation, but they often come up a bit short in the style department. One way to improve the appearance of a plain apron and create the look of a built-in tub is simply to build and tile a short wall in front of the tub. All it takes is a little simple framing and a few square feet of tile.

The basic strategy is to construct a 2 × 4 stub wall in front of the tub apron and then tile the top and front of the wall. One design option is to try and match existing tile, but it's unlikely you'll be able to find the exact tile unless it's relatively new. Choosing complementary or contrasting tile is usually a better bet. Specialty tile, such as listellos, pencils, and accent tile, can have a big impact without breaking the bank because you're covering such a small area. Ask your tile retailer to direct you to families of tile with multiple shapes and accessories.

Be sure to include a waterproof backer (cementboard is recommended) and get a good grout seal, since the stub wall will be in a wet area.

Tools & Materials ▸

- Stud finder
- Tape measure
- Circular saw
- Drill
- Laser or carpenter's level
- Tile cutting tools
- Utility knife
- Grout float
- Grout sponge
- Buff rag
- Foam brush
- 2 × 4 lumber
- Construction adhesive
- Screws (2½", 3")
- Cementboard
- Tile
- Thinset mortar
- Carbide paper or wet stone
- Wide painter's tape
- Grout
- Silicone caulk
- Grout sealer
- Notched trowel
- Rubbing alcohol
- Caulk gun
- Tile spacers
- Eye protection

An ordinary tub apron does little to inspire in a bathroom, but a tiled apron wall is a fine way to add interest.

How to Build a Tiled Tub Deck

1

Measure the distance of the tub rim from the floor, as well as the distance from one wall to the other at the ends of the tub. Allowing for the thickness of the tiles, create a layout for the project and draw a detailed plan, spacing the studs 16" apart on center.

2

Cut the 2 × 4s to length for the base plate and top plate (58½" long as shown). Cut the studs (five 11" pieces as shown). Set the base plate on edge and lay out the studs, spacing them 16" on-center. Make sure the first and last studs are perfectly parallel with the end of the base plate, then drive two 2½" screws through the base plate and each stud.

3

Draw a placement line on the floor using a permanent marker. Spread a generous bead of construction adhesive on the bottom of the base plate. Align the base plate with the placement line and set it into position. Put concrete blocks or other weights between the studs to anchor the base plate to the flooring and let the adhesive cure according to manufacturer's instructions.

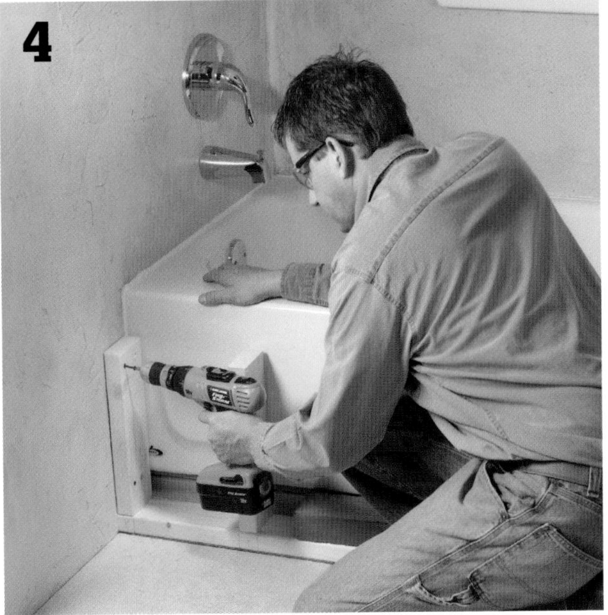

4

Drive two or three 2½" screws through the studs and into the room walls at each end of the stub wall. If the stub wall does not happen to line up with any wall studs, at least drive two 3" deck screws toenail style through the stub wall and into the room wall sole plate.

(continued)

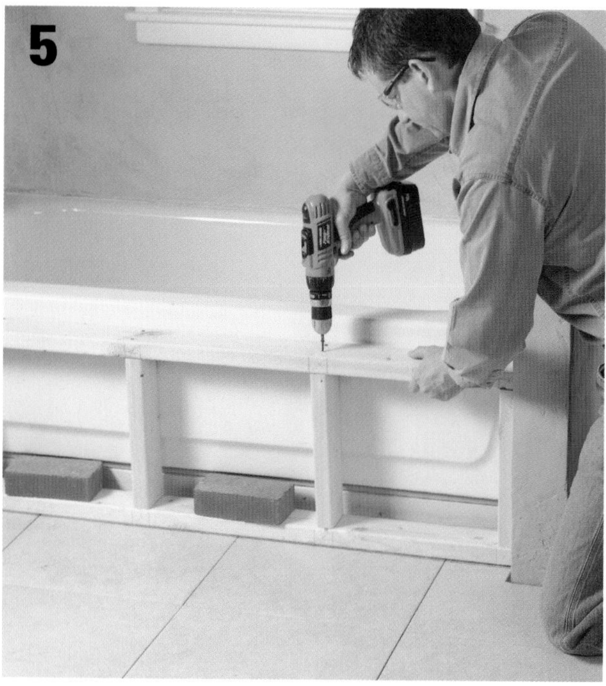

Set the top plate on the stub wall and attach it using two 2½" screws for each stud. Offset the screws slightly to increase the strength of the assembly. The top of the stub wall should be 2½" below the top of the tub.

Cut cementboard to fit the front (14½" as shown). With the factory-finished edge of the cementboard at the top of the wall, attach the cementboard to the studs using cementboard screws.

Cut cementboard to fit the top of the stub wall (3½"). With the factory-finished edge facing the tub edge, attach the cementboard to the top plate using cementboard screws.

Design the layout and mark reference lines (see page 139) on the wall. Draw horizontal and vertical reference lines for the corner tile (used to transition from vertical to horizontal at the top stub wall edge) and the coved base tile (if your project includes them). Lay out tile along the floor, including spacers.

Start tiling at the bottom of the wall. Lay out the bottom row of tile on the floor, using spacers if necessary. Adjust the layout to make end tiles balanced in size. Mark and cut the tiles as necessary, and then smooth any sharp edges with carbide paper or a wet stone. Mix a small batch of thinset mortar and install the base tiles by buttering the backs with mortar.

Beginning at the center intersection of the vertical field area, apply mortar using a notched trowel to spread it evenly. Cover as much area as required for a few field tiles. Install the field tiles, keeping the grout lines in alignment.

Finish installing the field tiles up to the horizontal line marking the accent tile location.

Apply thinset mortar to the backs of the accent tiles and install them in a straight line. The grout lines will likely not align with the field tile grout lines.

(continued)

Dry-lay corner tiles to create a rounded transition at the top edge of the wall. Install these before you install the field tiles in the top row of the wall face or on the top of the stub wall (corner tiles are virtually impossible to cut if your measurements are off). Dry-lay the top row of tiles. Mark and cut tile if necessary.

Fill in the top course of field tile on the wall face, between the accent tiles and the corner tiles. If you have planned well you won't need to trim the field tiles to fit. If you need to cut tiles to create the correct wall height, choose the tiles in the first row of field tiles.

Remove the dry-laid row of tile along the top of the wall. Shield the edge of the tub with painter's tape, then spread thinset adhesive on the wall and begin to lay tile. Keep the joints of the field tiles on the top aligned with the grout joints of the field tile on the face of the wall.

Mix a batch of grout and use a grout float to force it into the joints between the tiles. Keep the space between the top field tiles and the tub clear of grout to create space for a bead of silicone caulk between the tub and tile.

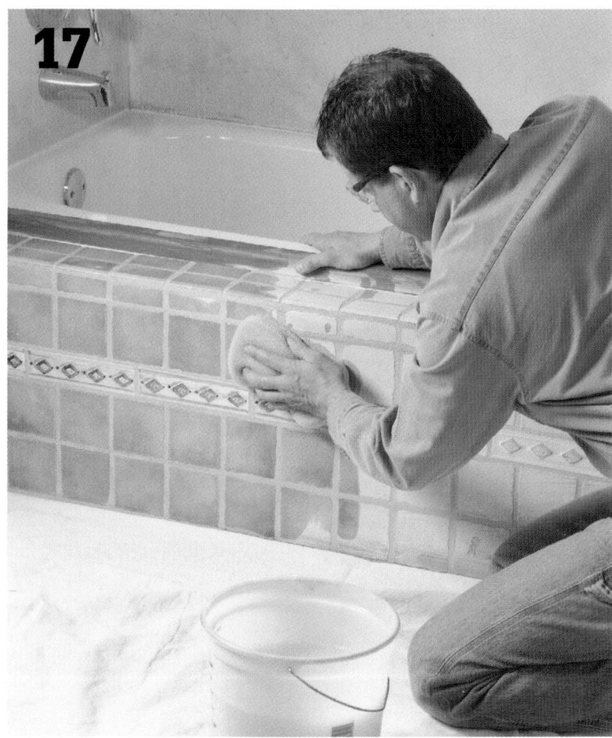

Remove excess grout and clean the tile using a damp sponge. Rinse the sponge often.

After 24 hours, clean the area where the tile and tub meet with rubbing alcohol, then put tape on the edge of the tub and the face of the tile. Apply clear silicone caulk into the gap, overfilling it slightly.

Smooth the caulk with a moistened plastic straw or a moistened fingertip to create an even finish. Make sure this spot is well-sealed, as it is a prime spot for water to penetrate into the tub wall.

When the grout has cured completely (consult manufacturer's directions), apply grout sealer to the joints.

This unique room feature is a showcase for beautiful tile work. A niche can be added to just about any wall, including a room divider wall that is built specifically to support the niche.

Tile Wall Niche

A wall niche—a small recessed area between studs—provides ideal display space and creates a focal point in a room. Typical recessed niches require that you cut into the wall, which can be a little intimidating. An easier answer is to build outward from the wall, as we do here.

The "columns" that form the sides of our niche are plain wood boxes that are built in a workshop and then installed. Quartz tile is attached to the columns after installation, and contrasting wall tiles are added to the wallspace between the columns. Finally, glass shelves are installed between the tiled columns to complete the project. The finished look is textural, natural, and sophisticated.

When designing your project, consider the size of the tile and grout lines to create a plan that requires the fewest possible cut tiles. If it's not possible to complete an area (such as a column or the background) with full tile, plan to cut equal-size tiles for each side so the full tiles are centered. If it is not possible for you to attach both boxes to wall studs, use sturdy hollow wall anchors or toggle bolts to secure one of the boxes.

Tools & Materials ▸

- Tape measure
- Stud finder
- Circular saw
- Drill
- Long driver bit or bit extender
- Bar clamps
- Pry bar
- Hammer
- Laser or carpenter's level and chalk line
- Awl
- ¼" carbide-tip bit
- ¼" notched trowel
- Grout float
- Grout sponge
- Buff rag
- Foam brush
- Needlenose pliers
- Rubber mallet
- 1¼" screws
- Construction adhesive
- Wide painter's tape
- Sheet plastic
- Tile
- Thinset mortar
- Tile spacers
- Grout
- Latex additive
- Shelf pins (4 per shelf)
- Teflon tape
- Glass shelves
- Grout sealer
- Lumber (1 × 2, 1 × 6, 1 × 8)
- Caulk gun
- Tile-cutting tools
- Eye protection

How to Build a Tiled Wall Niche

Use a stud finder to locate the studs in the area and mark them. Measure the area and draw a plan on graph paper.

If there are baseboards in the construction area, remove them using a pry bar and hammer. Tape down sheet plastic in the construction area, as close to the wall as possible.

(continued)

Cut four 1 × 6 and four 1 × 8s to length (108 inches for our project). On two of the 1 × 8s, drill ¾-inch holes centered every 10" down the length of each board. On the remaining two 1 × 8s, drill pilot holes centered every 10".

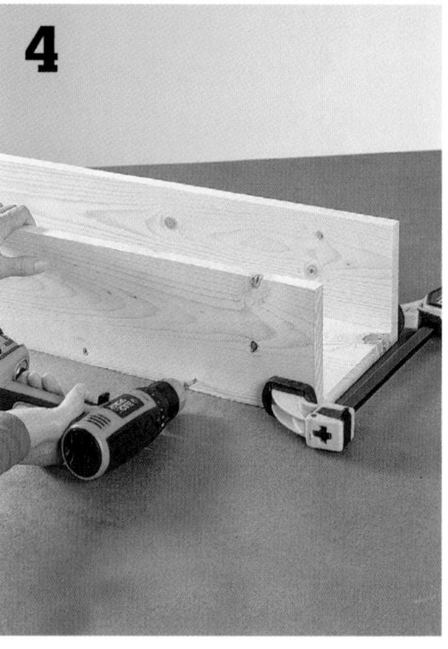

Place one 1 × 8 (one with pilot holes) on the work surface and position a 1 × 6 on edge beside it. Clamp the boards together and drive a 1¼" screw every 6" to join them. Put a second 1 × 6 on the work surface and clamp to assembly as shown. Drive screws every 6 in. to join the pieces.

Complete the box by adding a 1 × 8 (with ¾" holes in it) to the opposite side of the assembly and fasten it as described. Build a second, identical box.

Shoot a vertical line on the wall with the laser level. Spread a bead of construction adhesive on the back (1 × 8 with pilot holes) of the first box. With a helper, align the outside edge of the box. Using a long magnetic driver bit or bit extender, drive an 1¼" screw through each pilot hole (and into stud). Install the second box on the other side of the niche. *Note: When you cannot hit a stud, use toggle bolts.*

Mark the reference lines (see page 139). If necessary, tack a 1 × 2 batten in position to support the second row of tile above the floor. If tiles have to be cut for this row, mark and cut all of them.

Mix a small batch of thinset mortar. Spread the mortar on a small section of wall, then set the tiles into it. If tile is not self-spacing, insert spacers as you work. When all other tile is set, remove the battens and set the bottom row.

Repeat Step 8 to set tile on first one box and then the other. Let the mortar cure, according to manufacturer's instructions.

If there are spacers between tiles, use needlenose pliers to remove them. Grout the tile in the center of the niche. If necessary, grout the tile on the columns. Let the grout set and then wipe away excess with a damp sponge.

On the inside edges of each column, measure and mark the location for the shelf pins. Use a laser level to check and adjust the marks. Using an awl and hammer, create a dimple at each mark, then use a carbide-tipped ¼" bit to drill the holes.

Wrap the peg of each shelf pin with Teflon tape. (The tape will seal the hole and keep moisture from getting behind the tile.) Tap a pin into each hole, using a rubber mallet if necessary. Position the glass shelves.

Retrofit Accent Strip

Many of us live with tile we don't particularly like. It's easy to see why: builders and remodelers often install simple, neutral tile in an effort not to put off future buyers. Older homes sometimes have tile that's not quite vintage, but certainly no longer stylish. Or, a previous owner might just have had different taste. Because tile is so long-lasting, new styles and trends often overtake it and make it look dated. Here's a bit of good news: there's a choice beyond simply living with it or tearing out perfectly good tile to start over.

Removing a section of boring tile and replacing it with some decorative accent tile can transform a plain wall into one that makes a unique design statement. And while a project like this requires a bit of demolition, it can be done with very little mess and fuss. Because it involves breaking the seal of the wall surface, it's a better choice for a tiled wall that gets little exposure to water (as opposed to a shower wall or tub deck).

The new tile you install will need to be grouted, and the new grout will undoubtedly be a different color. The only way to blend the new tile into the old is to regrout the entire area. If the project involves only one wall and the same grout color is still available, it is necessary to remove the grout surrounding the tile on the project wall. If you are tiling two or more walls, regrout the whole room.

This project is easier if you don't have to cut any existing tile. Cutting tile is not especially difficult if you do, but it's always best to know what you're getting into before committing to a project.

Tools & Materials ▸

Tape measure
Grout saw
Grout scraper
Flathead screwdriver
Straightedge
Utility knife
Drill
¼" notched trowel
Grout float
Grout sponge
Buff rag
Needlenose pliers
Drop cloth
Grease pencil
Masking tape
Safety glasses
Wallboard screws
Cementboard
Thinset mortar
Mosaic medallion or decorative tile
Tile spacers
Grout
Dust mask
Wallboard tape

How to Embellish a Tiled Wall

Measure the decorative tiles and draw a detailed plan for your project. Indicate a removal area at least one tile larger than the space required. If it will be necessary to cut tile, create a plan that will result in symmetrical tiles.

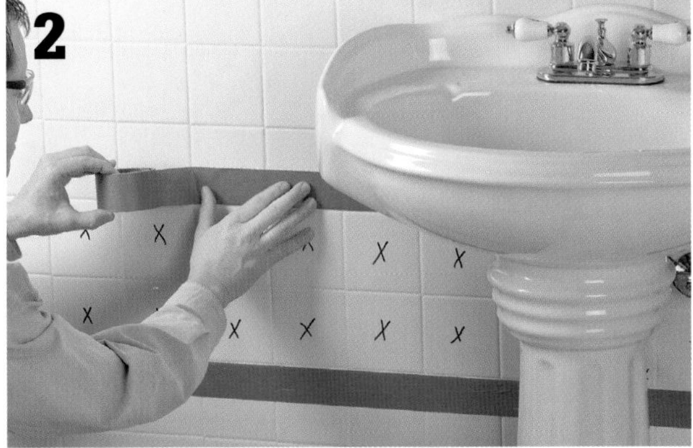

Protect the floor with a drop cloth. So you can patch the tile backer, you'll need to remove a section of tile that's a minimum of one tile all around the project installation area. Using a grease pencil, mark the tiles to be removed, according to the plan drawing. Put masking tape on the edges of the bordering tiles that will remain to keep them from being scratched or otherwise damaged by the grout saw. If you will be reinstalling some of the old tiles, protect them as well.

(continued)

Wearing eye protection and a dust mask, use a grout saw to cut grooves in all of the grout lines in the removal area. If the grout lines are soft this will only take one or two passes. If the grout is hard, it may take several. Using a grout scraper, remove any remaining material in the joint. Angle the tools toward the open area to protect the tile.

With a flathead screwdriver, pry up the edges of the tile at the center of the removal area. Wiggle the blade toward the center of the tile and pry up to pop it off. (For large areas, see page 131 for another removal method.)

Draw cutting lines on the drywall that are at least ½" inside the borders of the area where you removed tiles. Using a straightedge and utility knife, carefully cut out the old drywall. *Note: If the tile comes off very easily and the tile backer is not damaged, you may be able to scrape it clean and reuse it.*

Cut cementboard strips that are slightly longer than the width of the opening. Insert the strips into the opening and orient them so the ends are pressed against the back surface of the tile backer. Drive wallboard screws through the edges of the old tile backer and into the strips to hold them in place.

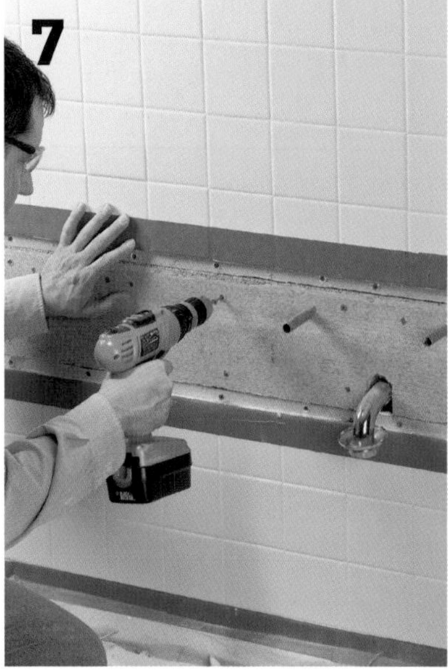

Cut a cementboard patch to fit the opening in the tile backer. Place the patch in the opening and drive wallboard screws through the cementboard and into the backer strips. Also drive screws at any stud locations.

Cover the edges with wallboard tape. Mix a small batch of thinset mortar. Apply the mortar using a notched trowel to spread it evenly.

Gently press the accent tiles into the adhesive, smoothing it from the center toward the edges. Let the mortar cure as directed.

Use a damp sponge to soak the protective sheet on the tile. Once wet, slide the sheet off and throw it away.

Mix a batch of grout and fill the joints between tile on the entire wall, one section at a time. Clean the tile with a damp sponge (inset). Occasionally rinse the sponge in cool water.

Design Suggestions ▸

Inserts add interest, texture, and color to tile designs. This piece combines tumbled stone with marble in a delicate floral motif.

This stone insert adds a contemporary flair to a simple tile design.

Fireplace Surround

Tile dresses a fireplace surround in style—any style you like. From simple ceramic to elegant cut stone to handmade art tile, anything goes. As long as it's sturdy enough to withstand significant swings in temperature, almost any tile will work.

Although the project shown here starts with unfinished wallboard, you can tile over any level surface that isn't glossy. If you're tiling over old tile or brick, go over the surface with a grinder, then apply a thin coat of latex-reinforced thinset mortar to even out any irregularities. To rough up painted surfaces, sand them lightly before beginning the project.

The tile shown here is flush with the face of the firebox, which then supports it during installation. If necessary, tack level battens in place to support the weight of your tile during installation.

You can finish the edges of the surround with wood cap rail trim, as shown here, bullnose tile, or other trim tile.

Tools & Materials ▸

Level
Drill
Hammer
Nail set
Notched trowel
Grout float
2 × 4 lumber
Mantel
Tile
Tile spacers
Masking tape
Grout
Cap rail trim
Wood putty
Sponge
Tape measure
Tile-cutting tools
Buff cloth
Buildup strips
Eye protection
Cementboard
Utility knife
Wallboard
Joint compound
Fiberglass seam tape
Wallboard knife
Scrap 2 × 4
Carpet scrap
Mallet
Trim (1 × 2, 1 × 3, 1 × 4)
6d and 4d finish nails
Pneumatic brad nailer
Sander
Wood-finishing materials
Latex-reinforced thinset mortar

Because tile is not flammable it makes a beautiful first line of defense around a fireplace opening.

How to Tile a Fireplace Surround

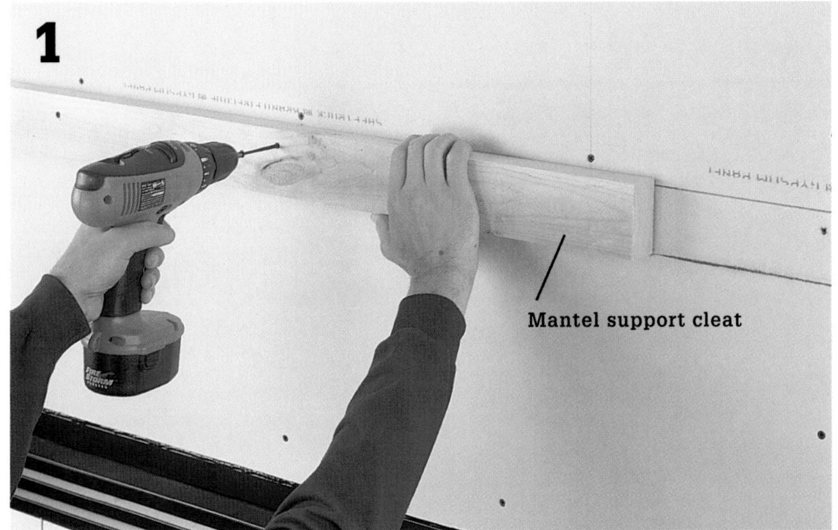

To install the mantel, measure up from the floor and mark the height of the support cleat. Use a level to draw a level line through the mark. Mark the stud locations just above the level line. Position the cleat on the line, centered between the frame sides, and drill a pilot hole at each stud location. Fasten the cleat to the studs with screws provided by the manufacturer.

Paint the areas of wallboard that won't be tiled. Finish the mantel as desired, then fit it over the support cleat and center it. Drill pilot holes for 6d finish nails through the top of the mantel, about ¾" from the back edge. Secure the mantel to the cleat with four nails. Set the nails with a nail set, fill the holes with wood putty, then touch up the finish.

Dry-fit the tile around the front of the fireplace. You can lay tile over the black front face, but do not cover the glass or any portion of the grills. If you're using tile without spacer lugs, use spacers to set the gaps (at least ⅛" for floor tile). Mark the perimeter of the tile area and make any other layout marks that will help with the installation. Pre-cut tiles.

(continued)

Mask off around the tile, then use a notched trowel to apply latex-reinforced thinset mortar to the wall, spreading it evenly just inside the perimeter lines. Set the tiles into the mortar, aligning them with the layout marks, and press firmly to create a good bond. Install spacers as you work. Install all of the tile, then let the mortar set completely.

Mix a batch of grout and spread it over the tiles with a rubber grout float. Drag the float across the joints diagonally, tilting it at a 45° angle. Make another pass to remove excess grout. Wait 10 to 15 minutes, then wipe away excess grout with a damp sponge, rinsing frequently. Let the grout dry for one hour, then polish the tiles with a dry cloth. Let the grout dry completely.

Cut pieces of cap rail trim to fit around the tile, mitering the ends. If the tile is thicker than the trim recesses, install buildup strips behind the trim using finish nails. Finish the trim to match the mantel. Drill pilot holes and nail the trim in place with 4d finish nails. Set the nails with a nail set. Fill the holes with wood putty and touch up the finish.

How to Install a Tile Surround with a Wood Border

A lovely ceramic tile and cherry fireplace surround frames a ventless gas fireplace in this basement rec room.

Cut cementboard into strips equal in width to the dimension of your tiled surround and attach them to the 2 × 4 nailers bordering the framed firebox opening. It is generally a good idea to predrill for cementboard screws, especially with narrower strips.

Patch around the cementboard, if necessary, with regular wallboard. If you are installing the surround in a damp area, such as a basement, use moisture-resistant wallboard.

Apply joint compound and fiberglass seam tape over seams and cover screwheads with compound (see pages 132 to 133). Sand the compound smooth.

(continued)

Touch up paint around the tile installation area as needed.

Apply a mortar bed for the tile surround using a notched trowel (a ¼" square-notch trowel is typical but check the recommendations on the thinset package label). Apply only as much mortar as you can tile in about 10 min. Treating each leg of the square surround separately is a good strategy.

Press the surround tiles into the mortar bed and set them by pressing with a short piece of 2 × 4 wrapped in a soft cloth. Most tiles (12 × 12 glass tiles in a mosaic pattern are shown here) have spacing nubs cast into the edges so setting the gaps between tiles or tile sheets is automatic. If your tiles do not have spacing nubs, use plastic tile spacers available at your tile store. Let the thinset mortar dry overnight once you've finished setting the tiles. See page 26 if you need to cut tiles.

Apply dark-tinted grout to the tiles using a grout float. Let the grout harden slightly and then buff off the residue with a soft, clean cloth. For more information on grouting, see page 141.

Begin adding surround trim. Here, 1 × 4 cherry casing is being attached to wall stud locations. The side casings should be slightly off the floor (if you have not installed flooring yet account for the floor covering thickness) and butted against the tile surround. If you have planned properly, there will be wall studs behind the casing. *Note: We chose 1 × 4 cherry because it is attractive, but also because you can usually buy it dimensioned, planed, and sanded on all sides at the lumber yard. If you have woodworking equipment, use any lumber you like.*

Add built-up head casing. The head casing should overhang the side casings by an inch or so. We used a built-up technique to add some depth and profile to the head casing. First, attach a full-width 1 × 4 to the wall. Then, install a 1 × 3 so the ends and top are flush with the ends and top of the 1 × 4. Finally, install a cherry 1 × 2 in the same manner.

Cut and install the mantel board. We used another piece of 1 × 4 cherry the same length as the head casings, but if you have access to woodworking tools consider a thicker board for a little more presence. Or, face-glue two 1 × 4s together.

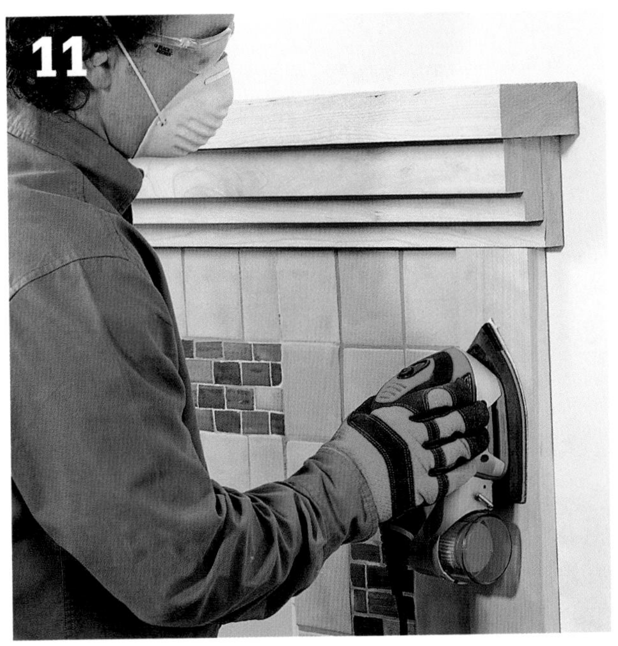

Finish-sand all the cherry and then apply a light wood stain. After the stain dries, topcoat with a cherry-tone or light mahogany wipe-on varnish that will even out the uneven coloration typical with cherry. Fill nail holes with cherry-tinted wood putty.

Countertops

Tile countertops are a cook's dream—resistant to heat and stains, easy to clean, and extremely durable. Fortunately, the process of building one is much easier than most people would imagine. The projects included in this chapter lead you through constructing the countertop itself as well as tiling it, and all the way through setting tile on a bi-level countertop and backsplash.

Edge treatments are integral parts of a countertop design. Consider trim tile, wood, and other materials for your edges and create a layout that complements the treatment you choose.

When designing a countertop, remember that larger tiles produce fewer grout lines to keep clean and more stable surfaces. For work areas, flat tiles are better than tiles with rounded or beveled edges because bowls and pans rock on rounded edges.

Before selecting natural stone tile for countertops, research your choice carefully. Some natural stone stains and scratches easily and requires more maintenance than you might wish to invest in a countertop. Be especially careful about choosing porous stone, which is difficult to keep clean in a kitchen or bathroom environment.

In this chapter:

Tile Countertop

Ceramic and porcelain tile remain popular choices for countertops and backsplashes for a number of reasons: these materials are available in a wide range of sizes, styles, and colors, are durable and repairable, and some tile—not all—is reasonably priced. With careful planning, tile is also easy to install, making a custom tile countertop a great do-it-yourself project.

The best tile for most countertops is glazed ceramic or porcelain floor tile. Glazed tile is better than unglazed because of its stain resistance, and floor tile is better than wall tile because it is thicker and more durable. While glaze protects tile from stains, the porous grout between tiles is still quite vulnerable. To minimize staining, use a grout that contains a latex additive or mix your own grout using a liquid latex additive. After the grout cures fully, apply a quality grout sealer, and reapply the sealer once a year thereafter. Also, choosing larger tiles reduces the number of grout lines to maintain. Although the selection is a bit limited, if you choose 13 × 13-inch floor tile, you can span from the front to the back edge of the countertop with a single seam.

The countertop in this project has a substrate of ¾-inch exterior-grade plywood that's cut to fit and fastened to the cabinets. The plywood is covered with a layer of plastic (for a moisture barrier) and a layer of ½-inch-thick cementboard. The overall thickness of the finished countertop is about 1½ inches. Two layers of ¾-inch exterior-grade plywood without cementboard is also an acceptable substrate. You can purchase tiles made specifically to serve as backsplashes and front edging. While the color and texture may match, these tiles usually come in only one length, making it difficult to align grout lines with the field tiles. You can solve this problem by cutting your own edging and backsplash tiles from field tiles.

Tools & Materials ▸

Tape measure
Circular saw
Drill with masonry bit
Utility knife
Straightedge
Stapler
Drywall knife
Framing square
Notched trowel
Grout float
Sponge
Corner bracket
Caulk gun
Ceramic tile
Tile spacers
¾" (CDX) plywood
4-mil polyethylene sheeting
Packing tape
½" cementboard
1¼" deck screws
Fiberglass mesh tape
Thinset mortar
Grout
Silicone caulk
Silicone grout sealer
Cementboard screws
Metal ruler
Eye protection
Wood scraps
Wet tile saw (available for rent)

Ceramic or porcelain tile makes a durable countertop that is heat-resistant and relatively easy for a DIYer to create. By using larger tiles, you minimize the number of grout lines (and the cleaning that goes with them).

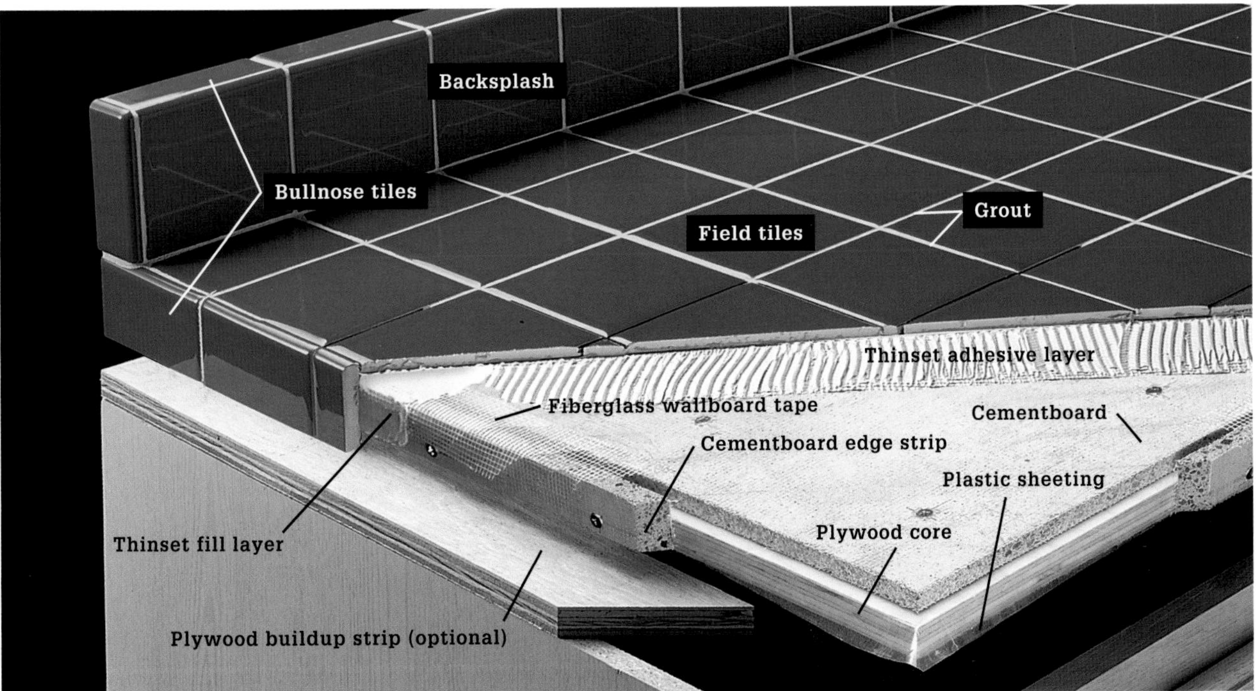

A ceramic tile countertop made with wall or floor tile starts with a core of ¾" exterior-grade plywood that's covered with a moisture barrier of 4-mil polyethylene sheeting. Half-inch cementboard is screwed to the plywood, and the edges are capped with cementboard and finished with fiberglass mesh tape and thinset mortar. Tiles for edging and backsplashes may be bullnose or trimmed from the factory edges of field tiles.

Options for Backsplashes & Countertop Edges

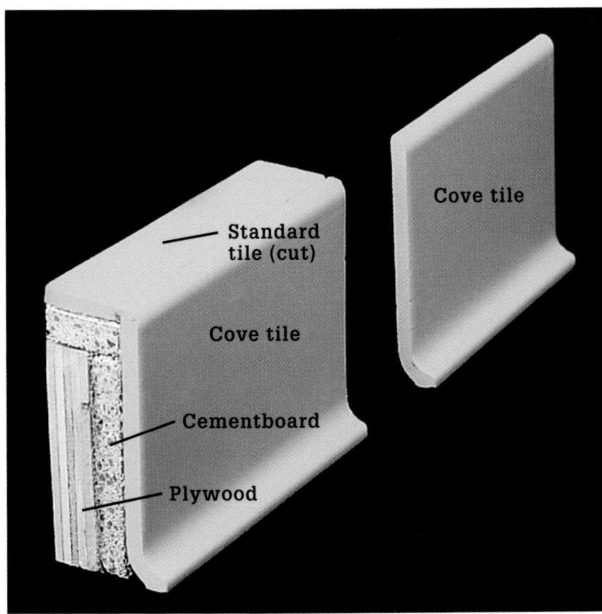

Backsplashes can be made from cove tile attached to the wall at the back of the countertop. You can use the tile alone or build a shelf-type backsplash using the same construction as for the countertop. Attach the plywood backsplash to the plywood core of the countertop. Wrap the front face and all edges of the plywood backsplash with cementboard before laying tile.

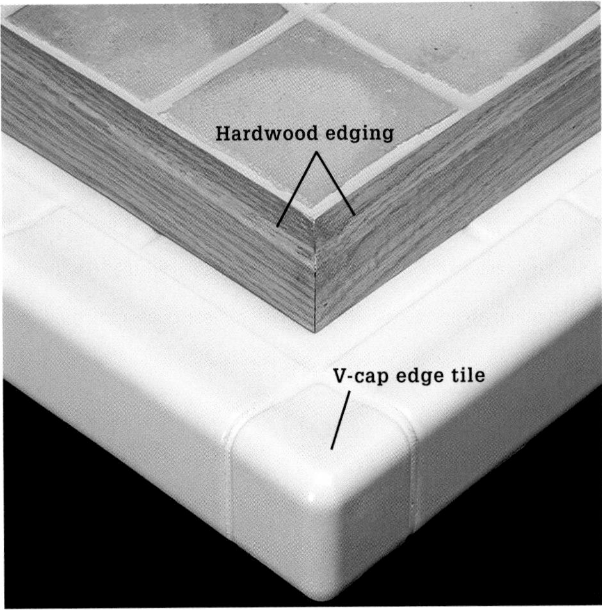

Edge options include V-cap edge tile and hardwood strip edging. V-cap tiles have raised and rounded corners that create a ridge around the countertop perimeter—good for containing spills and water. V-cap tiles must be cut with a wet saw. Hardwood strips should be prefinished with at least three coats of polyurethane finish. Attach the strips to the plywood core so the top of the wood will be flush with the faces of the tiles.

Tips for Laying Out Tile ▸

- You can lay tile over a laminate countertop that's square, level, and structurally sound. Use a belt sander with 60- or 80-grit sandpaper to rough up the surface before setting the tiles. The laminate cannot have a no-drip edge.

  If you're using a new substrate and need to remove your existing countertop, make sure the base cabinets are level front to back, side to side, and with adjoining cabinets. Unscrew a cabinet from the wall and use shims on the floor or against the wall to level it, if necessary.
- Installing battens along the front edge of the countertop helps ensure the first row of tile is perfectly straight. For V-cap tiles, fasten a 1 × 2 batten along the reference line using screws. The first row of field tile is placed against this batten. For bullnose tiles, fasten a batten that's the same thickness as the edging tile, plus ⅛" for mortar thickness, to the face of the countertop so the top is flush with the top of the counter. Bullnose tiles should be aligned with the outside edge of the batten. For wood edge trim, fasten a 1 × 2 batten to the face of the countertop so the top edge is above the top of the counter. The tiles are installed against the batten.
- Before installing any tile, lay out the tiles in a dry run using spacers. If your counter is L-shaped, start at the corner and work outward. Otherwise, start the layout at a sink to ensure equally sized cuts on both sides of the sink. If necessary, shift your starting point so you don't end up cutting tile segments that are too narrow.

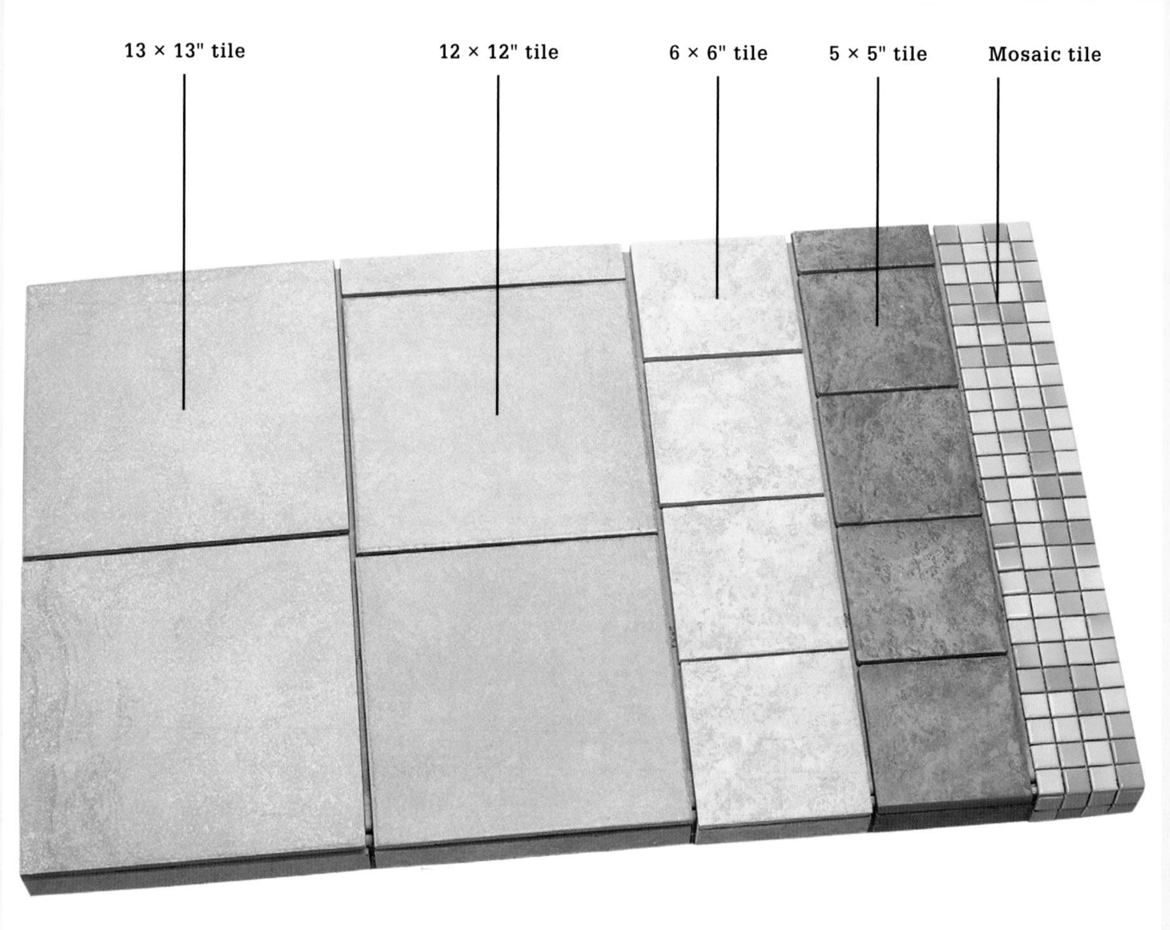

The bigger the tile the fewer the grout lines. If you want a standard 25"-deep countertop, the only way to get there without cutting tiles is to use mosaic strips or 1" tile. With 13 × 13" tile, you need to trim 1" off the back tile but have only one grout line front to back. As you decrease the size of your tiles, the number of grout lines increases.

How to Build a Tile Countertop

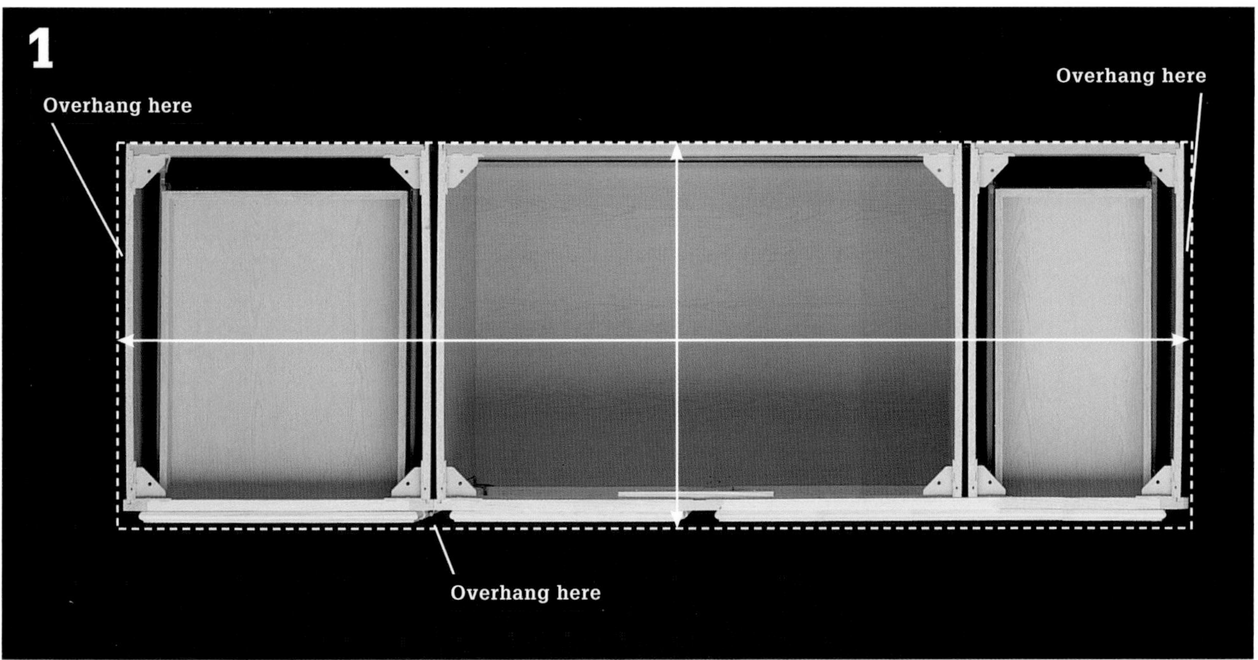

Determine the size of the plywood substrate by measuring across the top of the cabinets. The finished top should overhang the drawer fronts by at least ¼". Be sure to account for the thickness of the cementboard, adhesive, and tile when deciding how large to make the overhang. Cut the substrate to size from ¾" plywood using a circular saw. Also make any cutouts for sinks and other fixtures.

Set the plywood substrate on top of the cabinets, and attach it with screws driven through the cabinet corner brackets. The screws should not be long enough to go through the top of the substrate.

Cut pieces of cementboard to size, then mark and make the cutout for the sink. Dry-fit them on the plywood core with the rough sides of the panels facing up. Leave a ⅛" gap between the cementboard sheets and a ¼" gap along the perimeter.

(continued)

Option: Cut cementboard using a straightedge and utility knife or a cementboard cutter with a carbide tip. Hold the straightedge along the cutting line, and score the board several times with the knife. Bend the piece backward to break it along the scored line. Back-cut to finish.

Lay the plastic moisture barrier over the plywood substrate, draping it over the edges. Tack it in place with a few staples. Overlap seams in the plastic by 6", and seal them with packing tape.

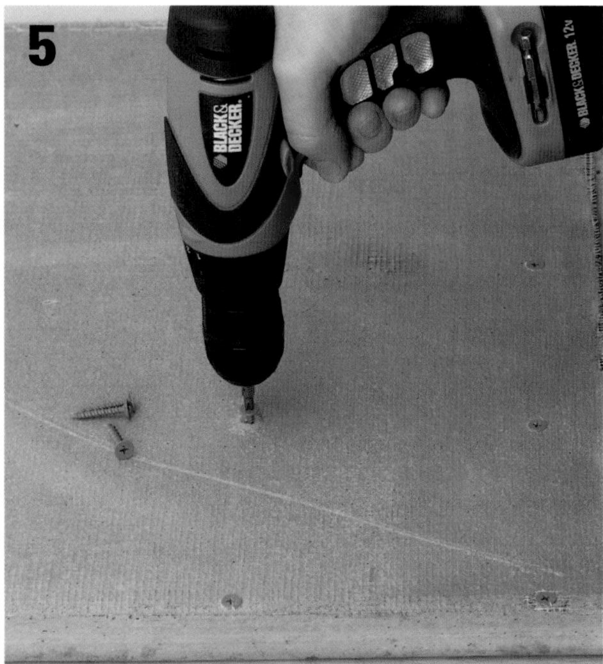

Lay the cementboard pieces rough-side up on top of the moisture barrier and attach them with cementboard screws driven every 6". Drill pilot holes using a masonry bit, and make sure all screw heads are flush with the surface. Wrap the countertop edges with 1¼"-wide cementboard strips, and attach them to the core with cementboard screws.

Tape all cementboard joints with fiberglass mesh tape. Apply three layers of tape along the front edge where the horizontal cementboard sheets meet the cementboard edging.

Fill all the gaps and cover all of the tape with a layer of thinset mortar. Feather out the mortar with a drywall knife to create a smooth, flat surface.

Determine the required width of the edge tiles. Lay a field tile onto the tile base so it overhangs the front edge by ½". Hold a metal ruler up to the underside of the tile and measure the distance from it to the bottom of the subbase. The edge tiles should be cut to this width (the gap for the grout line causes the edge tile to extend the subbase that conceals it completely).

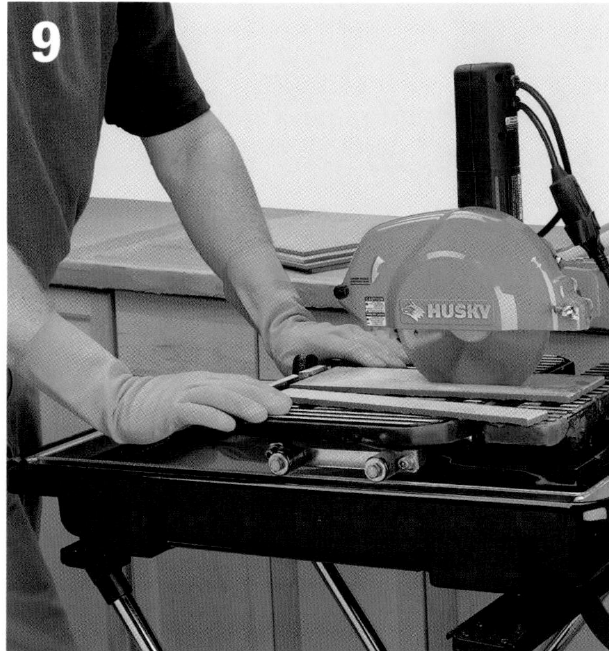

Cut edge tiles to the determined width using a wet saw. It's worth renting a quality wet saw for tile if you don't own one. Floor tile is thick and difficult to cut with a hand cutter (especially porcelain tiles).

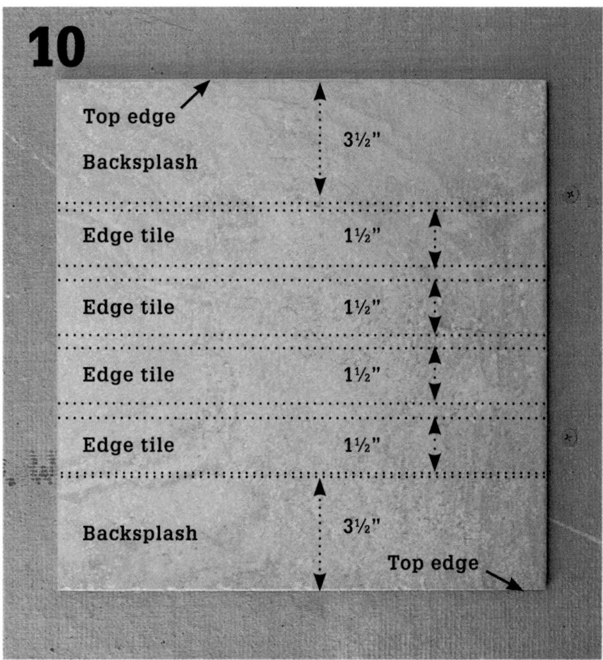

Cut tiles for the backsplash. The backsplash tiles (3½" wide in our project) should be cut with a factory edge on each tile that will be oriented upward when they're installed. You can make efficient use of your tiles by cutting edge tiles from the center area of the tiles you cut to make the backsplash.

(continued)

Dry-fit tiles on the countertop to find the layout that works best. Once the layout is established, make marks along the vertical and horizontal rows. Draw reference lines through the marks and use a framing square to make sure the lines are perpendicular.

Small Floor Tiles & Bullnose Edging ▸

Lay out tiles and spacers in a dry run. Adjust the starting lines, if necessary. If using battens, lay the field tile flush with the battens, then apply the edge tile. Otherwise, install the edging first. If the countertop has an inside corner, start there by installing a ready-made inside corner or by cutting a 45° miter in the edge tile to make your own inside corner.

Place the first row of field tile against the edge tile, separating the tile with spacers. Lay out the remaining rows of tile. Adjust the starting lines if necessary to create a layout using the smallest number of cut tiles.

Use a ⅜" square notched trowel to apply a layer of thinset mortar to the cementboard. Apply enough for two or three tiles, starting at one end. Hold the trowel at roughly a 30° angle and try not to overwork the mortar or remove too much.

Set the first tile into the mortar. Hold a piece of the edge against the countertop edge as a guide to show you exactly how much the tile should overhang the edge.

Cut all the back tiles for the layout to fit (you'll need to remove about 1" of a 13 × 13" tile) before you begin the actual installation. Set the back tiles into the thinset, maintaining the gap for grout lines created by the small spacer nubs cast into the tiles. If your tiles have no spacer nubs, see the option.

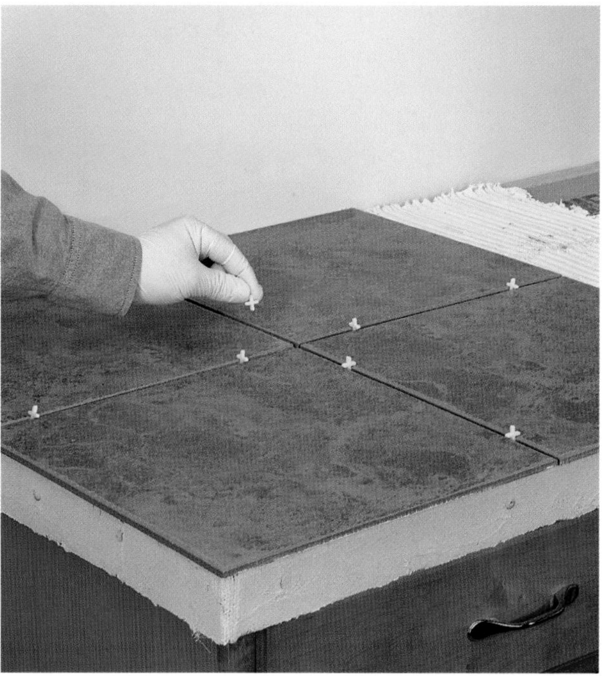

Option: To maintain even grout lines, some beginning tilers insert plus-sign-shaped plastic spacers at the joints. This is less likely to be useful with large tiles like those shown here, but it is effective. Many tiles today feature built-in spacing lugs, so the spacers are of no use. Make sure to remove the spacers before the thinset sets. If you leave them in place they will corrupt your grout lines.

(continued)

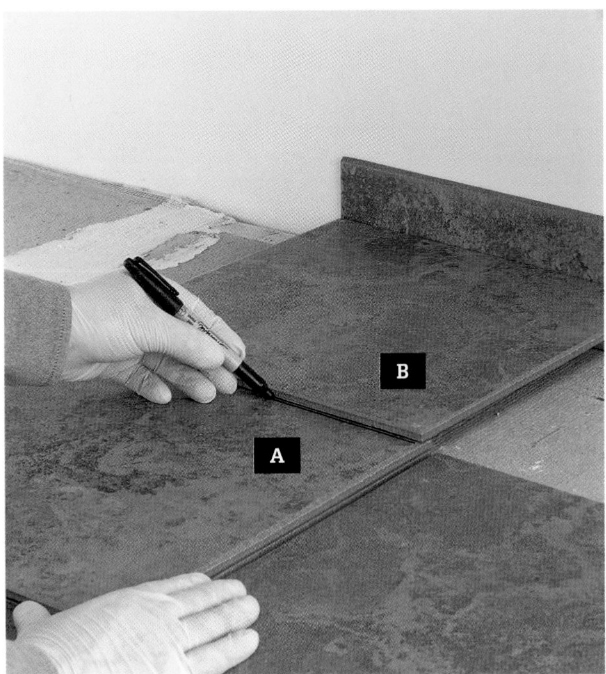

Tip: To mark border tiles for cutting, allow space for the backsplash tiles, grout, and mortar by placing a tile against the back wall. Set another tile (A) on top of the last full tile in the field, then place a third tile (B) over tile (A) and hold it against the upright tile. Mark and cut tile (A) and install it with the cut edge toward the wall. Finish filling in your field tiles.

To create a support ledge for the edge tiles, prop pieces of 2 × 4 underneath the front edge of the substrate overhang using wood scraps to prop the ledge tightly up against the substrate.

Apply a thick layer of thinset to the backside of the edge tile with your trowel. This is called "buttering" and it is easier and neater than attempting to trowel adhesive onto the countertop edge. Press the tiles into position so they are flush with the leading edges of the field tiles.

Butter each backsplash tile and press it into place, doing your best to keep all of the grout lines aligned. Allow the mortar to set according to the manufacturer's recommendations.

Mix a batch of grout to complement the tile (keeping in mind that darker grout won't look dirty as quickly as lighter grout). Apply the grout with a grout float.

Let the grout dry until a light film is created on the countertop surface, then wipe the excess grout off with a sponge and warm, clean water. See grout manufacturer's instructions on drying tiles and polishing.

Run a bead of clear silicone caulk along the joint between the backsplash and the wall. Install your sink and faucet after the grout has dried (and before you use the sink, if possible).

Wait at least one week and then seal the grout lines with a penetrating grout sealer. This is important to do. Sealing the tiles themselves is not a good idea unless you are using unglazed tiles (a poor choice for countertops, however).

Granite Tile Countertop

Solid granite countertops are hugely popular in kitchen décor today, and for good reason: they are beautiful, sturdy, and natural. However, they are also expensive and nearly impossible for a do-it-yourselfer to install. There is a way, however, for an enterprising DIY-er to achieve the look and feel of natural granite, but at a fraction of the price: granite tile countertops.

You have two basic product options with granite tile. Standard granite tiles consist of field tiles and edge tiles with square edges and are installed just like normal ceramic or porcelain tiles and finished with thin edge tiles to create the nosing. You can use granite tiles that are installed with front tiles that feature an integral bullnose that better imitates the look of solid granite. Typically, granite tiles fit together more snugly than ceramic tiles. And, you can choose grout that's the same color as the tiles for a near-seamless finished appearance.

Layout is the most important step in any tile project. If tiles need to be cut to fit, it is best to cut the tiles at the center of the installation or the sets of tiles at both ends. This creates a more uniform look. Granite tile can be installed over laminate countertop (not post-form) if you remove the nosing and backsplash first. The laminate substrate must be in good condition with no peeling or water damage.

Tools & Materials ▸

- ⅝" exterior grade plywood
- ¼" cementboard
- Cementboard screws
- Granite tiles
- Tile wet saw with diamond blade
- Honing stone
- Cordless drill with ½" masonry bit
- Modified thinset mortar
- 2 × 4 lumber scrap
- Circular saw
- Jigsaw
- Compass
- Utility knife
- Straightedge
- ¼" notched trowel
- Unsanded grout
- Stone sealer
- Rubber gloves
- Mallet
- Wood screws
- Scrap carpet
- Eye protection

Granite tiles are installed in much the same way as ceramic tiles, but the ultra-narrow gaps and matching grout mimic the appearance of solid polished granite.

How to Install Granite Tile Countertops

Remove the countertops. From inside the base cabinets, remove the screws holding the countertops to the cabinets. Unscrew take-up bolts on mitered sections of the countertop. Use a utility knife to cut through the caulk, if present. Countertops should lift off easily, but if they don't, you can use a prybar to carefully pry them away from the base cabinets. *Note: In some cases you can install these tiles over old laminate countertops (see previous page).*

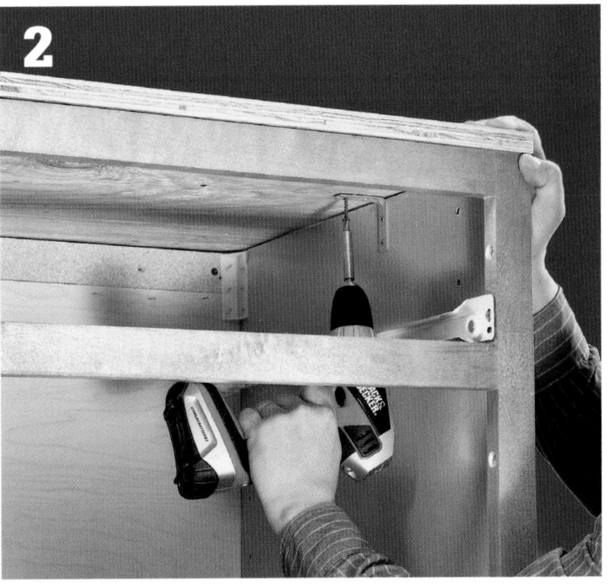

Prepare and install the subbase. Measure the cabinet bank from outside edges to outside edges on all sides and cut a piece of ⅝"-thick exterior grade plywood to fit. The edges of the plywood should be flush with the outside edges of the cabinet tops. Screw the plywood to the cabinet braces from underneath.

Make the sink cutout. To create cutting lines, place the sink upside down in the desired location. Trace the edges of the sink and remove it. To create support for the drop-in sink flange, use a compass to trace new cutting lines inside the traced lines (usually ⅝"). See the manufacturer's instructions to confirm dimensions (some sinks come with a template for making the cutout. Use a jigsaw to cut out the sink opening.

Install the tile underlayment. Granite tile, like ceramic tile, requires a cementboard or denseboard underlayment layer. Cut the material (see page 174) to the same dimension as the plywood subbase and lay the cementboard over the plywood with the edges flush. From inside the sink base, trace around the sink cutout with a marker. Remove the underlayment and make the cutout with a jigsaw fitted with a carbide blade.

(continued)

Attach the cementboard underlayment to the subbase. First, apply a ⅛"-thick layer of modified thinset to the top of the plywood using a ¼" notched trowel. Screw the cementboard to the plywood with cementboard screws. Space the screws 4" to 5" apart across the entire surface.

Cut (as needed) and lay out the tiles, beginning with an inside corner if you have one. Arrange tiles for the best color match. Tiles abut directly, with no space for grout. Cut the tiles as necessary to fit. Cut self-edged tiles edge side first. Cut the tiles with the polished side up. Use a fine honing stone to relieve the cut edge to match the manufactured edges.

Variations for Corners & Angles ▸

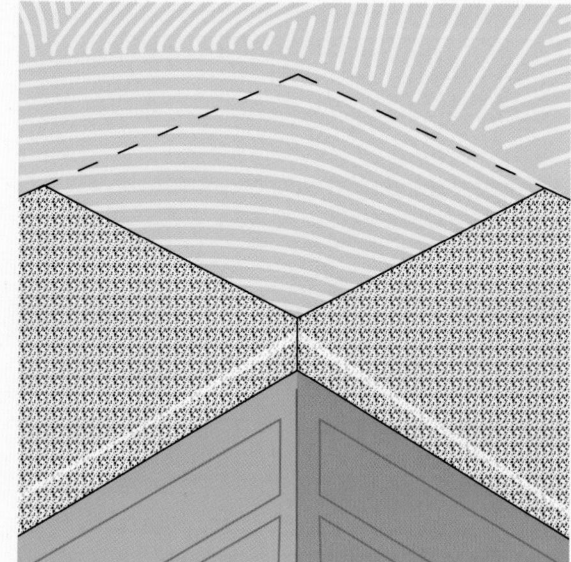

Mitered inside corners are a bit tricky to cut because the mitered point needs to align with the starting point of the bullnose edge. This has the effect of making the corner set back roughly an inch.

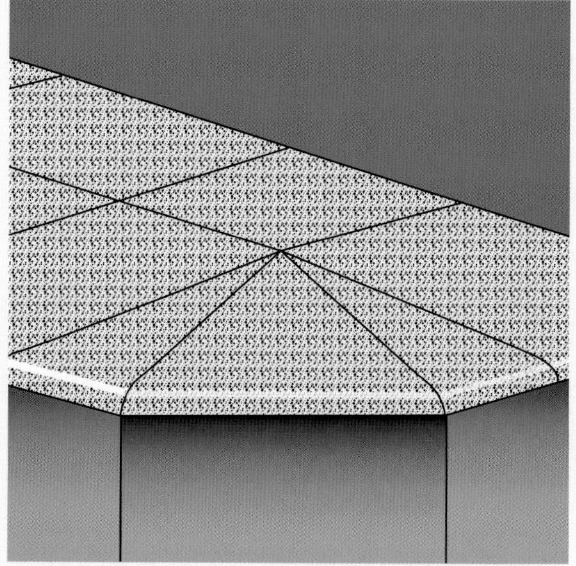

Kitchen islands often have corners that do not form a right angle. In such cases, you can avoid a sharp angle on the countertop by cutting a triangular bullnose piece to fill in.

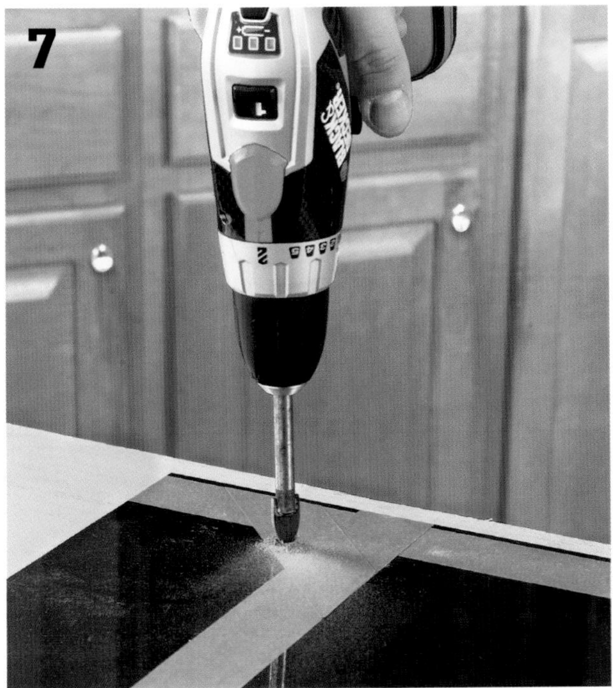

Round the inside corner cuts. Even though the flange of the sink shown here will cover the inside corners in the sink cutout, take care to make a gentle rounded corner cut by drilling at the corner with a ½" masonry bit. Perpendicular corner cuts can lead to cracking. Finish the straight legs of the cutout with a tile saw or a jigsaw with a masonry blade.

Start laying tiles. Use modified thinset and a ¼" trowel. If you have an inside corner in your countertop, begin there. Apply thinset at the inside corner, enough to place four or five tiles. Set the left and right inside corner pieces and the first 12 × 12 field tile.

Continue setting tiles. Apply the thinset mortar to an area big enough for two to four tiles and place the tiles. Use a 2 × 4 covered with carpeting to set the tiles. Push down on tiles to set, and also across the edges to ensure an even face.

Apply grout and seal. After the thinset has dried for at least 24 hours, grout with an unsanded grout. When the grout has dried, seal with natural stone sealer.

Tiled Backsplash

There are few spaces in your home with as much potential for creativity and visual impact as the space between your kitchen countertop and your cupboards. A well-designed backsplash can transform the ordinary into the extraordinary. Tiles for the backsplash can be attached directly to wallboard or plaster and do not require backerboard. When purchasing the tile, order 10 percent extra to cover breakage and cutting. Remove the switch and receptacle coverplates and install box extenders to make up for the extra thickness of the tile. Protect the countertop from scratches by covering it with a drop cloth during the installation.

Tools & Materials ▸

- Level
- Tape measure
- Pencil
- Tile cutter
- Notched trowel
- Rubber grout float
- Rubber mallet
- Sponge
- Story stick
- Tile spacers (if needed)
- Wall tile
- Mastic adhesive
- Masking tape
- Grout
- Caulk
- Drop cloth
- Caulk gun
- Scrap 2 × 4
- Carpet scrap
- Buff cloth

Mosaic Backsplash ▸

Break tiles into fragments and make a mosaic backsplash. Always use sanded grout for joints wider than ⅛".

Contemporary glass mosaic sheets create a counter-to-cabinet backsplash for a waterproof, splash-proof wall with high visual impact.

How to Install a Tile Backsplash

Make a story stick by marking a board at least half as long as the backsplash area to match the tile spacing.

Starting at the midpoint of the installation area, use the story stick to make layout marks along the wall. If an end piece is too small (less than half a tile), adjust the midpoint to give you larger, more attractive end pieces. Use a level to mark this point with a vertical reference line.

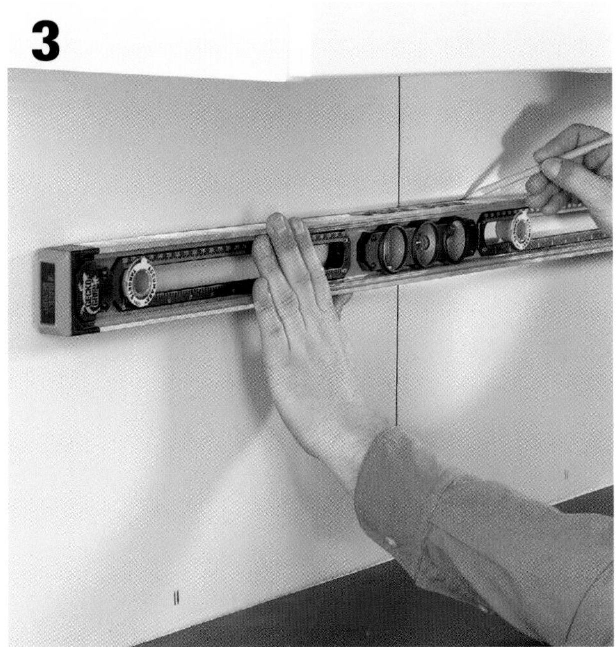

While it may appear straight, your countertop may not be level and therefore is not a reliable reference line. Run a level along the counter to find the lowest point on the countertop. Mark a point two tiles up from the low point and extend a level line across the entire work area.

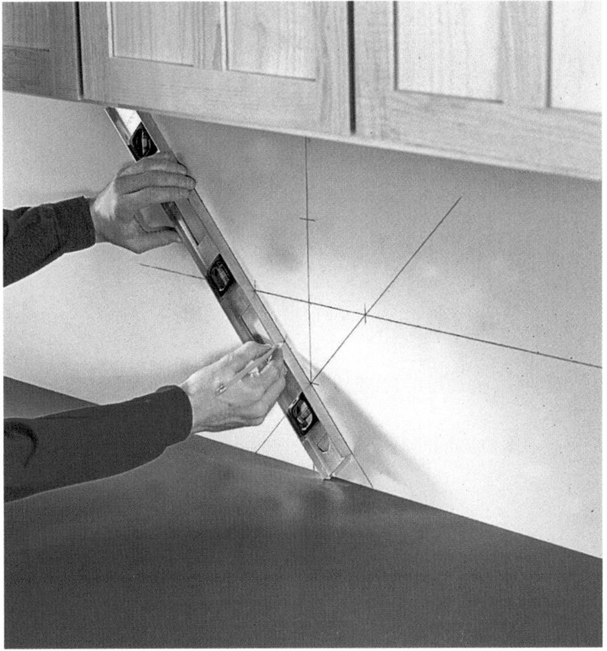

Variation: Diagonal Layout. Mark vertical and horizontal reference lines, making sure the angle is 90°. To establish diagonal layout lines, measure out equal distances from the crosspoint, and then connect the points with a line. Additional layout lines can be extended from these as needed.

(continued)

Apply mastic adhesive evenly to the area beneath the horizontal reference line using a notched trowel. Comb the adhesive horizontally with the notched edge.

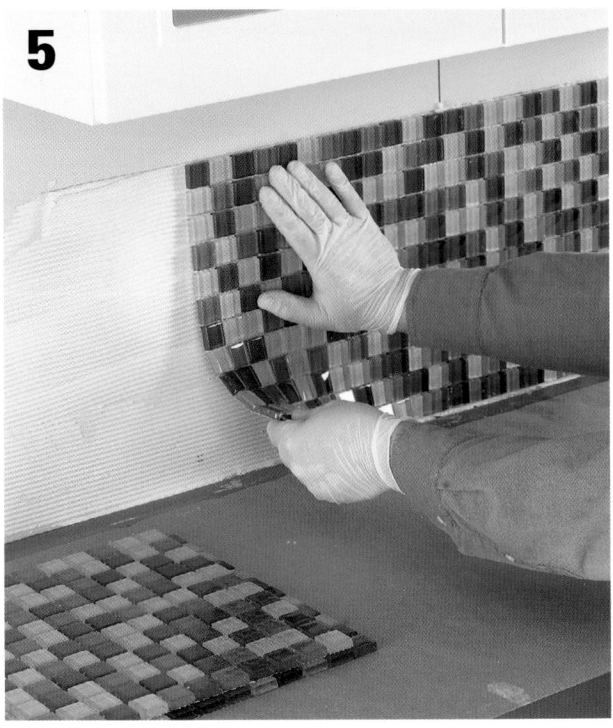

Press tiles into the adhesive with a slight twisting motion. If the tiles are not self-spacing, use plastic spacers to maintain even grout lines. If the tiles do not hang in place, use masking tape to hold them in place until the adhesive sets.

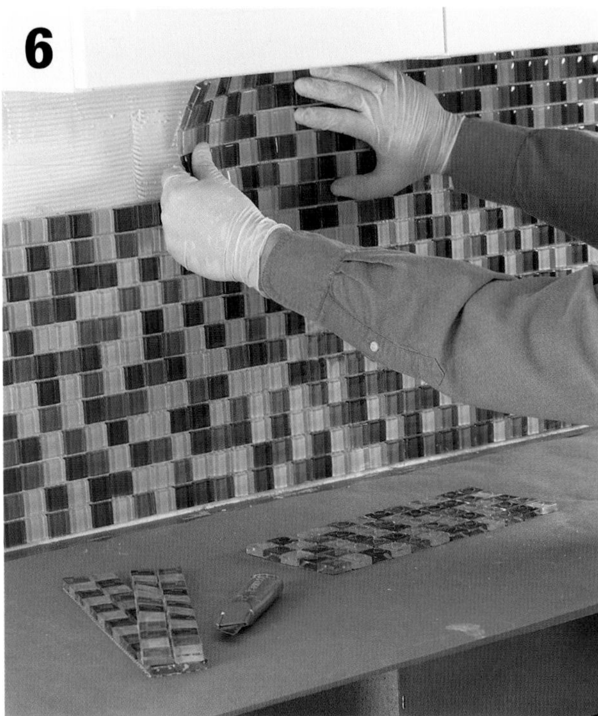

Install a whole row along the reference line, checking occasionally to make sure the tiles are level. Continue installing tiles below the first row, trimming tiles that butt against the countertop as needed.

Install an edge border if it is needed in your layout. Mosaic sheets normally do not have bullnose tiles on the edges, so if you don't wish to see the cut edges of the outer tiles, install a vertical column of edge tiles at the end of the backsplash area.

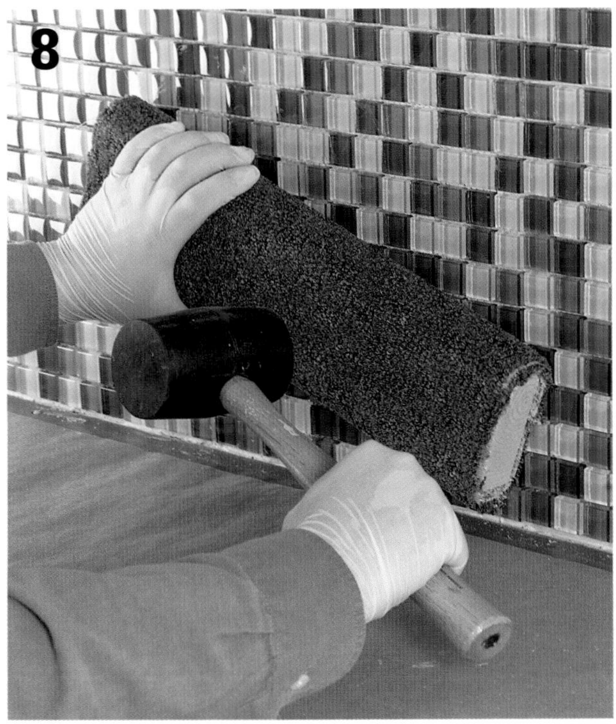

When the tiles are in place, make sure they are flat and firmly embedded by laying a beating block against the tile and rapping it lightly with a mallet. Remove the spacers. Allow the mastic to dry for at least 24 hours, or as directed by the manufacturer.

Mix the grout and apply it with a rubber grout float. Spread it over the tiles, keeping the float at a low 30° angle, pressing the grout deep into the joints. *Note: For grout joints 1/8" and smaller, be sure to use a non-sanded grout.*

Wipe off excess grout, holding the float at a right angle to the tile, working diagonally so as not to remove grout from the joints.

Clean excess grout with a damp sponge. When the grout has dried to a haze, buff the tile clean with a soft cloth. Apply a bead of caulk between the countertop and the tiles.

Tiled Island

Islands are one of the most requested kitchen features. People love them for many reasons, including their value as bi-level counter space. In most cases, the lower level is used as work space and the upper as casual dining space. The upper level provides a little camouflage for the work space, something that's especially welcome in open-plan kitchens where meal preparation areas are visible from social spaces.

When planning casual dining space, remember that designers suggest at least 24 inches per person. For the work space, remember that standard design guidelines recommend at least 36 inches of uninterrupted work space to the side of a sink or cooktop.

On work surfaces, mosaic and other small tile is rarely the best choice. Larger tile requires fewer grout lines, always a good idea when it comes to cleaning and maintenance. But there is no rule that all three elements of a bi-level island have to use the same material. In fact, projects like this offer wonderful opportunities to mix materials, colors, and textures. Choose floor tile or tile made especially for counters and then branch out when it comes to the backsplash, where wall tile and mosaics work beautifully.

Tools & Materials ▸

Tape measure
Circular saw
Drill
Utility knife
Straightedge
Stapler
Wallboard knife
Framing square
Notched trowel
Tile cutter
Grout float
Sponge
Foam brush
Caulk gun
1 × 2 hardwood
2 × 4 lumber
Ceramic tile
Construction adhesive
Paint and primer
Tile spacers
Masking tape
¾" exterior-grade (CDX) plywood
½" cementboard
3" deck screws
Fiberglass mesh tape
Thinset mortar
Grout with latex additive
Silicone caulk
Grout sealer
L-brackets
6d finish nails
Wallboard screws
Pneumatic nailer
Shims
Paint roller and tray
Cabinet doors and hardware
Eye protection
Cementboard screws
Mosaic tile
Buff cloth

This island adds storage, countertop space, and seating to a kitchen, revealing the truly astonishing transformation this simple yet functional piece can achieve.

How to Build a Tiled Bi-Level Island

Build a 2 × 4 base for the island cabinet by cutting the 2 × 4s to length and joining them in a square frame that lays flat (wide sides down) on the floor. Use metal L-brackets to reinforce the joints. If you don't wish to move the island, fasten the frame to the floor in position with construction adhesive and/or deck screws.

Cut the bottom panel the same dimensions as the base frame from ¾" plywood. Attach it to the frame with finish nails. Then, cut the side panels to size and shape and fasten them to the edges with 6d finish nails and adhesive. Slip ¾" shims (scrap plywood works well) beneath the side panels before fastening them.

Cut the 2 × 4 cross supports to length and install them between the side panels at every corner, including the corners created by the L-shape cutout. Use 3" deck screws driven through the side panels and into the ends of the cross supports.

Prime and paint the cabinet interior and exterior.

(continued)

Build a face frame from 1 × 2 hardwood to fit the cabinet front. Attach it to the cabinet with 6d finish nails and hang the cabinet doors (we installed three 13"-wide overlay doors).

Cut strips of ¾" exterior plywood to make the subbases for the countertops and a backer for the backsplash. The lower counter subbase should overhang by 2" on the front and sides. The upper should overhang 2" on the sides and be centered on the cabinet front to back. Attach the backer and subbases with wallboard screws driven down into the 2 × 4 cross supports.

Cut 2" wide strips of plywood for buildup strips and attach to the undersides of the subbases with construction adhesive and screws.

Attach cementboard to the counter subbases, the backsplash, and tape seams; cover screw heads with thinset mortar (see pages 174 to 175).

Cut mosaic sheets to fit the backsplash area and attach them with thinset adhesive (see Tile Backsplash, page 184).

Cut the edge tiles and fasten them around the perimeter of the subbase with thinset mortar. The tiles should be flush or slightly below the bottoms of the buildup strips and project past the top surfaces so they will be level with the field tiles. If you are not using edge tiles with a bullnose top, install the tiles so they are level with the subbase surface and overhang them with the field tiles.

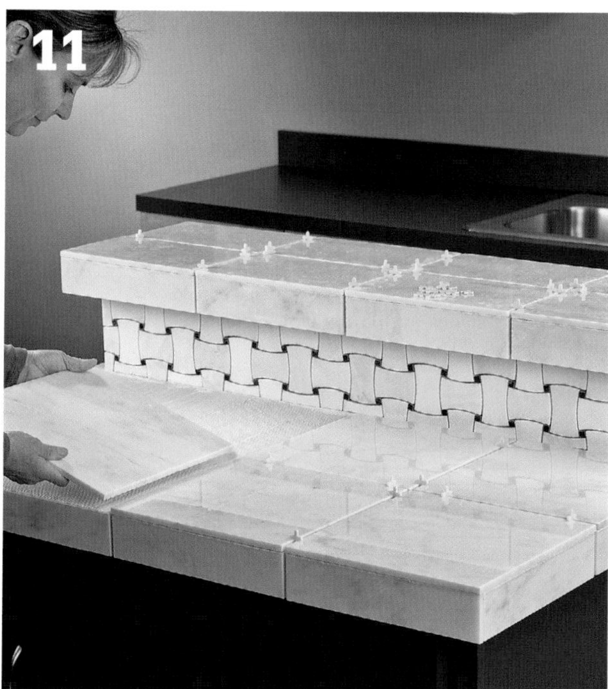

Install the field tiles for the countertops last (see Tile Countertop, pages 170 to 179).

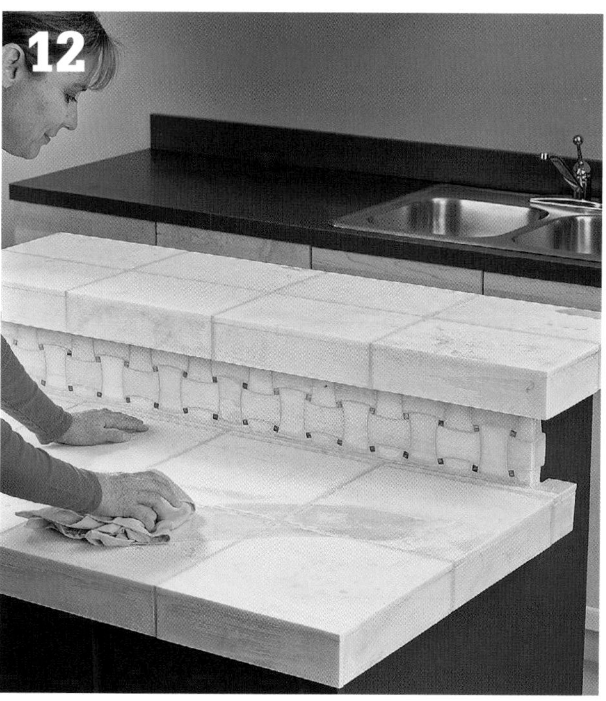

Choose a suitable grout color and apply it to the tile with a grout float. Buff off excess once it has dried. Seal the grout with grout sealer.

Outdoor Projects

Tile makes as much sense in your outdoor home as it does indoors. Its durability, ease of maintenance, and attractive appearance bring good things to patios, gardens, and outdoor kitchens, to name just a few places.

Tile set into a mortar bed can make a very durable exterior surface, but in colder climates with significant freeze/thaw cycles the tile will not last as well. It does not take much moisture in the tile or the bed to cause tile popouts or cracking when the temperature dips. In a cold climate you will likely have better luck installing tile by bonding it to a sturdy concrete subbase (patio or steps) with exterior-rated construction adhesive. You may need to re-glue a tile occasionally, but you will have much less trouble with popouts and fracturing. Use tinted latex caulk between the tiles instead of sanded grout.

In this chapter:

Tiled Steps

In addition to the traditional tricks for improving your home's curb appeal—landscaping, fresh paint, pretty windows—a tiled entry makes a wonderful, positive impression. To be suitable for tiling, stair treads must be deep enough to walk on safely. Check local building codes for specifics, but most require that treads be at least 11 inches deep (from front to back) after the tile is added.

Before you start laying any tiles, the concrete must be free of curing agents, clean, and in good shape. Make necessary repairs and give them time to cure. An isolation membrane can be applied before the tile. This membrane can be a fiberglass sheet or it can be brushed on as a liquid to dry. In either case, the membrane separates the tile from the concrete, which allows the two to move independently and protects the tile from cracking due to settling or shifting of the concrete.

Choose exterior-rated, unglazed floor tile with a skid-resistant surface. Tile for the walking surfaces should be at least ½-inch thick. Use bullnose tiles at the front edges of treads (as you would on a countertop) and use cove tiles as the bottom course on risers.

Tools & Materials ▸

- Pressure washer
- Masonry trowel
- 4-ft. level
- Straightedge
- Tape measure
- Tile cutter or wet saw
- Tile nippers
- Square-notched trowel
- Needlenose pliers
- Grout float
- Grout sponge
- Caulk gun
- Masonry patching compound
- Thinset mortar with latex bonding adhesive
- Isolation membrane
- Tile spacers
- Buckets
- Plastic sheeting
- Field tile
- Bullnose tile
- Grout
- Latex tile caulk
- Grout sealer
- 2 × 4 lumber
- Carpet scrap
- Cold chisel or flat-head screwdriver
- Wire brush
- Broom or vacuum
- Chalk
- Eye protection

How to Tile Concrete Steps

Use a pressure washer to clean the surface of the concrete. Use a washer with at least 4,000 psi and follow manufacturer's instructions carefully to avoid damaging the concrete with the pressurized spray.

Dig out rubble in large cracks and chips using a small cold chisel or flat-head screwdriver. Use a wire brush to loosen dirt and debris in small cracks. Sweep the area or use a wet/dry vacuum to remove all debris.

Fill small cracks and chips with masonry patching compound using a masonry trowel. Allow the patching compound to cure according to manufacturer's directions.

Option: If damage is located at a front edge, clean it as described above. Place a board in front and block the board in place with bricks or concrete blocks. Wet the damaged area and fill it with patching compound. Use a masonry trowel to smooth the patch and then allow it to cure thoroughly.

Test the surface of the steps and stoop for low spots using a 4-ft. level or other straightedge. Fill any low spots with patching compound and allow the compound to cure thoroughly.

(continued)

Spread a layer of isolation membrane over the concrete using a notched trowel. Smooth the surface of the membrane using the flat edge of a trowel. Allow the membrane to cure according to manufacturer's directions.

The sequence is important when tiling a stairway with landing. The primary objective is to install the tile in such a way that the fewest possible cut edges are visible from the main viewing position. If you are tiling the sides of concrete steps, start laying tile there first. Begin by extending horizontal lines from the tops of the stair treads back to the house on the sides of the steps. Use a 4-ft. level.

Mix a batch of thinset mortar with latex bonding adhesive and trowel it onto the sides of the steps, trying to retain visibility of the layout lines. Because the top steps are likely more visible than the bottom steps, start on top and work your way down.

Begin setting tiles into the thinset mortar on the sides of the steps. Start at the top and work your way downward. Try to lay out tile so the vertical gaps between tiles align. Use spacers if you need to.

Wrap a 2 × 4 in old carpet and drag it back and forth across the tile surfaces to set them evenly. Don't get too aggressive here—you don't want to dislodge all of the thinset mortar.

Measure the width of a riser, including the thickness of the tiles you've laid on the step sides. Calculate the centerpoint and mark it clearly with chalk or a high visibility marker.

Next, dry-lay the tiles on the stair risers. Because the location of the tops of the riser tiles affects the positioning of the tread and landing tiles, you'll get the most accurate layout if the riser tiles are laid first. Start by stacking tiles vertically against the riser. (In some cases, you'll only need one tile to reach from tread to tread.) Add spacers. Trace the location of the tread across the back of the top tile to mark it for cutting.

Cut enough tiles to size to lay tiles for all the stair risers. Be sure to allow enough space for grout joints if you are stacking tiles.

Trowel thinset mortar mixed with bonding adhesive onto the faces of the risers. In most cases, you should be able to tile each riser all at once.

Lay tiles on the risers. The bottom tile edges can rest on the tread, and the tops of the top tiles should be flush with or slightly lower than the plane of the tread above.

(continued)

Dry-lay tile in both directions on the stair landing. You'll want to maintain the same grout lines that are established by the riser tiles, but you'll want to evaluate the front-to-back layout to make sure you don't end up with a row of tiles that is less than 2" or so in thickness.

Cut tiles as indicated by your dry run, and then begin installing them by troweling thinset mortar for the bullnose tiles at the front edge of the landing. The tiles should overlap the top edges of the riser tiles, but not extend past their faces.

Set the first row of field tiles, maintaining an even gap between the field tiles and the bullnose tiles.

Add the last row of tiles next to the house and threshold, cutting them as needed so they are between ¼ and ½" away from the house.

Install tiles on the stair treads, starting at the top tread and working your way downward. Set a bullnose tile on each side of the centerline and work your way toward the sides, making sure to conceal the step-side tiles with the tread tiles.

Fill in the field tiles on the stair treads, being sure to leave a gap between the back tiles and the riser tiles that's the same thickness as the other tile gaps.

Let the thinset mortar cure for a few days, and then apply grout in the gaps between tiles using a grout float. Wipe away the grout after it clouds over. Cover with plastic, in the event of rain.

After a few weeks, seal the grout lines with an exterior-rated grout sealer.

Select (or have prepared) a pretinted caulk that's the same color as your grout. Fill the gap between the back row of tiles and the house with caulk. Smooth with a wet finger if needed.

Tiled Patio

Outdoor tile can be made of several different materials and is available in many colors and styles. Make sure the tiles you select are intended for outdoor use. A popular trend is to use natural stone tiles with different shapes and complementary colors, as demonstrated in this project. Tile manufacturers may offer brochures giving you ideas for modular patterns that can be created from their tiles.

When laying a modular, geometric pattern with tiles of different sizes, it's crucial that you test the layout before you begin and that you place the first tiles very carefullly. The first tiles will dictate the placement of all other tiles in your layout.

You can pour a new masonry slab on which to install your tile patio, but another option is to finish an existing slab by veneering it with tile—the scenario demonstrated here.

Outdoor tile must be installed on a clean, flat, and stable surface. When tiling an existing concrete slab, the surface must be free of flaking, wide cracks, and other major imperfections. A damaged slab can be repaired by applying a one- to two-inch-thick layer of new concrete over the old surface before laying tile.

Note: Wear eye protection when cutting tile and handle cut tiles carefully—the cut edges of some materials may be very sharp.

Tools & Materials ▸

- Tape measure
- Pencil
- Chalk line
- Tile cutter or wet saw
- Tile nippers
- Square-notched trowel
- 2 × 4 padded with carpet
- Paintbrush and roller
- Hammer
- Grout float
- Grout sponge
- Cloth
- Caulk gun
- Tile spacers
- Buckets
- Plastic sheeting
- Thinset mortar
- Modular tile
- Grout
- Grout additive
- Grout sealer
- Tile sealer
- Foam brush
- Trowel
- Eye protection

This compact tile patio creates a welcoming entry without consuming too much yard and garden space.

How to Tile a Patio Slab

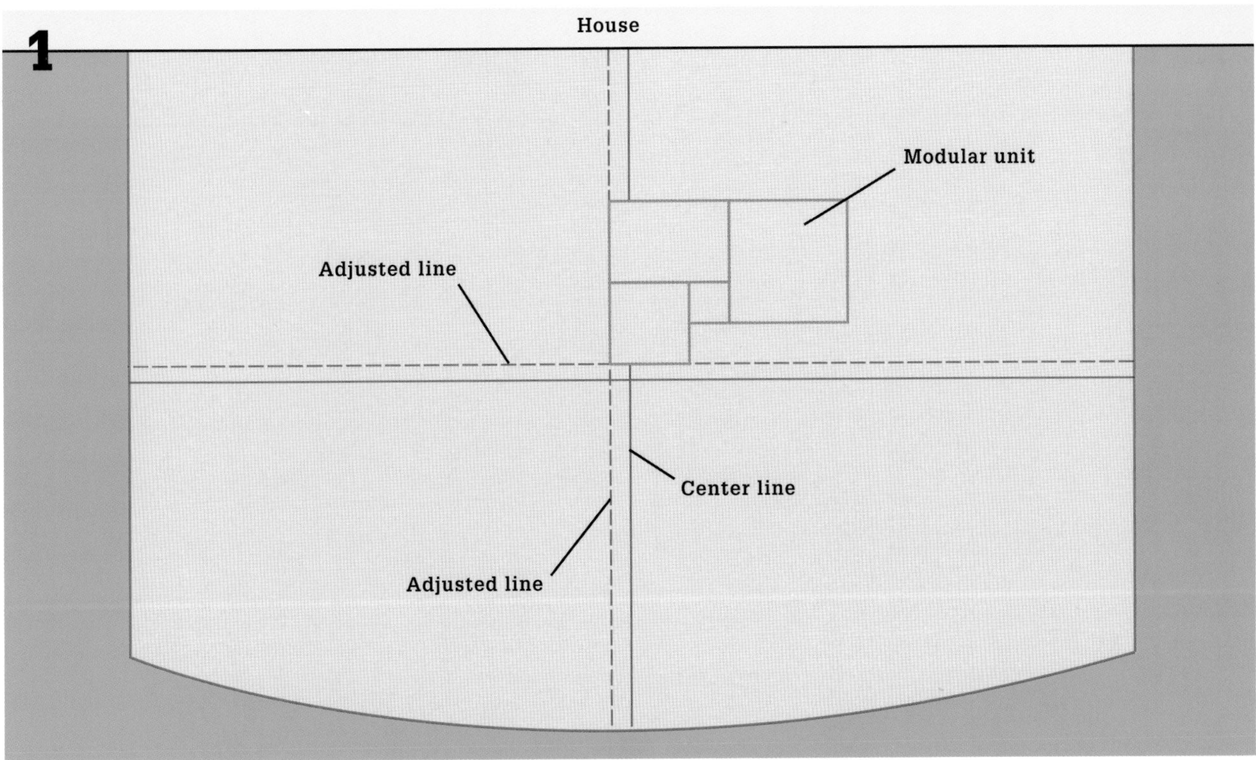

To establish a layout for tile with a modular pattern, you must carefully determine the location of the first tile. On the clean and dry concrete surface, measure and mark a centerline down the center of the slab. Test-fit tiles along the line—because of the modular pattern used here, the tiles are staggered. Mark the edge of a tile nearest the center of the pad, then create a second line perpendicular to the first and test-fit tiles along this line.

Make adjustments as needed so the modular pattern breaks evenly over the patio surface, and is symmetrical from side to side. You may need to adjust the position of one or both lines. The intersection of the lines is where your tile installation will begin. Outline the position of each group of tiles on the slab.

(continued)

Variation: To establish a traditional grid pattern, test-fit rows of tiles so they run in each direction, intersecting at the center of the patio. Adjust the layout to minimize tile cutting at the sides and ends, then mark the final layout and snap chalk lines across the patio to create four quadrants. As you lay tile, work along the chalklines and in one quadrant at a time.

Following manufacturer's instructions, mix enough thinset mortar to work for about 2 hrs. (start with 4 to 5" deep in a 5-gal. bucket. At the intersection of the two layout lines, use a notched trowel to spread thinset mortar over an area large enough to accommodate the layout of the first modular group of tiles. Hold the trowel at a 45° angle to rake the mortar to a consistent depth.

Set the first tile, twisting it slightly as you push it into the mortar. Align it with both adjusted layout lines, then place a padded 2 × 4 over the center of the tile and give it a light rap with a hammer to set the tile.

Position the second tile adjacent to the first with a slight gap between them. Place spacers on end in the joint near each corner and push the second tile against the spacers. Make certain the first tile remains aligned with the layout lines. Set the padded 2 × 4 across both tiles and tap to set. Use a damp cloth to remove any mortar that squeezes out of the joint or gets on tile surfaces. Joints must be at least ⅛"-deep to hold grout.

Lay the remaining tiles of the first modular unit using spacers to set gaps. Using a trowel, scrape the excess mortar from the concrete pad in areas you will not yet be working to prevent it from hardening and interfering with tile installation.

With the first modular unit set, continue laying tile following the pattern established. You can use the chalk lines for general reference, but they will not be necessary as layout lines. To prevent squeeze-out between tiles, scrape a heavy accumulation of mortar ½" away from the edge of a set tile before setting the adjacent tile.

Cutting Contours in Tile ▸

To make convex (left) or concave (right) curves, mark the profile of the curve on the tile, then use a wet saw to make parallel straight cuts, each time cutting as close to the marked line as possible. Use a tile nippers to break off small portions of tabs, gradually working down to the curve profile. Finally, use an angle grinder to smooth off the sharp edges of the tabs. Make sure to wear a particle mask when using the tile saw and wear sturdy gloves when using the nippers.

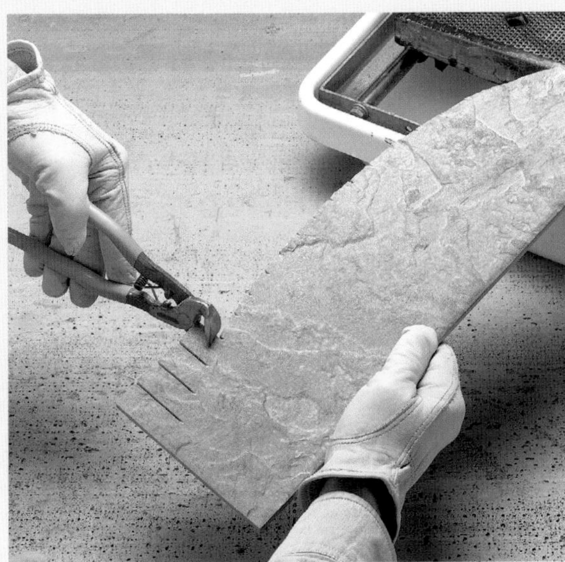

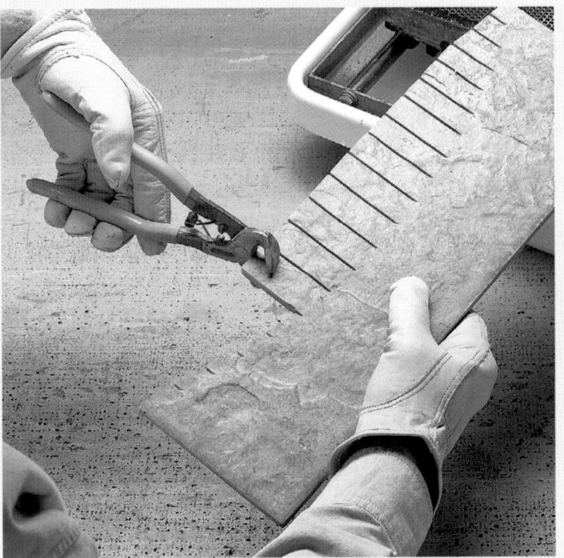

(continued)

After installing the tile, remove all the spacers, cover the tiled area with plastic, and let the thinset mortar cure according to the manufacturer's instructions. When tile has fully set, remove the plastic and mix grout, using a grout additive instead of water. Grout additive is especially important in outdoor applications, because it creates joints that are more resilient in changing temperatures.

Use a grout float to spread grout over an area that is roughly 10 sq. ft. Push down with the face of the float to force grout into the joints, then hold the float edge at a 45° angle to the tile surfaces and scrape off the excess grout.

Once you've grouted this area, wipe off the grout residue using a damp sponge. Wipe with a light, circular motion—you want to clean tile surfaces but not pull grout out of the joints. Don't try to get the tile perfectly clean the first time. Wipe the area several times, rinsing out the sponge frequently.

11

Once the grout has begun to set (usually about 1 hour, depending on temperature and humidity), clean the tile surfaces again. You want to thoroughly clean grout residue from tile surfaces because it is difficult to remove once it has hardened. Buff off a light film left after final cleaning with a cloth.

Grouting Porous Tiles ▸

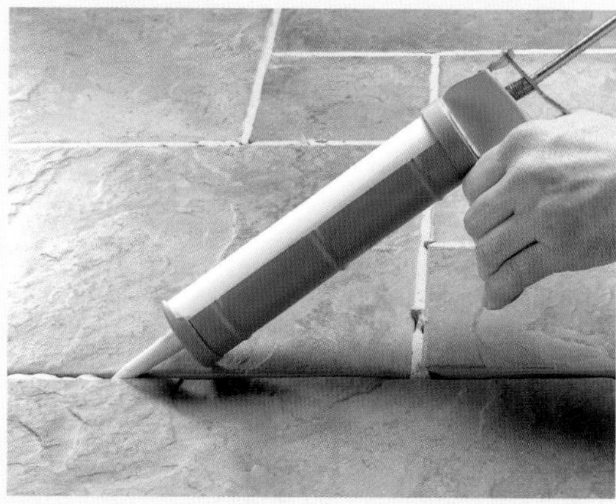

Some tiles, such as slate, have highly porous surfaces that can be badly stained by grout. For these tiles, apply grout by filling an empty caulk tube (available at tile stores and some building centers) with grout, and apply the grout to the joints with a caulk gun. Cut the tip to make an opening just large enough to allow grout to be forced out. Run the tip down the joint between tiles as you squeeze out the grout. Remove the grout that gets on the tile surface with a wet sponge. You may need to use your finger to force grout into the joint—protect your skin by wearing a heavy glove to do this.

Cover the pad with plastic and let the grout cure according to manufacturer's instructions. Once the grout has cured, use a foam brush to apply grout sealer to only the grout, wiping any spill-over off of tile surfaces.

Apply tile sealer to the entire surface using a paint roller. Cover the patio with plastic and allow the sealer to dry completely before exposing the patio to weather or traffic.

Creating a Ceramic Tile Fountain

A fountain is welcome in any landscape, and building and installing one is easier and much less expensive than you might imagine. Think of it: a colorful tile-covered fountain reflected in a small garden pond, water gently splashing on sparkling sea glass. And you can make one. Easily.

Start with a common chimney flue tile and a few square feet of colorful mosaic tiles. Add an inexpensive twelve-volt fountain pump and tiny submersible disc lights, which can be wired into any low-voltage system. Almost before you know it, you'll be ready to show off for the neighbors.

One note of caution: before adding accessories to your low-voltage system, make sure your transformer can handle the extra load.

Chimney flue tiles are available in many different sizes and can be purchased at most fireplace and masonry stores. Small precut sheets of expanded metal grate are available from most hardware stores and home centers.

Tools & Materials ▸

- Notched trowel
- Grout float
- Caulk gun
- Jigsaw or bolt cutters
- 18 × 18 × 24" chimney flue tile
- Bricks
- Metal L-brackets
- 18 × 18" expanded metal grate
- 12 sq. ft. of mosaic tile
- Thinset-mortar
- Grout
- Concrete block
- Construction adhesive
- Low-voltage fountain pump
- Low-voltage fountain lights
- Sea glass (approx. 4 lbs.)
- Silicone caulk

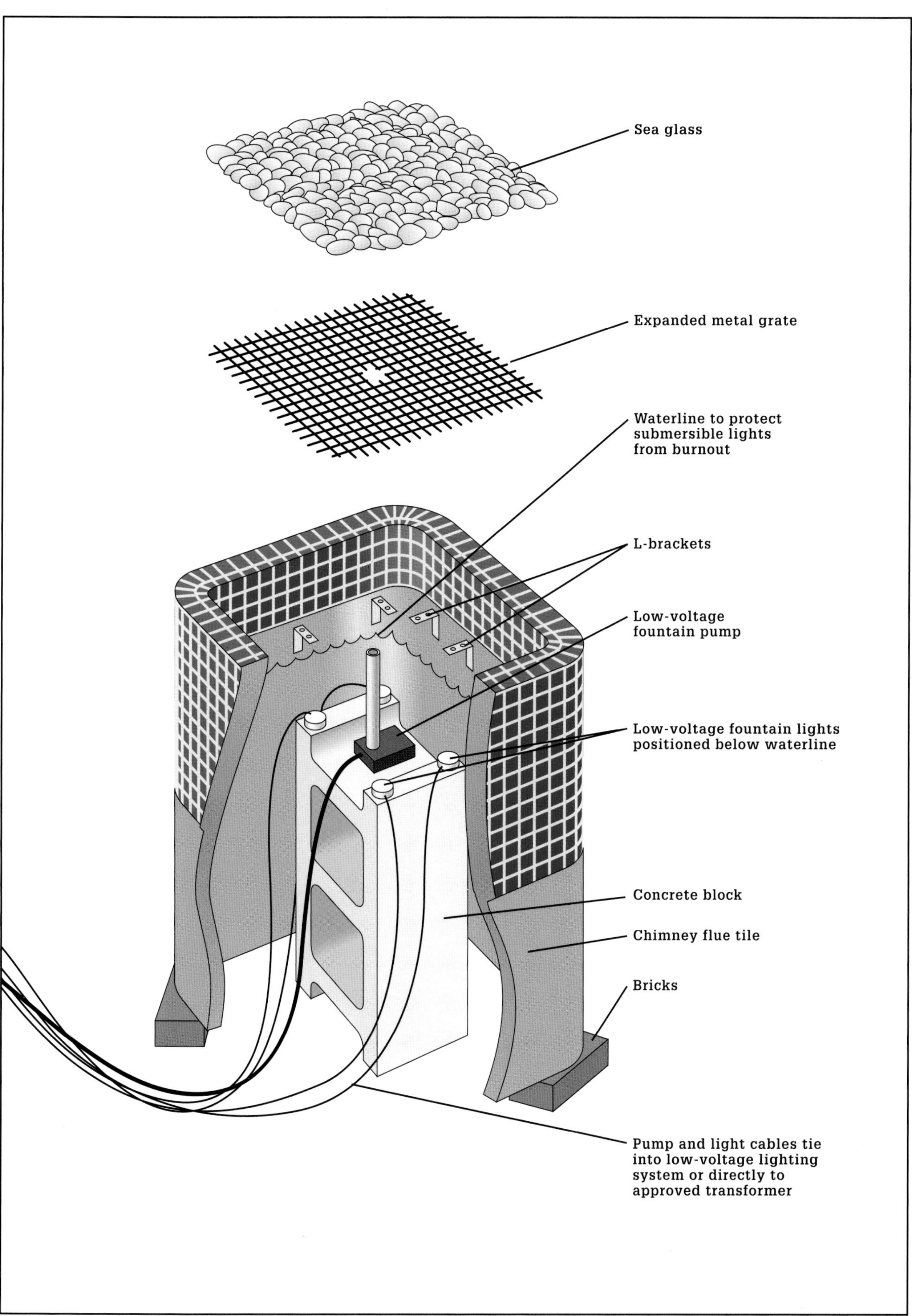
Sea glass
Expanded metal grate
Waterline to protect submersible lights from burnout
L-brackets
Low-voltage fountain pump
Low-voltage fountain lights positioned below waterline
Concrete block
Chimney flue tile
Bricks
Pump and light cables tie into low-voltage lighting system or directly to approved transformer

How to Create a Ceramic Tile Fountain

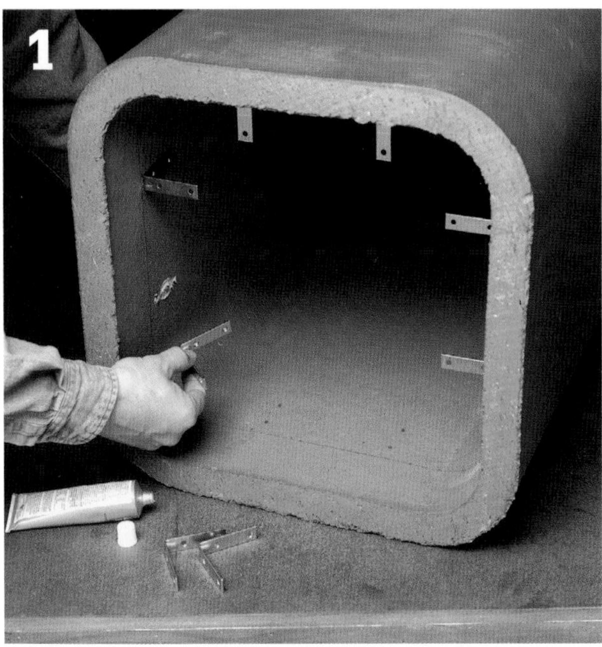

Draw a line on the inside of the flue tile, about 4" from the top. On each wall of the tile, position two L-brackets at the line and glue each bracket in place with construction adhesive.

Set tile on the outside of the flue tile and the inside down to the line. Working on one side of the flue at a time, spread thin-set mortar on the surface, then press the tile into place. Let the mortar dry according to manufacturer's directions. When the mortar is dry, grout the tile.

Position four bricks at the bottom of the water garden and set the flue tile on them. (The flue tile will be very heavy—recruit a helper or two for this.) Set a concrete block in the center of the flue tile and put the fountain pump on top of it.

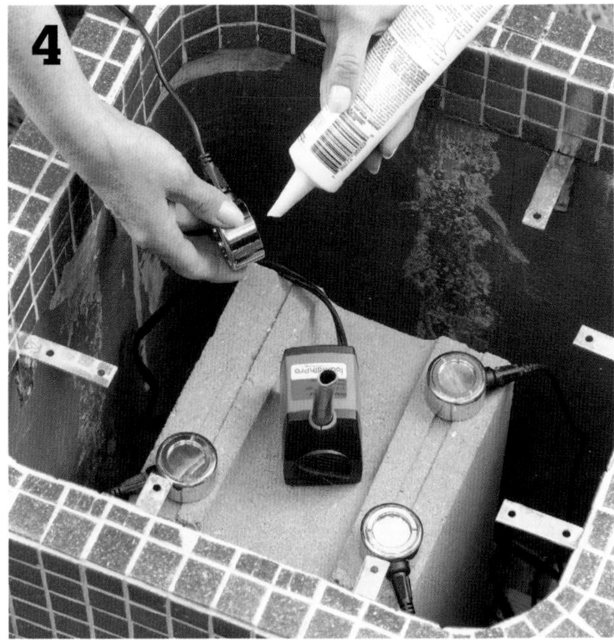

Set the lights in place, securing them to the concrete block with dabs of silicone caulk. Run the cables from the pump and lights out of the pond to the nearest fixture in your low-voltage lighting system. (If you don't have a low-voltage lighting system, run the cables to the transformer and plug the transformer into the nearest GFCI outlet.)

Connect the cables from the pump and lights to a cable from your low-voltage lighting system, using the simple connectors included with the pump. Add water to the pond and test the lights and pump. Adjust the operation of the pump as necessary. Dig a small, shallow trench and bury the cables.

If necessary, cut the expanded metal grate to fit inside the flue tile, using a jigsaw with a metal-cutting blade. In the center of the grate, use the jigsaw or a bolt cutter to expand a hole to approximately 2" in diameter. Insert the pump's discharge tube into this hole, then set the grate on top of the L-brackets in the flue tile. Mound the sea glass around the discharge tube. Use silicone to stick individual pieces of sea glass together, if necessary to hold them in place. Cover the remaining grate with a layer of sea glass.

Low-voltage Accessories ▸

If you have a low-voltage lighting system, add light fixtures to the area surrounding your garden pond and fountain. The extra light will focus even more attention on this lovely little fountain.

Before adding additional fixtures and accessories, make sure your transformer can handle the extra load. If not, run the pond lighting as a separate circuit or purchase a larger transformer to handle the load.

Decorative Projects

Decorative tile projects are just plain fun. Once you understand the basic techniques of tile decoration, the possibilities are limited only by your imagination, your time, and your budget.

In this chapter you'll find projects ranging from small items, such as decorative planters and an address marker to large ones, such as a tiled sink base. You'll learn how to frame a bathroom mirror with tile and how to create an artistic mosaic wall-hanging. In short, there's something in this chapter for all decorators—regardless of your skill level or experience.

You'll also find detailed instructions on how to make your own tile. This is an easy process, and one that can be shared with children of all ages. It does require access to a kiln and glazes, but with some advance notice, that can be arranged with retail pottery shops or studios. This is the type of project that requires experimentation and test runs. Try out different shapes and colors; work with traditional and non-traditional tools to create texture; blend glazes until you find a combination that pleases you.

As your skills and confidence grow, you'll discover that decorative tile projects make excellent gifts.

In this chapter:

Creating Mosaic Planters

The basic steps for adding tile to a planter are much the same as for adding tile to any other surface: plan the layout, set the tile, and grout. Fun and creativity come into the process when you turn your imagination loose with tile and container selection.

But don't limit yourself to tile—mix in other materials such as flat glass marbles or broken pieces of stained glass, mirror, and china. The designs can be as simple or as elaborate as you'd like.

Try a mosaic of daisies using bits of white stained glass for the petals, golden flat glass marbles for the centers, and broken tile bits for the background. Or maybe you'd prefer to use bits of green tile for a vine and leaves with purple flat glass marbles arranged like bunches of grapes. Add a background of broken china or broken stained glass, and you've got a beautiful handmade piece for only a few hours' work.

Select containers that have flat rims like the white planter shown below or that have a broad expanse of flat surface like the pot shown in the project on the following page. Try to match the style and colors of the planters to the design.

Tools & Materials ▸

- Snap cutter
- Tile nippers
- Putty knife
- Grout float
- Grout sponge
- 1" mosaic tile
- Tile mastic
- Grout
- Grout sealer
- Eye protection

A few pieces of broken-up mosaic tile can turn an ordinary pot into a garden showpiece.

How to Decorate Planters

Remove the mosaic tiles from their backing and experiment with designs and layouts. Cut tiles in half as necessary using a snap cutter. Use tile nippers to break some tiles into small pieces.

Draw an irregular border around the planter, ranging from 1½ to 2" wide. Use a putty knife to spread mastic within the border and position the tile, alternating between the whole and half tiles all the way around the planter.

Fill in the remaining portion of the border with pieces of broken tile. Let the mastic dry according to manufacturer's directions. Grout the tile. If the planter will be used outdoors, apply grout sealer after the grout has fully cured.

Bathroom Mirror Frame

The vast majority of bathrooms in new homes today come equipped with flat, boring mirrors. There's nothing wrong with these mirrors, but there's not much right with them, either. Framing a mirror with ceramic or glass tile transforms it from flat to fabulous, and the whole project takes only a few hours.

The process is extremely simple. In fact, shopping for the tile can be the most difficult part of the project. If you're tiling the rest of the bathroom at the same time, you'll want to combine trim pieces that match or complement the field tile. If the room has no other tile, you can mix and match to your heart's content, going as bold or as subtle as you like.

There are two ways you can go about tiling a mirror frame: apply the tile directly to the mirror; or tile around the mirror and butt up to the edges. We chose to remove the mirror, attach the tiles around the perimeter, and then rehang the mirror. If you're rehanging a mirror, take care to make sure the hanger and anchor you use are quite sturdy, as the mirror will have gained a good deal of weight.

Tools & Materials ▸

- Tape measure
- Permanent marker
- Wet saw
- Tile spacers
- Putty knife
- Grout float
- Grout sponge
- Foam paintbrush
- Caulk gun
- Straightedge
- Heavy brown paper or cardboard
- Chair rail and mosaic tile
- Windshield adhesive
- Wide painter's tape
- Grout with latex additive
- Grout sealer
- Eye protection
- Laser or carpenter's level

Tiled Mirror Designs ▸

In this project, tile is added only to the mirror. The mirror is framed by a mosaic of shards and small pieces of glass tile. Mosaic projects are incredibly easy to do and really add a lot to a small room like this one.

In new construction or major remodeling projects, place the mirror so the trim tile can be attached to the wall rather than to the mirror.

How to Frame a Bathroom Mirror

Measure the mirror and cut a template from a piece of heavy brown paper or cardboard. Put the template on the floor or a large work surface. Dry lay the tile around it, using spacers if the tiles are not self-spaced.

Mark any tiles that must be cut to produce full tiles at the corners. (If it's absolutely necessary to trim corner tiles, make them all equal lengths.) Miter the one end of each corner tile at a 45° angle.

Dry lay the outermost row of chair rail tiles. Check corner miters of chair rail to make sure everything is cut properly and aligned on the mirror as desired.

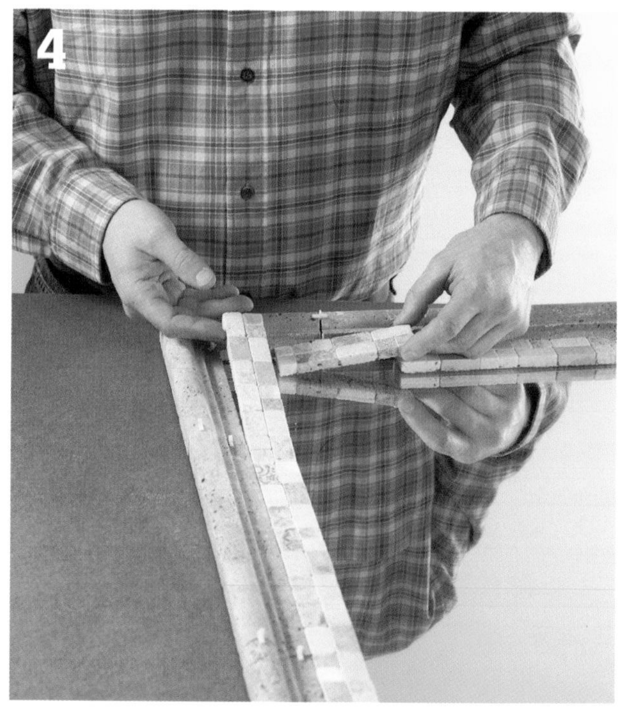

Starting in the left-hand corner, dry lay the next couple of rows of field tile. For accurate placement, include spacers. Make sure tiles match in corners.

Now that the chair rail and two rows of field tile are aligned, dry lay the final row of pencil tiles. Cut tiles, as necessary, to fit onto mirror as planned. Once all tiles fit as planned, remove all but the first row of chair rail tile.

Starting at the top left-hand corner, apply adhesive to the back of the tile using a small putty knife. Set the tile on the mirror and twist it a little to secure it in place.

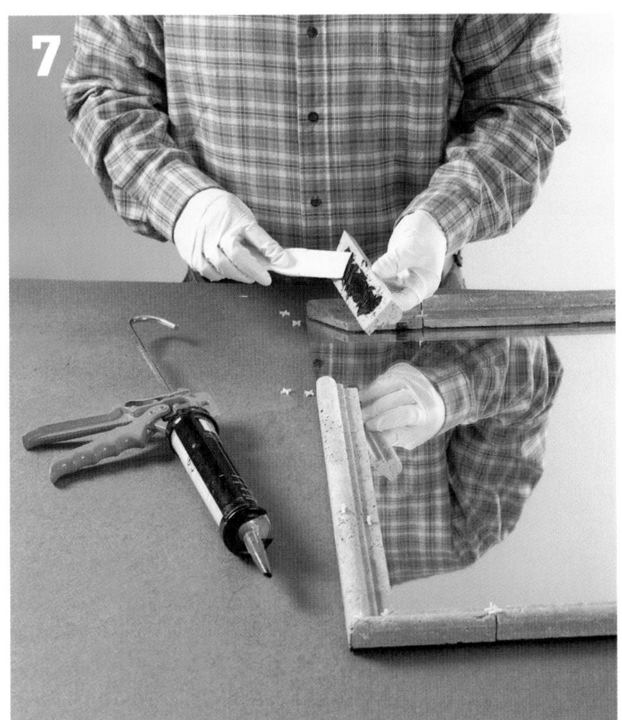

Continue to set the tiles in each corner and then work around the entire perimeter, fastening each tile with adhesive. Once the chair rail is secure, move on to the next row. Repeat this process until all rows are secured to the mirror.

Prepare a small batch of grout and fill all the tile joints. Clean and buff the tile. Allow grout to set completely according to manufacturer recommendation.

Address Marker Mosaic

Broken tile and broken china combine beautifully for mosaics of all sorts. Here they're put to work on an address marker, a quick and easy project and a good way to use leftover tile.

Cut the base material for the marker in the shape shown here or create your own. No matter what shape you choose, use exterior-grade plywood and seal the grout after it has cured according to the manufacturer's directions. With those precautions, your address marker will remain attractive for many years.

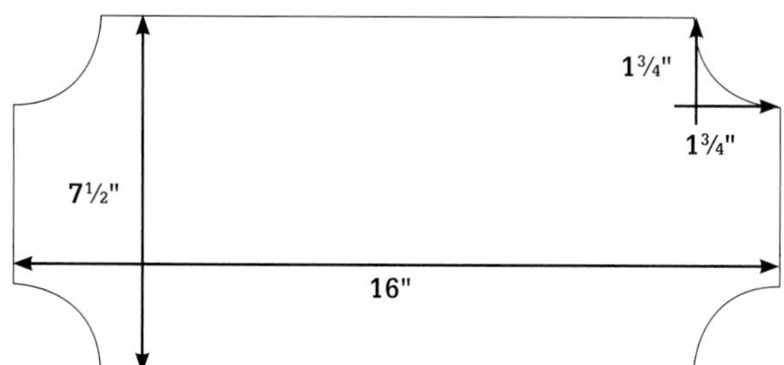

Tools & Materials ▸

- Jigsaw
- Paintbrush
- Rubber mallet
- Tile nippers
- Rotary tool
- Hot glue gun
- Grout float
- Drill
- Grinding disc
- Caulk gun
- Grout sealer
- ¾" exterior-grade plywood
- Wood sealer
- 4" number stencils
- Tile and plates
- Hot glue or silicone caulk
- Grout
- Slot hangers and screws
- Tape measure
- Paper bag
- Eye protection
- Foam brush

A unique address marker fashioned from shards of broken tile makes an interesting and inviting statement to visitors.

How to Make an Address Marker

Enlarge and photocopy the pattern on the opposite page. Trace the pattern onto plywood and cut it out using a jigsaw. Apply a coat of wood sealer and let it dry. Mark the center and draw parallel placement lines on the plywood, then plan the placement of the numbers. Trace the numbers onto the plywood, then draw a 1¼" border around the outside edge.

Use a rotary tool and a grinding disc to polish away the ridge on the back of each plate. One at a time, place the plates in a heavy paper bag and roll the top closed. Rap the bag with a rubber mallet to break the plate. Wear safety goggles. Break the tiles in the same manner.

Lay out the pieces within the number outlines, using tile nippers to reshape pieces as necessary. Use hot glue or silicone caulk to secure the tile to the plywood. Fill in the background with pieces of china.

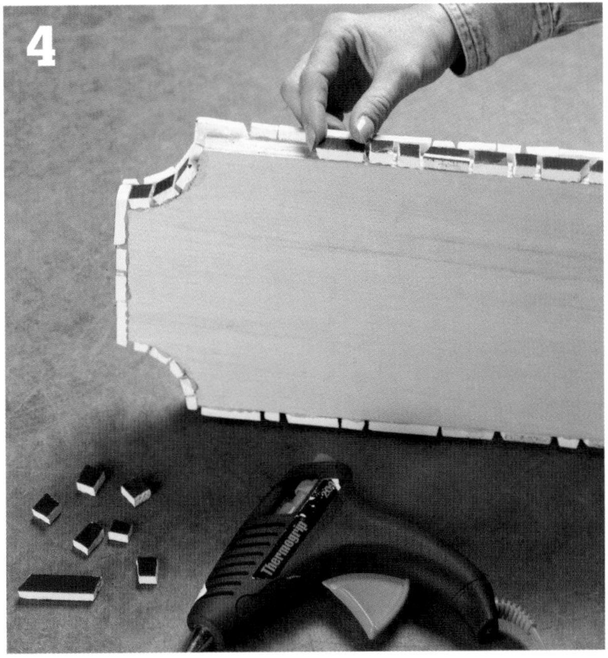

Turn the marker on edge and add tile to all the edges. Grout the tile, let it dry thoroughly, and seal the grout with grout sealer. Attach two slot hangers to the back of the mosaic.

Mosaic Wall Hanging

Unlike most tile projects, a wall-hanging doesn't need to be watertight or have structural strength, so a project like this gives you the chance to play with tile and other complementary materials. You can use tile fragments, broken dishes, pieces of mirror, and even pieces of glass.

These days it can be difficult to find small pieces of masonite in building centers or home stores. However, many art supply stores offer pieces framed out for painting projects, and these work wonderfully for this project.

Sea glass is a lovely addition to a mosaic, but it's relatively difficult to find and can be expensive to buy. We solved that problem by creating our own, which gave us more colors than the limited choices of brown and green typically available in stores.

In addition to free-form projects, such as the one shown here, you can combine the techniques from the original floor mosaic project (pages 100 to 105) with the ones shown here to create a different type of mosaic.

How to Create a Mosaic Wall-hanging

Tools & Materials ▸

Safety glasses
Rubber mallet
Tile nippers
Rock tumbler
Square-notched trowel
Grout float
Grout sponge
Tile
Old dishes
Glass bottles
Tile mastic
Artist's masonite
Grout
Cloth
Paper bag
Gloves

Sort through the materials you've collected and decide what to use. Wearing safety glasses, put tile, dishes, or bottles inside a heavy-duty paper bag and hit them with a rubber mallet. Use tile nippers to tailor china or tile pieces, as necessary.

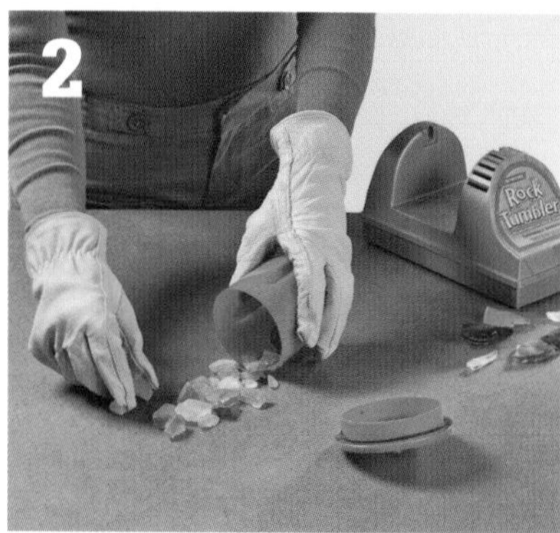

Following manufacturer's directions, tumble pieces of glass in a rock tumbler to smooth the edges and give them the look of sea glass. *Note: It will take several days to create an appreciable amount of tumbled glass.*

Draw reference lines on the masonite and spread tile mastic on one section using a square trowel. Embed the glass, tile, and other materials in the mastic on that section. Continue working in small sections until the masonite is covered.

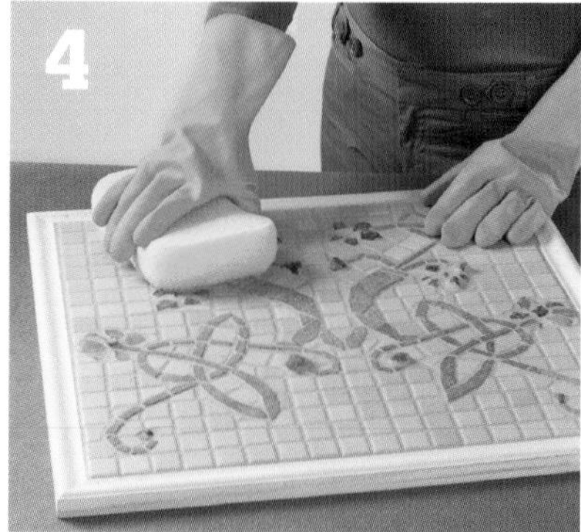

Mix a small batch of grout and spread it over the surface of the mosaic. Let the mosaic dry a few minutes, then wipe the surface with a damp grout sponge. Let the mosaic dry, then buff away any grout film with a clean, dry cloth.

Pansy
Snapdragon
Tall Maximum Blend

Tiled Sink Base

From its treadle sewing machine base to its handmade tile and hand-thrown sink, this project is unique. Other versions of this project could be made with commercially available tile and one of the many bowl-type sinks on the market.

It isn't necessary to use a sewing machine stand, either. Many interesting or vintage pieces will work for the base. Don't destroy a valuable antique—instead, look for a stand with no top or a small chest with a badly damaged top. You'll need to remove the top anyway in order to add a plywood and cementboard core that can stand up to daily exposure to water.

After you choose a base, select a bowl-type sink basin and a specially designed faucet, either wall- or counter-mounted. Tile the wall around a wall-mounted faucet, and make cutouts for a counter-mounted faucet. Even with a counter-mounted faucet such as the one shown here, you may want to add a small backsplash (see page 184).

If you don't like the idea of raw plywood being visible from beneath the sink, paint the bottom of the plywood before beginning to assemble the core. Coordinate the paint color with the tile and sink, so your project looks attractive from any angle.

Tools & Materials ▸

- Circular saw
- Drill and hole saw
- Jigsaw
- Utility knife
- Heavy-duty stapler
- Wallboard knife
- Framing square
- Notched trowel
- Grout float
- Grout sponge
- Foam brush
- Caulk gun
- Tape measure
- ¾" exterior-grade plywood
- 4-mil plastic sheeting
- Packing tape
- ½" cementboard
- Fiberglass mesh tape
- 1½" cementboard screws
- Thinset mortar
- Tile
- Grout and latex additive
- Caulk
- Salvaged base
- Bowl-type sink basin
- Faucet
- Drain hardware
- L-brackets or angle-irons
- Eye protection
- Wood screws
- Grout sealer
- Tile spacers
- Tile-cutting tools

How to Make a Tiled Sink Base

Measure the base and the sink and determine a size for the plywood core. Cut the core to size.

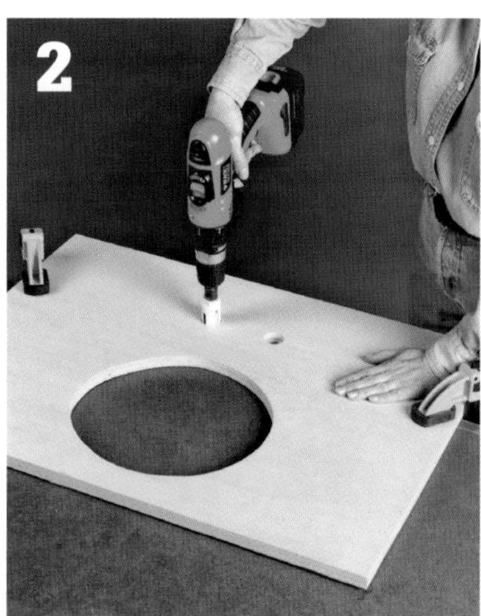

Mark a cutout for the sink on the plywood. Drill entrance holes, then use a jigsaw to make the cutout. Use the template supplied with the faucet to mark those cutouts. Use a hole saw to make the faucet cutouts.

Cut cementboard to match the dimensions of the plywood core, then use the plywood as a template to mark the cutouts on the cementboard.

(continued)

Lay plastic sheeting over the plywood core, draping it over the edges. Tack the plastic in place with staples. If you use more than one piece, overlap the seams by 6" and seal them with packing tape.

Set the plywood core on top of the base and attach it with screws driven through the base and into the core. Use angle irons or L-brackets if necessary with the base you've selected. Make sure the screws don't go through the top of the plywood.

Position the cementboard (rough-side up) on the core and attach it with 1½" screws. Make sure the screw heads are flush with the surface. Cut 1¼"-wide cementboard strips and attach them to the edges of the core with screws.

Tape all joints with fiberglass mesh tape. Apply three layers of tape along the edge where the top meets the edging. Fill all gaps and cover all of the tape with a layer of thinset mortar. Feather out the mortar to create a smooth, flat surface.

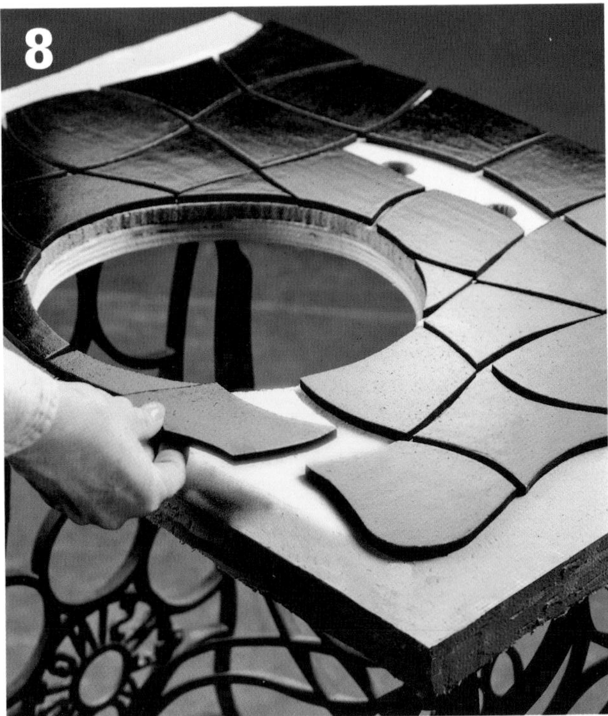

Dry-fit tiles to find the layout using spacers. Once the layout is established, make marks along the vertical and horizontal rows. Draw reference lines through the marks and use a framing square to make sure the lines are perpendicular.

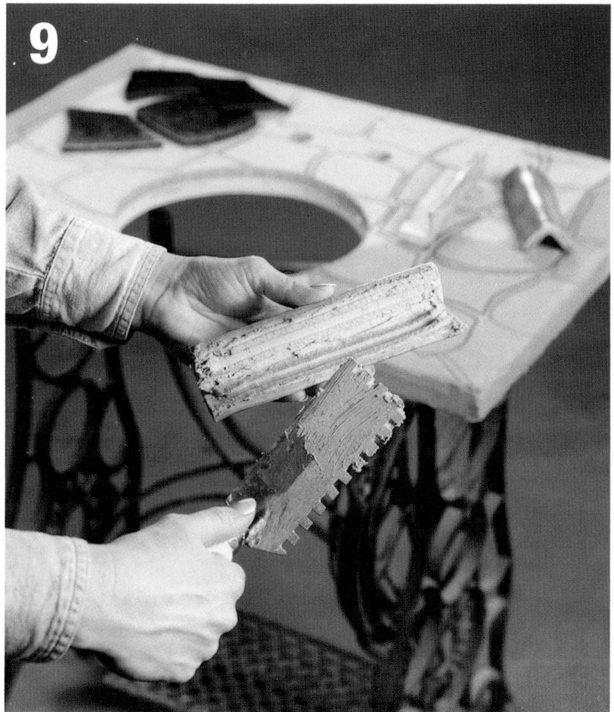

Set the edge tiles and let them dry. Install the field tiles and let them dry. Cut tile as necessary. (See pages 170 to 179 for more information on setting tile on a countertop.)

Mix a batch of grout with a latex additive and apply it with a rubber grout float. Wipe away excess grout with a damp sponge. When the grout has cured, apply sealer with a foam brush.

Apply a bead of caulk to the side of the sink, just below the lip of the ridge. Set the sink into the cutout, resting the ridge of the sink at the lip of the cutout. Make sure the joint between the sink and the counter is filled with caulk.

Install the faucet and drain hardware, following manufacturer's instructions.

Handmade Tile

Making ceramic tile from scratch is a therapeautic art for many people, requiring patience and plenty of time. After forming, the tile has to air dry for two to three weeks and then needs to be fired in a kiln twice before it's ready to be used. Before committing to the project, find a hobby shop or ceramic supply store where you can have your tile fired. Talk with the staff to find out how much the firings will cost and how much in advance they must be scheduled.

Measure the area where you plan to use the tile, and calculate how many tiles you'll need for the project. It's a good idea to make more tiles than you'll need to account for defective pieces. Also, be sure to check the manufacturer specifications for shrinkage (or test your chosen clay for shrinkage before committing to a large purchase). Talk with the staff at the ceramic store to figure out how much clay you'll need to buy to produce the number of tiles you need. If the tile will be used in a kitchen or near a bathroom sink, choose food-safe glazes for them.

While you're still in the exploratory phase, experiment with glazes and decorative possibilities. First, buy some low-fire clay and play with ways to make impressions. Next, buy several white or off-white matte-finish, glazed tiles. Paint glaze on the test tile in thin layers and have them fired. When you're satisfied with the results, you're ready to make your own tile.

Tools & Materials ▸

- Straightedge
- Utility knife
- Rolling pin
- Clay squeegee
- Craft knife
- Spatula
- Paintbrushes
- Stiff cardboard
- Paring knife
- Blanket or bubblewrap
- Canvas
- Low-fire clay
- Seashells or other imprinting objects
- Plywood scraps
- Low-fire glazes
- Ruler or measuring tape

Create your own custom tiles from clay and have them fired at a local ceramics store.

How to Make Handmade Tile

On a piece of stiff cardboard, draw a template for the tile. Measure carefully and allow for shrinkage. (For example, a 4⅝ × 4⅝" template should produce a 4 × 4" tile, factoring in a 12% shrinkage rate.) Measure diagonally from corner to corner; when the diagonals are precisely equal, the template is square. Cut out the template using a straightedge and utility knife.

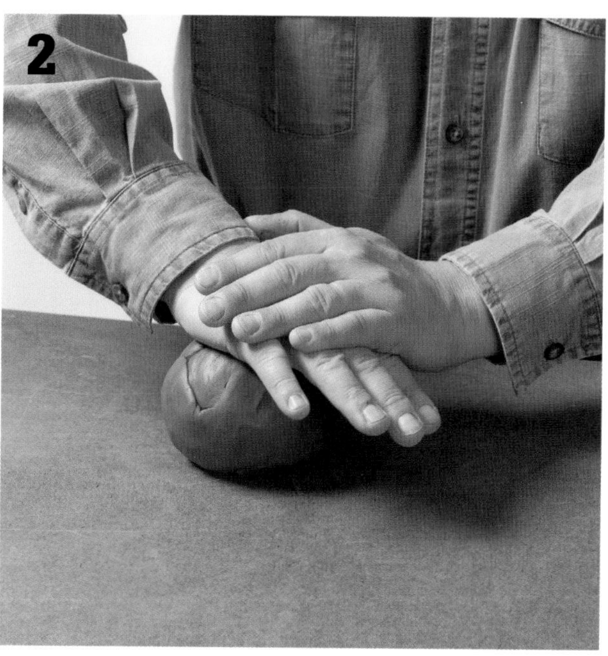

Take out a 1 lb. chunk of clay and pat it into a ball. Close the bag securely to prevent the remaining clay from drying out. Put the clay on a smooth work surface and pound it with the palm of your hand, flattening the ball. (Don't fold the clay over itself—this traps air in the clay.)

Cover the clay with a piece of canvas. Roll out the clay to a uniform thickness. Change directions as you roll the clay so the clay particles will be evenly distributed. If all the clay particles go the same direction, the tile will shrink unevenly as it's fired. Lay two ½" plywood scraps on the table as guides (inset).

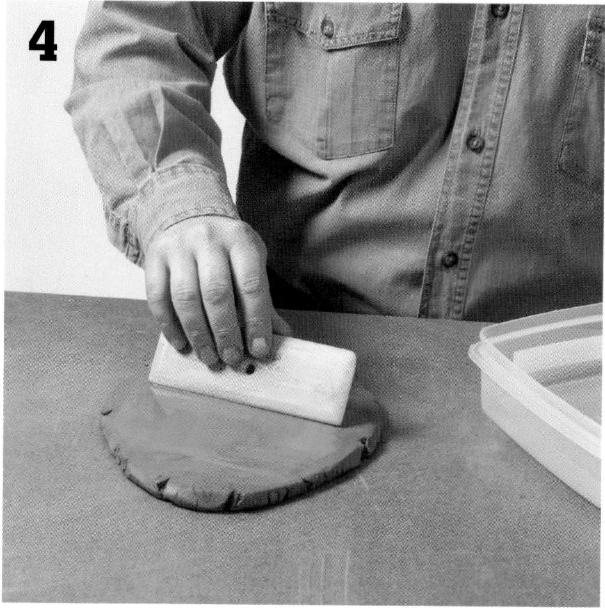

Dip the edge of a clean squeegee in water. Take the canvas off the clay and pull the squeegee across the clay, smoothing the surface. Work in one direction only, and rinse the squeegee as often as necessary to keep the edge clean.

(continued)

Carefully place the template on the clay. Holding it firmly against the clay with one hand, use a craft knife to cut around the template. Pull the extra clay away from the tile and run the knife around the edges again.

Scoot the tile to the side to make sure it's not stuck to the work surface. Wet your index finger and use it to smooth the corners and sides of the tile. Gently press a clean shell into the clay to create the desired design.

Pick up the tile with a spatula and set it on a scrap of plywood to dry. If the tile has gotten distorted, nudge it back into shape.

Continue cutting out tile. Set them out of direct sunlight to dry.

Dry the tiles for a day or two, until they're the consistency of leather. Using a paring knife, trim any bulging edges. Allow the tiles to dry completely, which should take two to three weeks. If the air is extremely dry, the tile may dry too quickly, causing cracking. Lay a cloth over them to slow down the drying process.

Put the tiles on a sturdy tray or piece of flat plywood and wrap it in a blanket or bubble wrap. Carefully transport the dried tile to a kiln for firing.

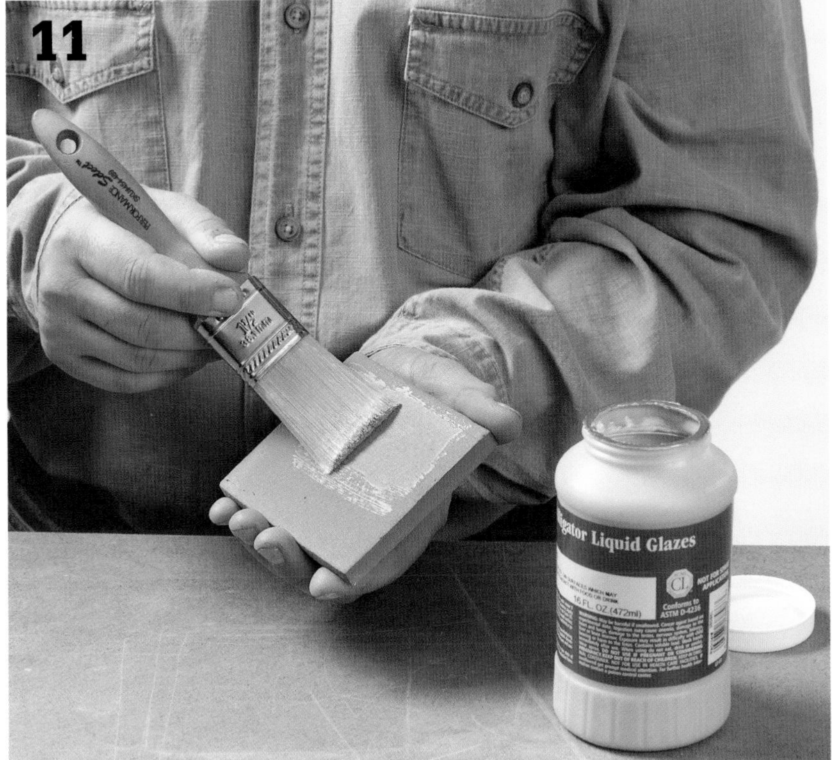

Brush two or three thin coats of glaze onto the fired (and cool) tile. Let the glaze dry to touch between coats. Have the tile fired a second and final time.

Tiled Garden Bench

Here's a splendid example of the term "return on investment." Four decorative tiles and a handful of coordinated accent tiles produce quite an impact. In fact, those accents and a few dozen 4 × 4-inch tiles transform a plain cedar bench into a special garden ornament. And you can complete this entire project over one weekend.

Making this tiled benchtop requires some creativity and a fair amount of tile cutting, but the result is both interesting and beautiful.

Tools, Materials, & Cutting List

Tools

Tape measure
Circular saw
Drill
Stapler
Power or hand miter saw (optional)
Utility knife
Chalk line
Cloth
¼" notched trowel
Needlenose pliers
Grout float
Sponge
1½" blocks
Tile-cutting tools
Paintbrush
Eye protection

Materials

Plastic sheeting
Galvanized deck screws (2", 3")
1¼" cementboard screws
Clear wood sealer
Field and accent tile
Thinset mortar
Tile spacers
Grout
Grout sealer
150-grit sandpaper

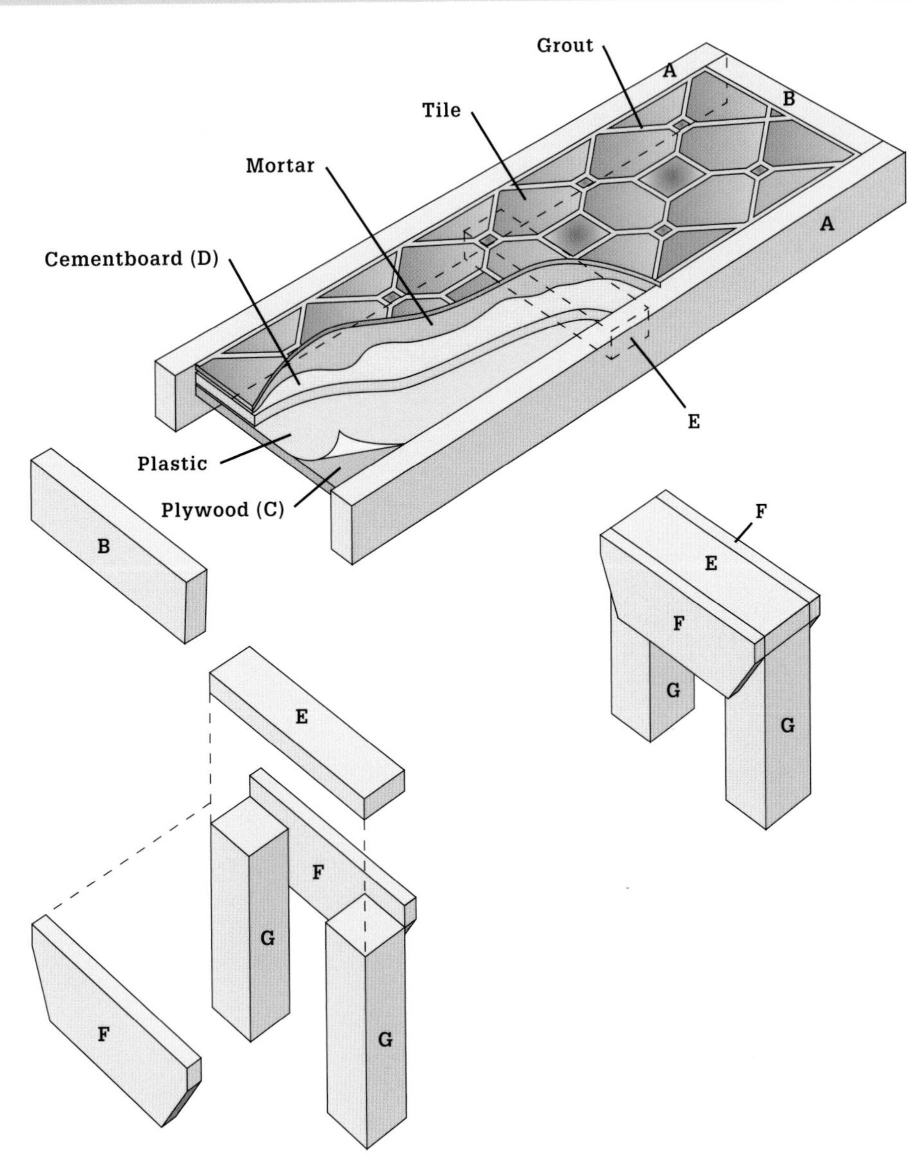

Cutting List

KEY	PART	DIMENSION	PCS.	MATERIAL
A	Sides	1½ × 3½ × 51"	2	Cedar
B	Ends	1½ × 3½ × 16"	2	Cedar
C	Core	15 × 48"	1	¾" ext. plywood
D	Core	15 × 48"	1	¾" cementboard
E	Stretchers	1½ × 3½ × 16"	3	Cedar
F	Braces	1½ × 5½ × 16"	4	Cedar
G	Legs	3½ × 3½ × 13"	4	Cedar

How to Make a Tiled Garden Bench

Cut two sides and two ends, then position the ends between the sides so the edges are flush. Make sure the frame is square. Drill ⅛" pilot holes through the sides and into the ends. Drive 3" screws through the pilot holes.

Cut three stretchers. Mark the sides, 4½" from the inside of each end. Using 1½" blocks beneath them as spacers, position the stretchers and make sure they're level. Drill pilot holes and fasten the stretchers to the sides with 3" screws.

Cut one 15 × 48" core from ¾" exterior-grade plywood and another the same size from cementboard. Staple plastic sheeting over the plywood, draping it over the edges. Lay the cementboard rough-side up on the plywood and attach it with 1¼" cementboard screws driven every 6". Make sure the screw heads are flush with the surface.

Position the bench frame upside down and over the plywood/cementboard core. Drill pilot holes and then drive 2" galvanized deck screws through the stretchers and into the plywood.

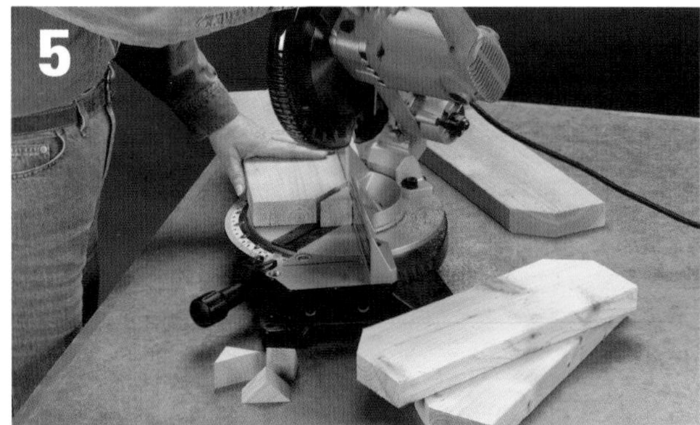

Cut four braces from a cedar 2 × 6. Mark the angle on each end of each brace by measuring down 1½" from the top edge and 1½" along the bottom edge. Draw a line between the two points and cut along that line using a power or hand miter saw or a circular saw.

On each brace, measure down ¾" from the top edge and draw a reference line across the stretcher for the screw positions. Drill ⅛" pilot holes along the reference line. Position a brace on each side of the end stretchers and fasten them with 3" screws driven through the braces and into the stretchers.

Cut four 13" legs from a 4 × 4. Position each leg between a set of braces and against the sides of the bench frame. Drill pilot holes through each brace and attach the leg to the braces by driving 3" screws through the braces and into the leg. Repeat the process for each leg. Sand all surfaces with 150-grit sandpaper, then seal all wood surfaces with clear wood sealer.

Snap perpendicular reference lines to mark the center of the length and width of the bench. Beginning at the center of the bench, dry-fit the field tiles, including spacers. Set the accent tiles in place and mark the field tile for cutting.

Cut the field tile and continue dry-fitting the bench top, including the accent and border tiles. When you're satisfied, remove the tile and apply thinset mortar over the cementboard using a notched trowel.

Set the tile into the thinset mortar, using a slight twisting motion. Continue adding thinset and setting the tile until the bench top is covered. Remove the spacers. Let the mortar dry according to manufacturer's directions. (See pages 170 to 179 for more information on setting tile.)

Mix grout and use a grout float to force it into the joints surrounding the tile. Wipe excess grout away with a damp sponge. When the grout has dried slightly, polish the tiles with a clean, dry cloth to remove the slight haze of grout. Seal the grout joints with grout sealer when dry.

Repair Projects

Tile is extremely durable, but like any construction material, it requires maintenance and occasional repairs. This chapter leads you through the most common repair projects: replacing grout, removing and replacing a broken tile, and replacing accessories, such as a ceramic soap dish.

When it comes to tile, replacing grout is the most common repair project because the grout is the most vulnerable part of the installation. While a small crack or hole in a grout joint may not seem like a major issue, in floors and wet walls it allows water to seep behind the tile and can lead to serious damage over time. Like any other repair, taking care of grout issues while they're small prevents much larger problems later. This chapter gives you all the information you'll need to take excellent care of all your floor tile, wall tile, and its grout throughout your home.

In this chapter:

Maintaining Floor Tile

Although ceramic tile is one of the hardest floor coverings, problems can occur. Tiles sometimes become damaged and need to be replaced. Usually, this is simply a matter of removing and replacing individual tiles. However, major cracks in grout joints indicate that floor movement has caused the mortar beneath the tile to deteriorate. In this case, the mortar must be replaced in order to create a permanent repair.

Any time you remove tile, check the underlayment. If it's no longer smooth, solid, and level, repair or replace it before replacing the tile. When removing grout or damaged tiles, be careful not to damage surrounding tiles. Always wear eye protection when working with a hammer and chisel. Any time you are doing a major tile installation, make sure to save extra tiles. This way, you will have materials on hand when repairs become necessary.

Tools & Materials ▸

- Hammer
- Cold chisel
- Eye protection
- Putty knife
- Square-notched trowel
- Rubber mallet
- Grout float
- Thinset mortar
- Replacement tile
- Grout
- Bucket
- Grout pigment
- Grout sealer
- Grout sponge
- Floor-leveling compound
- Carbide-tipped grout saw
- Sand paper
- Cleaning tools
- Wood block
- Carpet scrap
- Vacuum
- White vinegar

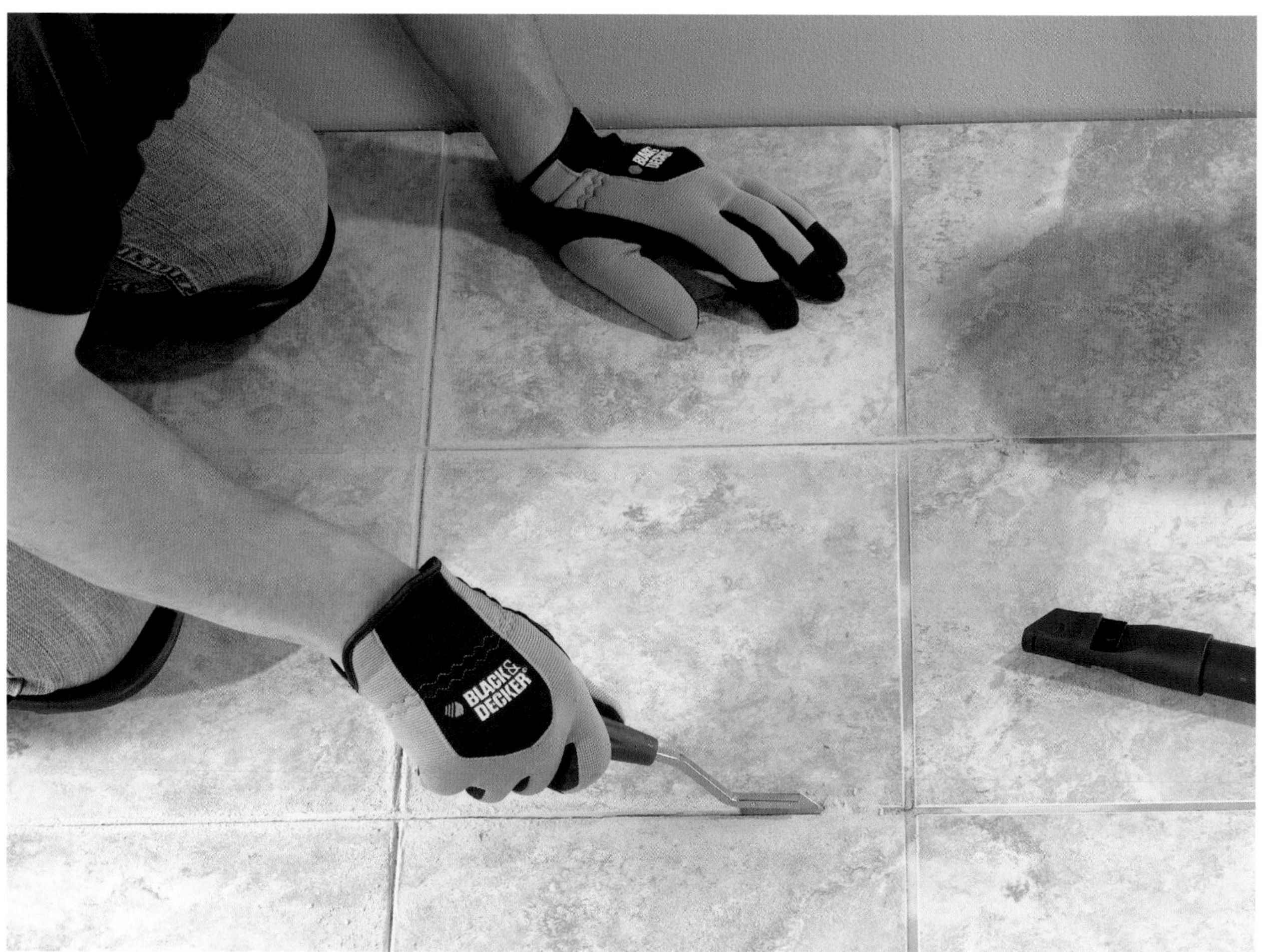

Regrouting tile may feel like a repair project (and not a very fun one at that), but it really is more of an ongoing maintenance issue. Failed or failing grout will allow moisture underneath tiles and can cause entire floors to fail.

How to Replace a Floor Tile

With a carbide-tipped grout saw, apply firm but gentle pressure across the grout until you expose the unglazed edges of the tile. Do not scratch the glazed tile surface. If the grout is stubborn, use a hammer and nail set to first tap the tile (step 2).

If the tile is not already cracked, use a hammer to puncture the tile by tapping a nail set or center punch into it. Alternatively, if the tile is significantly cracked, use a chisel to pry up the tile.

Insert a chisel into one of the cracks and gently tap the tile. Start at the center and chip outward so you don't damage the adjacent tiles. Be aware that cementboard looks a lot like mortar when you're chiseling. Remove and discard the broken pieces. Be sure to wear eye protection.

Use a putty knife to scrape away old thinset mortar; use a chisel for poured mortar installation. If the underlayment is covered with metal lath, you won't be able to get the area smooth; just clean it out the best you can. Once the mortar is scraped from the underlayment, smooth the rough areas with sand paper. If there are gouges in the underlayment, fill them with epoxy-based thinset mortar (for cementboard) or a floor-leveling compound (for plywood). Allow the area to dry completely.

Set a new tile into the empty spot. Use a notched trowel to apply thinset mortar to the back of the tile before setting it into place. Make sure all debris is cleaned from the floor. Rap on a carpet-covered wood block with a mallet to set the tile.

Fill in around the new tile with grout that matches the grout already on the floor. Because most grout darkens over time, choose a shade that's a bit darker than the original color.

Regrouting Tile

The process of removing old grout and filling the cleaned joints with new grout is the same for most ceramic and porcelain tile installations (including floors, walls, and countertops). For improved adhesion and waterproofing, use a polymer-modified grout mix.

It's important to note that regrouting is an appropriate repair only for tile that is securely bonded to its substrate. Several loose tiles in one area indicate that the mortar has failed or there are problems (usually moisture-related) with the substrate. If multiple tiles are loose, retiling the floor may be your only option. If a tile job is generally in good shape and you can find a perfect color match with your old grout, you can regrout only the affected areas. Otherwise, it will look best to replace all of the grout within an area.

Carbide-blade grout saws are used to remove failing grout.

Failed grout allows water underneath tiles, which causes the damage to spread rapidly. If the grout lines in your tile floor are crumbling or a few tiles are loosened, the best solution is to regrout the entire floor.

How to Regrout Floor Tile

Scrape out the old grout with a grout saw or other tool, being careful not to scratch the tile faces or chip the edges. You may choose to regrout only the filed grout lines for a quick fix, but for more pleasing results and to prevent color variation in the grout lines, remove the grout around all tiles and regrout the entire floor.

Wash the tiled floor with a 1:1 mix of white vinegar and water, paying special attention to the areas around the tile joints. Vacuum the floor first to get rid of all debris.

Apply new grout. Prepare grout mix according to the instructions on the package and then pack fresh grout deep into the joints using a rubber grout float. Hold the float at a 30° angle to the tiled surface.

Wipe diagonally across the tiles and grouted joints to remove excess grout and smooth the joints. Seal the grout joints with grout sealer after they've dried for a week or so. *Note: Sealing all the grout joints will help new grout lines blend with old grout if you're only doing a partial regrouting.*

Grout Colorant

Available in a wide variety of colors, grout colorant is a topically-applied, water-based paint that is specially designed to recolor, rejuvenate, and seal existing grout mortar joints.

Grout colorant bonds well to sanded grout mortar making it an ideal solution for rejuvenating old ceramic tile flooring. For applications around porous or pitted tiles, use masking tape to prevent the edges of the tile from absorbing the colorant. Lighter colorants applied over darkened grout joints may require more than one application.

To begin, clean the work area thoroughly, removing bond-inhibiting grease, oil, and calcium deposits from the surface of the tile and grout. Rinse with clean water and allow it to fully dry. Properly prepared, grout joints will be porous and readily absorb water.

A foam brush applicator is used to carefully work the colorant into the grout joints. Remove excess colorant immediately from the edges of surrounding tile using a damp rag. Dry colorant can be removed using a damp, white nylon scrub pad.

Tools & Materials ▸

- Grout colorant
- Masking tape
- Foam brushes
- White scrub pad
- Disposable rags
- Cleaning products
- Toothbrush

Grout that is in good condition but has simply become stained or discolored can be refreshed quickly and easily with an application of grout colorant.

How to Apply Grout Colorant

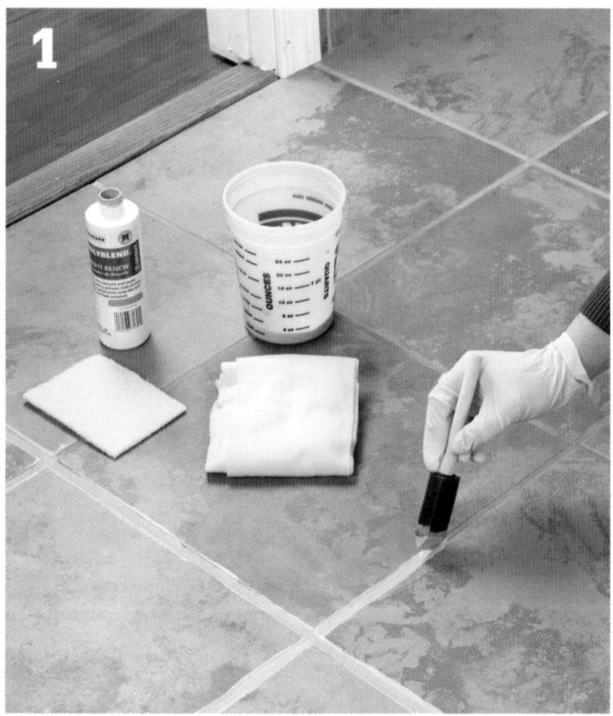

Apply grout colorant in thin coats to the grout joints using a foam brush. Clean the tiles and grout thoroughly first, and make sure the grout lines are dry.

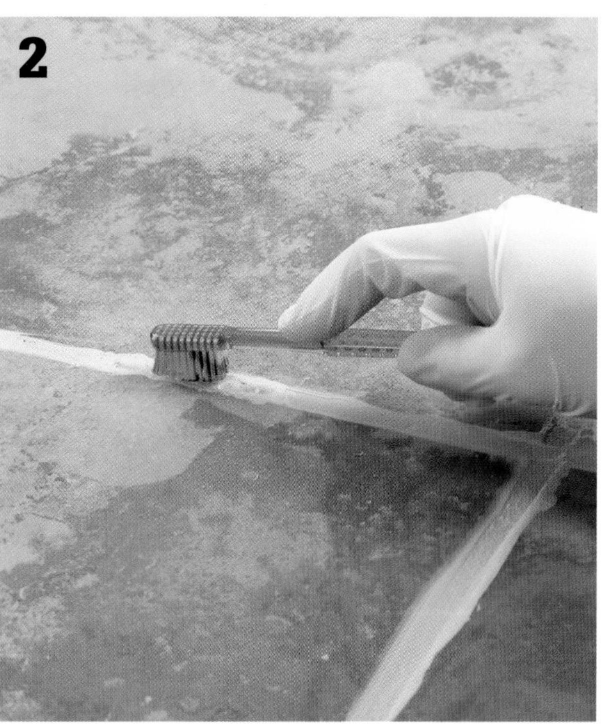

Work the colorant into the the grout with an old (but clean!) toothbrush.

Use a damp rag or white nylon scrub pad to remove excess colorant from the edges of surrounding tile. Allow the grout colorant to dry completely.

Colorizing Grout ▸

Grout colorant can transform an old tile floor into a vibrant new floor at very little cost. It is sold in a variety of colors. If your local building center doesn't carry it, check with a tile shop.

Repairing Wall Tile

As we've said throughout this book, ceramic wall tile is durable and nearly maintenance-free, but like every other material in your house, it can fail or develop problems. The most common problem with ceramic tile involves damaged grout. Failed grout is unattractive, but the real danger is that it offers a point of entry for water, especially in rooms like bathrooms. Given a chance to work its way beneath grout, water can destroy a tile base and eventually wreck an entire installation. It's important to regrout ceramic tile as soon as you see signs of damage.

Another potential problem for wall tile installations is damaged caulk. In tub and shower stalls and around sinks and backsplashes, the joints between the tile and the fixtures are sealed with caulk. The caulk eventually deteriorates, leaving an entry point for water. Unless the joints are recaulked, seeping water will destroy the tile base and the wall.

In bathrooms, towel rods, soap dishes, and other accessories can work loose from walls, especially if they weren't installed correctly or aren't supported properly. For maximum holding power, anchor new accessories to wall studs or blocking. If no studs or blocking are available, use special fasteners, such as toggle bolts or molly bolts, to anchor the accessories directly to the surface of the underlying wall. To hold screws firmly in place in ceramic tile walls, drill pilot holes and insert plastic sleeves, which expand when screws are driven into them.

Tools & Materials ▸

- Awl
- Utility knife
- Notched trowel
- Grout float
- Hammer
- Chisel
- Small pry bar
- Eye protection
- Replacement accessory
- Tile adhesive
- Masking tape
- Grout
- Cloth or rag
- Silicone or latex caulk
- Sponge
- Surface-mounting hardware
- Tile-cutting tools
- Replacement tile

How to Regrout Wall Tile

Use an awl or utility knife to scrape out the old grout completely, leaving a clean bed for the new grout.

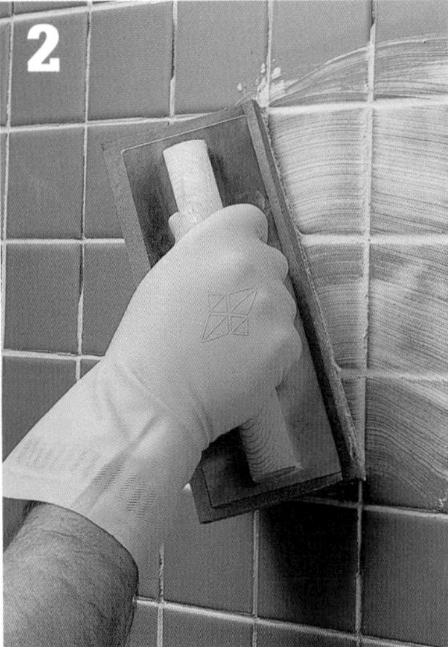

Clean and rinse the grout joints, then spread grout over the entire tile surface, using a rubber grout float or sponge. Work the grout well into the joints and let it set slightly.

Wipe away excess grout with a damp sponge. When the grout is dry, wipe away the residue and polish the tiles with a dry cloth.

How to Replace Built-in Wall Accessories

Carefully remove the damaged accessory. Scrape away any remaining mortar or grout. Apply dry-set tile adhesive to the back side of the new accessory, then press it firmly in place.

Use masking tape to hold the accessory in place while the adhesive dries. Let the mortar dry completely (12 to 24 hrs.), then grout and seal the area.

How to Replace Surface-mounted Accessories

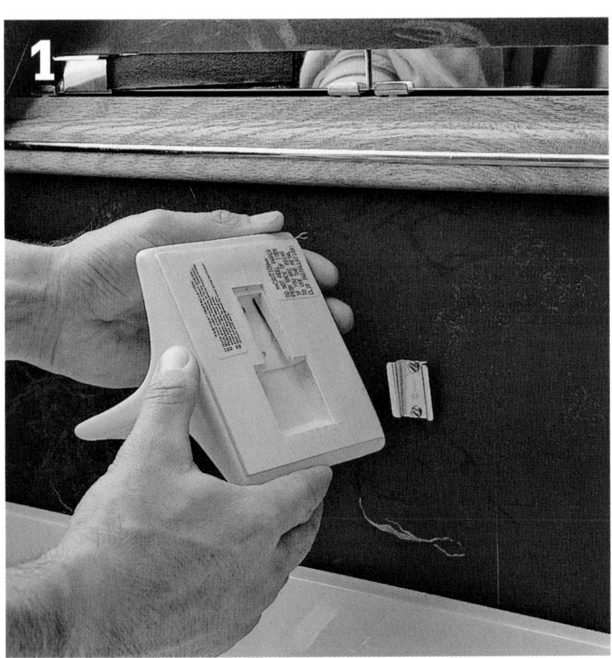

Lift the accessory up and off the mounting plate. If the mounting plate screws are driven into studs or blocking, simply hang the new accessory. If not, add hardware such as molly bolts, toggle bolts, or plastic anchor sleeves.

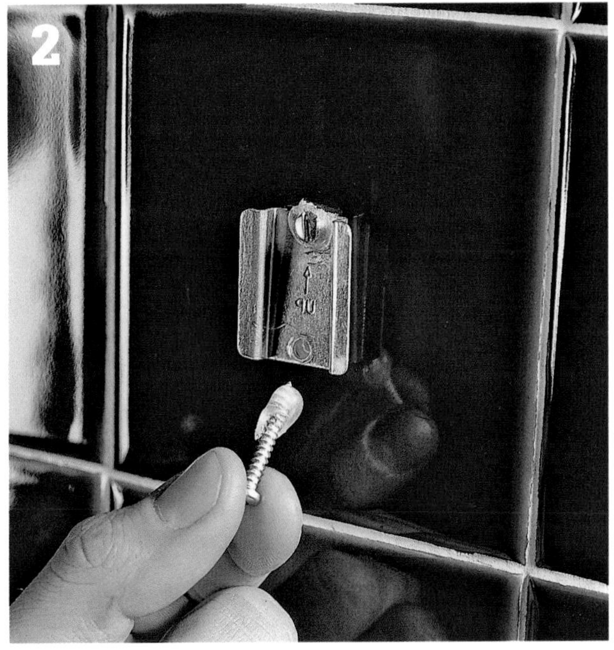

Put a dab of silicone caulk over the pilot holes and the tips of the screws before inserting them. Let the caulk dry, then install the new fixture on the mounting plate.

How to Remove & Replace Broken Wall Tiles

Carefully scrape away the grout from the surrounding joints using a utility knife or an awl. Break the damaged tile into small pieces using a hammer and chisel. Remove the broken pieces, then scrape away debris or old mortar from the open area.

If the tile to be replaced is a cut tile, cut a new one to match. Test-fit the new tile and make sure it sits flush with the field. Spread adhesive on the back of the replacement tile and place it in the hole, twisting it slightly. Use masking tape to hold the tile in place for 24 hrs. so the adhesive can dry.

Remove the tape, then apply premixed grout using a sponge or grout float. Let the grout set slightly, then tool it with a rounded object such as a toothbrush handle. Wipe away excess grout with a damp cloth.

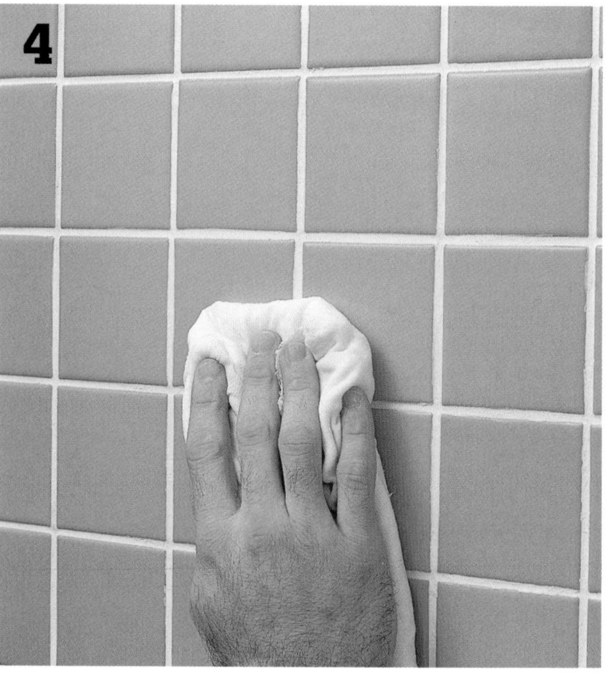

Let the grout dry for an hour, then polish the tile with a clean, dry cloth.

Replacing Caulk ▸

Replace all of the old caulking along the tub or shower edges at the floor, and essentially anywhere a surface meets another surface. Don't add a new layer of caulk over the old. This just makes a mess and may hide areas where the old caulk is failing without providing an adequate water seal.

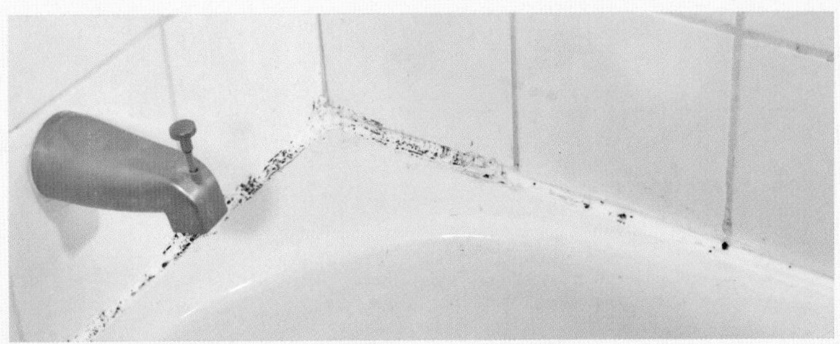

Just about any dated tub or shower can benefit from a thorough cleaning and recaulking of its seals.

How to Replace Caulk

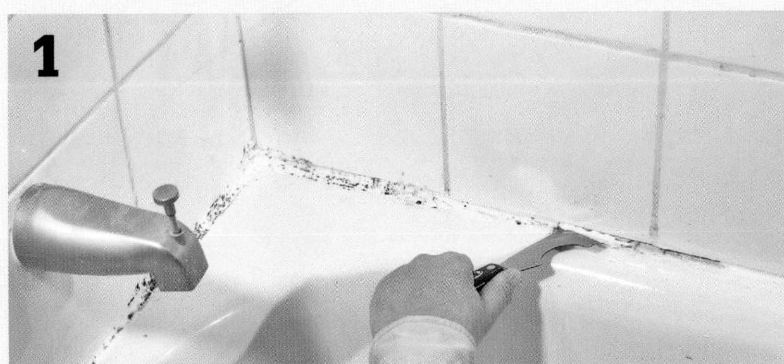

1

A 5-in-1 tool works better than a putty or utility knife for removing caulk. Use the tool's razor-sharp tooth to slice caulk from crevices.

2

Scrub the area with denatured alcohol to remove grime and film from the area.

3

Filling—but not overfilling—the joint is the key to a neat caulk job. Smooth the freshly applied caulk with a damp finger using a very light touch.

Cleaning Tile & Grout ▸

You spent a considerable amount of time and money on your new tile installation, so it is only natural that you want to take good care of your investment. Fortunately, tile is a low-maintenance product and with proper care it will look new for many years to come.

Purchase a dust mop and sweep your floors daily. Place mats in doorways and through walkways to help collect dirt and grime and shake them out frequently. In showers and tub tile surrounds, use a squeegee or towel to wipe excess water off walls after each use. This will help to prevent spotting and the formation of stain-causing mildew.

Dirt and grime will often accumulate in the textured surfaces of tile and grout. A plastic scrub brush and a little elbow grease will remove most stubborn dirt deposits. Household floor-cleaning machines with rotating brushes will safely scrub tile flooring and grout clean. Avoid using steam cleaners though, as the hot steam can damage grout and remove topically applied colorants or sealers.

Long term use of many tile cleaning products can actually harm tile and grout. A quality cleanser should be pH balanced, non-abrasive, and safe for tile surfaces and grout. Most are not. Natural stone and cementitious grouts are especially vulnerable to cleaning products that contain acid. These types of products should never be used to clean natural stone and their use on ceramic tile and grout should be limited.

Tile Maintenance

To determine if your grout needs to be resealed, test the existing sealer by putting a few drops of water on a grout line. If the water beads up, the sealer is still working. If the water absorbs into the grout, it needs to be resealed.

For heavy stains on natural stone tile, apply poultice made for cleaning porous stone materials. Cover the stain with the poultice, then tape plastic over it. Let the poulitice set according to the manufacturer's instructions, then remove it.

Glossary

American National Standards Institute (ANSI) — A standards-making organization that rates tile for water permeability.

Art tiles — Hand-finished tiles with designs, pictures or patterns. Art tiles are often used to accent a large tile layout.

Back buttering — Spreading mortar on the back of a tile before pressing it onto the substrate.

Baseboard tile — Baseboard-shaped tiles used to replace wood baseboards.

Bullnose trim tile — Tile with one rounded edge that is meant to be left exposed.

Cement body tile — Tile made from concrete poured into forms.

Coefficient of friction — The measure of a tile's slip resistance. Tiles with high numbers are more slip resistant.

Decorative — Tile with designs, pictures, or relief. Decorative tiles are generally used as accents in a field of solid-color tiles.

Dry fit — Installing tile without mortar in order to test the layout.

Expansion joint — An expansion joint is a joint in a tile layout filled with a flexible material like caulk instead of grout. The expansion joint allows the tile to shift without cracking.

Field tiles — The main tile in a tile design. As opposed to trim or accent tiles.

Floor tile — Any type of tile designated for use on floors. It can generally also be used for walls or countertops.

Floor-warming systems — A system of heating elements installed directly under the floor material. Floor-warming systems are intended to provide supplemental radiant heat for a room.

Glass tile — Tile made of translucent glass. Glass tile is often used as accent tile.

Glazed ceramic — Tile made from refined clay that has been coated with a glaze and then fired in a kiln.

Grade — Ratings applied to some tile indicating the quality and consistency of manufacturing. Grade 1 tile is standard, suitable for most applications; grade 2 may have minor glaze and size imperfections; grade 3 tile is thin and suitable only for wall or decorative applications.

Grout — A dry powder, usually cement based, that is mixed with water and pressed into the joints between tiles. Grout also comes with latex or acrylic added for greater adhesion and impermeability.

Impervious — Tile that absorbs less than .5% of its weight in water.

Isolation membrane — Isolation membrane is a flexible material installed in sheets or troweled onto an unstable or damaged base floor, subfloor, or wall before installing tile. The isolation membrane prevents shifts in the base from damaging the tile above.

Joists — The framing members that support the floor.

Kiln — A high-temperature oven used to harden clay tile.

Liners — Narrow tiles used for adding contrasting lines to tile layouts.

Listello — A border tile, usually with a raised design. Also called listel.

Mastic or organic mastic — A type of glue for installing tile. It comes premixed and cures as it dries. It is convenient for wall tiles smaller than 6 × 6, but it is not suitable for floors.

Metal tile — Tile made of iron, stainless steel, copper, or brass. Metal tile is often used as accent tile.

Mortar or thin-set mortar — A mixture of portland cement and sand and occasionally a latex or acrylic additive to improve adhesion.

Mosaic tile — Small colored tiles used to make patterns or pictures on walls and floors.

Natural stone tile — Tile cut from marble, slate, granite, or other natural stone.

Non-vitreous — Very permeable tile. Non-vitreous tile absorbs more than 7% of its total weight in water. Not suitable for outdoor installations.

Porcelain Enamel Institute (PEI) — A tile industry group that issues ratings on tile's resistance to wear.

Porcelain tile — Tile made from refined white clay fired at high temperatures. Porcelain is usually dyed rather than glazed, and thus its color runs the tile's full thickness.

Quarry tile — Tile formed to look like quarried stone.

Reference lines — Lines marked on the substrate to guide the placement of the first row of tile.

Saltillo — Terra-cotta tile from Mexico. Saltillos have a distinctly rustic appearance.

Sealants — Sealants protect non- and semi-vitreous tile from stains and from water damage. Sealants are also important for protecting grout.

Self-spacing tile — Tile with attached tabs for maintaining even spacing.

Semi-vitreous — Moderately permeable tile. Absorbs 3-7% of its total weight in water. Not suitable for outdoor installations.

Spacers — Plastic lugs meant to be inserted between tiles to help maintain uniform spacing during installation.

Story stick — A length of 1 × 2 lumbar marked with the tile spacing for a specific layout.

Subfloor — The surface, usually made of plywood, attached to the floor joists.

Substrates or underlayment — A surface installed on top of an existing floor, subfloor, or wall. The substrate creates a suitable surface for installing tile. Substrate materials include cementboard, plywood, cork, backerboard, greenboard, or water-proofing membrane.

Terra-cotta tile — Tile made from unrefined clay. Terra-cotta is fired at low temperature. Its color varies greatly depending on where the source of the clay.

Trim tile — Tile with a finished edge for completing wall tile layouts.

V-cap tiles — V- or L-shaped tile for finishing the exposed edges of countertops.

Vitreous — Slightly permeable tile. Absorbs .5-3% of its total weight in water.

Wall tile — Tile intended for use on walls. It is generally thinner than floor tile and should not be used on floors or countertops.

Water absorption or permeability — The measure of the amount of water that will penetrate a tile when it is wet. Measurement ranges from non-vitreous to semi-vitreous to vitreous to impervious.

Waterproofing membrane — A flexible, water-proof material installed in sheets or brushed on to protect the subfloor from water damage.

Photo Credits

Courtesy of Ceramic Tiles of Italy
p. 8 (lower), 9 (top), 11 (top left)

Crossville Porcelain Store
p. 13 (top left)

Eric Roth
p. 12 (top)

Courtesy of Hakatai Enterprises, Inc.
p. 9 (lower, left and right)

Courtesy of Ikea Home Furnishings
p. 10 (lower right)

Angela Lanci-Macris
p. 11 (top right), 12 (lower)

Courtesy of National Kitchen & Bath Associations
p. 13 (lower)

Courtesy of Oceanside Glasstile ™
p. 10 (lower left), 24-25 (all)

Shutterstock
p. 56 (top), 57 (all), 58 (all), 59 (all), 124 (lower left), 125 (both), 126 (all), 127 (lower right)

Stephen Saks / Index Stock Imagery Inc.
p. 11 (lower)

Tim Street-Porter
p. 8 (top), 10 (top right)

Van Robaeys / Inside / Beateworks.com
p. 13 (top left)

Brian Vanden Brink
p. 10 (top left)

Resources

American Society of Interior Designers
202-546-3480
www.asid.org

Black & Decker
Power tools & Accessories
800-544-6986
www.blackanddecker.com

Ceramic Tiles of Italy
www.italiatiles.com

Clay Squared to Infinity
612-781-6409
www.claysquared.com

Construction Materials Recycling Association
630-585-7530
www.cdrecycling.org

Cool Tiles
1-888-TILES-88 (888-845-3788)
www.cooltiles.com

Crossville Porcelain Stone
931-484-2110
www.crossvilleceramics.com

Daltile
800-933-TILE
www.daltile.com

Energy & Environmental Building Alliance
952-881-1098
www.eeba.org

EuroTile Featuring Villi®Glas
866-724-5836
www.villiglasusa.com

Fireclay Tile, Inc.
408-275-1182
www.fireclaytile.com

Hakatai Enterprises, Inc.
888-667-2429
www.hakatai.com

IKEA Home Furnishings
610-834-0180
www.Ikea-USA.com

KPTiles
Kristen Phillips
248-853-0418
www.kptiles.com

Laticrete
Floor warming mats & supplies
800-243-4788
www.laticrete.com

Meredith Collection
330-484-1656
www.meredithtile.com

Montana Tile & Stone Co.
406-587-6114
www.montanatile.com

National Kitchen & Bath Association (NKBA)
800-843-6522
www.nkba.org

Oceanside Glasstile™
760-929-5882
www.glasstile.com

Red Wing Shoes Co.
Work shoes and boots shown throughout book
800-733-9464
www.redwingshoes.com

Snapstone
Floating Porcelain Tile System
877-263-5861
www.snapstone.com

The Tile Shop
888-398-6595
www.tileshop.com

Walker & Zanger, Inc.
www.walkerzanger.com

US Environmental Protection Agency, Indoor Air Quality
www.epa.gov/iedweb00/pubs/insidest.html

Measurement Conversions

Lumber Dimensions

NOMINAL - U.S.	ACTUAL - U.S. (IN INCHES)	METRIC
1 × 2	¾ × 1½	19 × 38 mm
1 × 3	¾ × 2½	19 × 64 mm
1 × 4	¾ × 3½	19 × 89 mm
1 × 5	¾ × 4½	19 × 114 mm
1 × 6	¾ × 5½	19 × 140 mm
1 × 7	¾ × 6¼	19 × 159 mm
1 × 8	¾ × 7¼	19 × 184 mm
1 × 10	¾ × 9¼	19 × 235 mm
1 × 12	¾ × 11¼	19 × 286 mm
1¼ × 4	1 × 3½	25 × 89 mm
1¼ × 6	1 × 5½	25 × 140 mm
1¼ × 8	1 × 7¼	25 × 184 mm
1¼ × 10	1 × 9¼	25 × 235 mm
1¼ × 12	1 × 11¼	25 × 286 mm

NOMINAL - U.S.	ACTUAL - U.S. (IN INCHES)	METRIC
1½ × 4	1¼ × 3½	32 × 89 mm
1½ × 6	1¼ × 5½	32 × 140 mm
1½ × 8	1¼ × 7¼	32 × 184 mm
1½ × 10	1¼ × 9¼	32 × 235 mm
1½ × 12	1¼ × 11¼	32 × 286 mm
2 × 4	1½ × 3½	38 × 89 mm
2 × 6	1½ × 5½	38 × 140 mm
2 × 8	1½ × 7¼	38 × 184 mm
2 × 10	1½ × 9¼	38 × 235 mm
2 × 12	1½ × 11¼	38 × 286 mm
3 × 6	2½ × 5½	64 × 140 mm
4 × 4	3½ × 3½	89 × 89 mm
4 × 6	3½ × 5½	89 × 140 mm

Metric Conversions

TO CONVERT:	TO:	MULTIPLY BY:
Inches	Millimeters	25.4
Inches	Centimeters	2.54
Feet	Meters	0.305
Yards	Meters	0.914
Square inches	Square centimeters	6.45
Square feet	Square meters	0.093
Square yards	Square meters	0.836
Ounces	Milliliters	30.0
Pints (U.S.)	Liters	0.473 (Imp. 0.568)
Quarts (U.S.)	Liters	0.946 (Imp. 1.136)
Gallons (U.S.)	Liters	3.785 (Imp. 4.546)
Ounces	Grams	28.4
Pounds	Kilograms	0.454

TO CONVERT:	TO:	MULTIPLY BY:
Millimeters	Inches	0.039
Centimeters	Inches	0.394
Meters	Feet	3.28
Meters	Yards	1.09
Square centimeters	Square inches	0.155
Square meters	Square feet	10.8
Square meters	Square yards	1.2
Milliliters	Ounces	.033
Liters	Pints (U.S.)	2.114 (Imp. 1.76)
Liters	Quarts (U.S.)	1.057 (Imp. 0.88)
Liters	Gallons (U.S.)	0.264 (Imp. 0.22)
Grams	Ounces	0.035
Kilograms	Pounds	2.2

Counterbore, Shank & Pilot Hole Diameters

SCREW SIZE	COUNTERBORE DIAMETER FOR SCREW HEAD (IN INCHES)	CLEARANCE HOLE FOR SCREW SHANK (IN INCHES)	PILOT HOLE DIAMETER	
			HARD WOOD (IN INCHES)	SOFT WOOD (IN INCHES)
#1	.146 (9/64)	5/64	3/64	1/32
#2	¼	3/32	3/64	1/32
#3	¼	7/64	1/16	3/64
#4	¼	⅛	1/16	3/64
#5	¼	⅛	5/64	1/16
#6	5/16	9/64	3/32	5/64
#7	5/16	5/32	3/32	5/64
#8	⅜	11/64	⅛	3/32
#9	⅜	11/64	⅛	3/32
#10	⅜	3/16	⅛	7/64
#11	½	3/16	5/32	9/64
#12	½	7/32	9/64	⅛

Index